General Headquarters
1914–1916
and its Critical Decisions

BY

GENERAL ERICH VON FALKENHAYN

The Naval & Military Press Ltd

Reproduced by kind permission of the Central Library,
Royal Military Academy, Sandhurst

Published by
The Naval & Military Press Ltd
Unit 10, Ridgewood Industrial Park,
Uckfield, East Sussex,
TN22 5QE England
Tel: +44 (0) 1825 749494
Fax: +44 (0) 1825 765701
www.naval-military-press.com
© The Naval & Military Press Ltd 2004

In reprinting in facsimile from the original, any imperfections are inevitably reproduced and the quality may fall short of modern type and cartographic standards.

General Headquarters
1914-1916
and its Critical Decisions

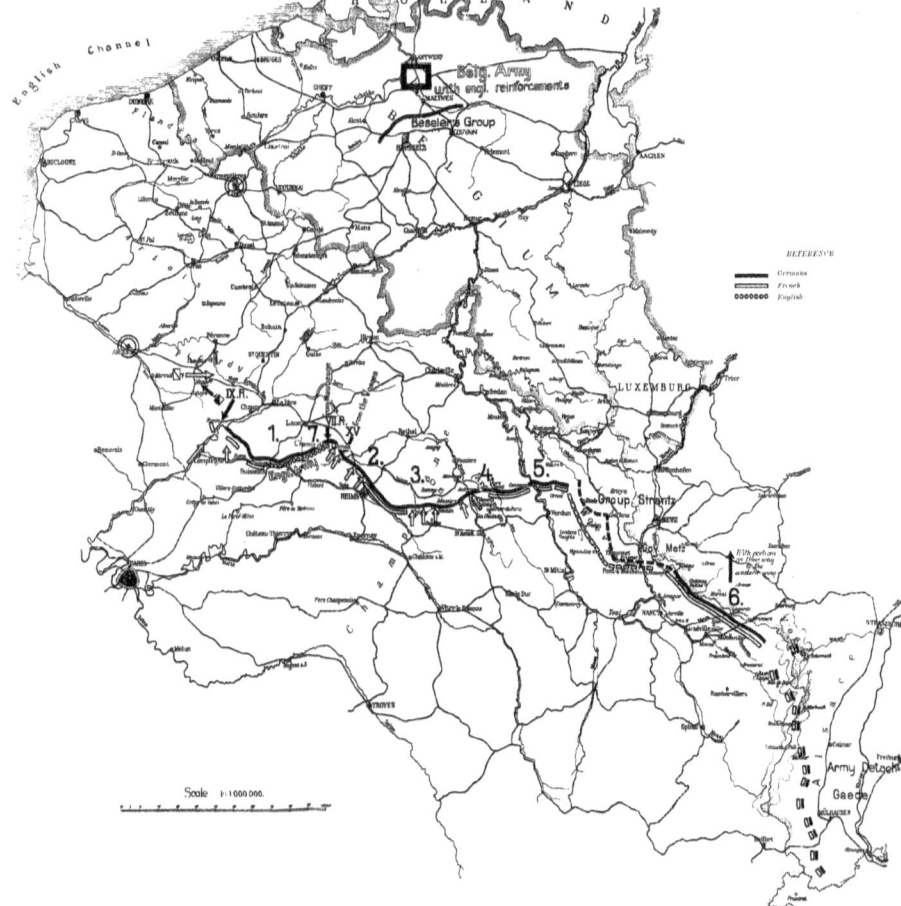

MAP 1

The Situation in the Western Theatre. Middle of September, 1914

PREFACE

THIS book is written in memory of all those who gave their lives and of those who suffered for the Fatherland.

It will not praise their deeds in detail. They need no herald for those who are living and want to see, and a stronger voice than mine will render to the coming generations the sublime song of German self-sacrifice, of German loyalty, and of German heroism in grave but glorious days.

But the book will attempt to set forth in an intelligible form, according to my knowledge at the time of their occurrence, those operative ideas by which the best of us were guided in battle and victory during the two years of the war when I was at the head of the General Staff.

My statements do not form a history of the war in the ordinary sense of the word. They touch upon the events of the war, and other occurrences connected with the latter, only in so far as is necessary to justify the decisions of the General Staff.

They are not written for or against anybody. A judgment is only given, or a deduction made, where it seemed unavoidable in order to explain my actions. I have purposely avoided all secondary matters, all digressions and amplifications. My other official activities will be dealt with separately later.

Rhetoric, self-adulation and lies, plunged Germany into the deepest abyss, when they stifled the sense of reality in our once strong and good people. The continuance of their rule threatens to make us slaves for ever. They shall at least find no place here, where is recorded our leadership in the mightiest struggle that ever a nation had to endure.

VON FALKENHAYN.

Berlin, August, 1919.

CONTENTS

                                                                                                  PAGE

I.—THE CHANGE OF CHIEF OF THE GENERAL STAFF . . .   1

    The idea and scope of General Headquarters—The relations between General Headquarters and the allied Headquarters—The most prominent members of the General Staff.

II.—THE GENERAL MILITARY SITUATION IN THE MIDDLE OF SEPTEMBER, 1914   9

    A dangerous weakening of the Western front in favour of the Eastern—A further withdrawal of the front rejected—The impossibility of resorting to an offensive campaign in the East and a defensive in the West—The Navy gives no active support for the time being—The importance of the permanent closing of the Dardanelles—Decision to support our Allies in Galicia—The gravity of the situation—England's plan of starvation.

III.—THE BATTLES OF THE YSER AND AROUND LODZ . .   25

    Failure of the advance against the San and the Vistula—The attack in Flanders continued—The Commander-in-Chief in the East decides on a flanking movement—The Ypres Battle—Principles of trench warfare—Division into Army Groups; its disadvantages.

IV.—THE PERIOD FROM THE BEGINNING OF TRENCH WARFARE IN NOVEMBER–DECEMBER, 1914, UNTIL THE RESUMPTION OF THE WAR OF MOVEMENT IN 1915   40

    Advantages and disadvantages of trench warfare—Increase of fighting units by decrease of fighting strengths—Supplementing war material and munitions in the winter of 1914–1915—Development of the Air Force—Turkey comes in—The deficiencies from which the Turkish Army suffered—The leaders in the East claim further reinforcements—The importance of Russia to the issue of the war—The winter offensive in the East is decided upon—The offensive in the East only leads to partial successes—Results of the battles in the Carpathians, and the Battle of Masurian Lakes—Relief attacks in the West—Situation in the Dardanelles—Italy's attitude—The submarine war.

CONTENTS

V.—THE BREAK-THROUGH AT GORLICE–TARNOW AND ITS CONSEQUENCES 73

    The situation on the Western Front in the spring of 1915—The condition of the Austro-Hungarian Army—Reflections before the decision to break through—Considerations before the break-through—Preparations for the break-through—Feints before the break-through—Relief attacks in the West—The effects of the break-through—Procedure with regard to Italy—Reflections on action against Italy—Decision to conduct a defensive war against Italy for the time being—Relations between Germany and Italy—The situation in Galicia at the end of May and the beginning of June, 1915—The offensive in Galicia is resumed.

VI.—OPERATIONS AGAINST RUSSIA IN THE SUMMER AND AUTUMN OF 1915. BEGINNING OF THE UNRESTRICTED SUBMARINE CAMPAIGN 104

    The situation in the East in the middle of 1915—Reflections on the situation in Galicia at the end of June, 1915—Formation of the Bug Army—The nature of the terrain in the Pripet area—Relief measures for the attacking group in Poland—Attitude of General Headquarters towards the intentions of the Commander-in-Chief in the East—Serious reverse of the fourth Austro-Hungarian Army at the beginning of July, 1915—Renewed relief measures for the attacking group—Woyrsch's passage of the Vistula; Mackensen's victory—The taking of Warsaw and Ivangorod—Discussion between General Headquarters and the Commander-in-Chief in the East—Mistakes in the conduct of operations—Separate operations on the part of the Austro-Hungarian Headquarters, as well as of the Commander-in-Chief in the East—Transport of troops to the Serbian frontier begins—The taking of Novo Georgievsk—The Russians reinforce near Vilna—The Vilna offensive of the Commander-in-Chief in the East begins—The Vilna operations come to a standstill—Discussion between General Headquarters and the Commander-in-Chief in the East—Position consolidated—Situation in the autumn of 1915—Peace feelers towards Russia—The intensification of the submarine campaign—America's proposal of mediation.

VII.—ATTEMPTS TO BREAK THROUGH IN THE WEST IN THE AUTUMN OF 1915 AND THE CAMPAIGN AGAINST SERBIA . 159

    Conclusion of the alliance with Bulgaria—Draft of operations against Serbia—French successes in the Champagne in the autumn of 1915—The enemies' massed attacks are broken—Arrival of reinforcements for the West only in the nick of time—German heroes in France in the autumn of 1915—Conditions of a break-through—Passage of the Danube in the autumn of 1915; operations in Serbia—Collapse of the Serbian Army—Greece's difficult position is taken into account—Serbian campaign a secondary operation—

CONTENTS

Bulgarian and Austro-Hungarian friction—The continuation of operations against Salonica abandoned—Position consolidated on the Greek frontier.

VIII.—THE POSITION AT THE END OF 1915 193

Rejection of the Austro-Hungarian proposal to attack Italy—The Austro-Hungarian Command refrains from operations against Italy—Reflections on an offensive against Rumania—We refrain from an attack on Rumania in the autumn of 1915—The Dardanelles are free—Plan of operations for 1916—Policy hinders the submarine campaign in 1916.

IX.—THE CAMPAIGN OF 1916 223

Position of the operations in the Meuse area, 1916—1916 Army Reserves—No hope of assistance in the West from our allies—Reflections on the direction of the attack and the preparations for it—Measures to cloak our intentions—The attack in the Meuse area begins—Successes on the west bank of the Meuse—Counter-attacks in the Meuse area—Big successes in the Meuse area—A Russian relief attack—Austro-Hungarian offensive in Italy—Failure of the Austro-Hungarian offensive; success of the Russian—Situation completely changed by the failure of our allies in Galicia—The Western reserves have to go to the East—The Russian offensive in Galicia—Preparatory measures against Rumania—Military situation in the Balkans in the middle of 1916—Military situation in Asia in the summer of 1916—The enemy offensive on the Somme begins—The Somme offensive—Moderate success of the enemy on the Somme—Military situation in the West at time of the Somme offensive—Excessive weakening of the Galician front ascertained—The powers of German leaders are extended—Measures against Rumania—The Polish question—Rumania's attitude becomes threatening—Counter-thrust by the Italians—Italy's and Rumania's declarations of war—Resignation of the Chief of the General Staff—The general situation at the end of August, 1916.

COMPARATIVE REVIEW OF THE RELATIVE STRENGTH OF THE OPPONENTS 293

INDEX 297

INDEX TO MAPS

MAP 1.—Situation in the Western Theatre of War
middle of September, 1914 . . . *Frontispiece*
,, 2.—Situation in the Western Theatre of War
middle of October, 1914 . . . *Facing page* 32
,, 3.—Attacks against the Wings of the Russian
Front, January–February, 1915 . . ,, ,, 64
,, 4.—Summer Campaign in the East, 1915 . ,, ,, 160
,, 5.—Operations in Serbia in the Autumn,
1915 . . . . ,, ,, 192
,, 6.—Brussiloff's Offensive in the Summer of
1916. . . . . ,, ,, 288

IN THE TEXT

PAGE
FIG. 1.—Situation in the East middle of September, 1914 . 17
,, 2.—Situation in the East beginning of November, 1914 . 32
,, 3.—Italian Theatre of War . . . . . 92 & 93
,, 4.—Battles on the Meuse, 1916 231
,, 5.—Battle of the Somme 264

General Headquarters, 1914-1916, and its Critical Decisions

CHAPTER I

THE CHANGE OF CHIEF OF THE GENERAL STAFF

ON the evening of the 14th of September, 1914, in Luxemburg, Lieut.-General von Falkenhayn, then Minister of War, was entrusted by His Majesty the Emperor and King with the post of Chief of the General Staff of the Army in the Field, in the place of the invalided General von Moltke.

The change was not universally made known forthwith. It took place, however, to the full extent of the duties of this post, so that from that day onwards until his resignation on the morning of August 29th, 1916, the General assumed sole responsibility for Germany's conduct of the war, whilst until the day of his appointment he had had neither indirect nor direct influence upon it.

The choice of this extraordinary form of procedure was due to his own wish. It did not seem fitting to disquiet any further the population at home, which was already sufficiently agitated by the events of the war, and by means of this change of leadership to give enemy

Critical Decisions at General Headquarters

propaganda further ostensible proof of the completeness of the victory obtained on the Marne, so long as there was any prospect of a speedy improvement in General von Moltke's health, enabling him to participate once more in the duties of his office in one form or another. This hope was not fulfilled. On November 3rd, 1914, the definitive appointment of Lieut.-General von Falkenhayn as Chief of the General Staff, retaining at the same time his position as Minister of War, was made known.

The General had himself proposed the temporary retention of this post in his hands.

This matter was decided by the memory of the unedifying relationship between the Minister of War and the General Staff in the War of 1870–1871, that had not been generally known, although it had existed as a matter of fact. Prompt dealing with the enormous demands, which, as was already clear at this early juncture, had to be made upon the capacity of the Ministry in the course of the war, and the necessity of effecting its intelligent, smooth, even intimate co-operation with the General Staff, made the unity of command absolutely desirable until the authorities were working easily together. It was mainly owing to this unity that the regulation of the question of raw materials introduced by the War Minister immediately after the outbreak of war, and the raising of strong new formations of troops, that was ordered at the same time, proceeded without interruption, as well as the fact that the reorganization and enormous increase of the production of war material, which were soon demanded by the War Minister, were effected without any hindrance in the shape of " departmental considerations."

During the first two years of the war the relationship thus established between the General Staff and the

Change of Chief of General Staff

War Ministry was never disturbed. Indeed, it did, on the whole, withstand all tests right up to the end of the war. There is no need to count the fruits of this arrangement. It may even be said that the temporary union of the posts of Chief of the General Staff and Minister of War in one hand at the beginning of the war was one of the most important premises for its prosecution in the face of an immeasurable superiority in armaments. When the posts were separated again in January, 1915, at the instigation of the Imperial Chancellor, von Bethmann-Hollweg, for perfectly justified constitutional reasons, co-operation was then so firmly established that it could hardly be endangered again. In addition to this the personality of the new Minister of War, Lieut.-General Wild von Hohenborn, guaranteed the maintenance of it. As former Quartermaster-General, the Minister was thoroughly conversant and in accord with the plans and intentions of his predecessor.

In connection with the foregoing, it will be useful, before beginning to discuss events, to explain both the idea of the " Supreme Command " and also the questions of its relations with the allied Army Commands.

On the basis of the Imperial Constitution the control of the whole of Germany's armed forces, and consequently the supreme command of the army, not only of that of the army in the field, but of all that could be regarded as belonging to the army—as well as of the navy—lay directly with the Emperor as Supreme War Lord. Thus the Supreme Command was centred in his person. His organs in the fulfilment of the duties of Supreme War Lord were the Prussian Chief of the General Staff of the Army for the land forces, and the German Chief of the Naval Staff for the sea forces, whereby it was tacitly accepted that the voice of the Chief of the General Staff would be the deciding factor in matters which touched the conduct of the war, both on sea and land.

In order to facilitate, or, rather, to render possible a regulated business procedure, the Emperor had conceded to the Chief of the General Staff the right to issue operative commands in his name.

As a result of this, and still more by historical development, the Chief of the General Staff had become the actual bearer of the authority of the Supreme Command, and in any case the only person who was responsible for its actions or omissions.

The natural premise was that he kept the Emperor currently informed of the events of the war, and secured his decision before taking important steps. This was done without exception during General von Falkenhayn's period of office. Not a single event of any importance was concealed from the Supreme War Lord, nor was any important measure taken which had not been previously submitted to him.

The domain of the Chief of the General Staff, in his capacity of representative of the Supreme War Lord in the Supreme Command, was limited only by the powers constitutionally conferred upon the highest officials of the Empire. Thus—and it is worth mentioning in this connection—the conduct of the policy of the Empire, which was incumbent upon the Imperial Chancellor, and the conduct of the army administration, which was the War Minister's duty, remained independent of one another. This illuminates the importance, which has been indicated, of the temporary fusion of the offices of War Minister and Chief of the General Staff in the circumstances which the war had pro-

Change of Chief of General Staff

duced, and which had not been foreseen to their full extent.

The execution of the allied idea of attaining the same object by instituting a special Commander-in-Chief, who would have been above both the Minister of War and the Chief of the General Staff, did not come into question in a strong but constitutional Monarchy, such as was the Prussian. The Commander-in-Chief already existed in the person of the Emperor, and even if he was often claimed by other business, he never allowed his duties as Commander-in-Chief to be put in the background.

On the other hand, it is not intended to suggest that the activities of the Minister of War, after the separation of the posts, or those of the Imperial Chancellor, would be effected without the co-operation of the Chief of the General Staff, although not always in accordance with the wishes of the latter. Politics and army administration were so closely bound up with the command of the army in this fight for existence that they could not be separated from it. Wherever this did happen, misfortune was always the result. The Chief of the General Staff had to occupy himself with them often enough, particularly with politics. Apart from a few unavoidable exceptions, however, he severely avoided taking any part in their execution; for he was convinced, and he was strengthened in this conviction in the main by his experience during the period in which he conducted affairs as Minister for War and Chief of the General Staff, that no man could have the strength to attend for any length of time to other offices besides the affairs of General Headquarters. This view has certainly not been refuted by events during the latter course of the war.

It may be maintained that the German solution, as

described here, of the problem of leading a great modern State in war was a successful one in principle. No better existed anywhere among our enemies.

Whether the solution proved itself in actual life depended, to be sure, as in all things in this imperfect world, primarily upon the men who had to put these principles into practice.

The problem of the conduct of an allied war had not been settled between Germany and Austria-Hungary either before the war or after its outbreak. The reasons why this had been omitted, in spite of the experiences of former allied wars, are not known. After the change in the Chief of the General Staff an alteration of the existing state of affairs was not considered opportune, because an unfavourable effect upon the internal conditions in the Austro-Hungarian Army and in the Dual Monarchy was feared, all the more so because both the latter were already shaken by the reverses at the front. If an alteration had been compelled then, a change of personnel in the leading posts of the allied army command could have been expected with certainty, and in its train a change of system would have been probable. In time of war a change of this kind is always such a risky undertaking, with the gigantic mechanism of a national army of to-day, that it was inadmissible except under the most compelling necessity, and especially as the present leaders were known in Germany, their virtues as well as their faults, and it was uncertain who could take their places. Finally the change did not seem to be urgent. Germany's allies were forced by the pressure of the military situation to subordinate any particular wishes of their own to the common ends.

Change of Chief of General Staff

In order to bring their views into harmony with one another, the German and the Austro-Hungarian Command, which latter was officially styled the Imperial and Royal Supreme Army Command, had to settle each point as it came up. That the German G.H.Q.'s view carried most weight in such cases was only natural in view of the relative strength of the forces.

This system of commands worked satisfactorily, chiefly owing to far-reaching consideration on Germany's part, until Austria-Hungary was tempted by the improvement in her position during the winter of 1915–16 to go her own ways. This led to unhealthy symptoms which soon became so marked that the system had to be abandoned towards the end of General von Falkenhayn's period of office, and the way had to be prepared for the formal acknowledgment of the German Command as the "Supreme Military Command" by all allies. Further opportunity will offer itself of dealing more closely with the development which led to this.

No difficulties ever arose in the relations of the German Command with the Bulgarian and Turkish Commands. They were always ready to consider Germany's wishes.

It has been remarked that the responsibility for the measures of General Headquarters reposed solely with the Chief of the General Staff. Of course he was only able to bear this enormous burden because he had around him a circle of selected men as his collaborators, who must be regarded as belonging to G.H.Q. Their names ought not to be absent from a work which deals with the activities of G.H.Q.

Immediately under the Chief of the General Staff were the chiefs of departments in the General Staff: Colonels Tappen—Operations Section—and von Dommes,

Critical Decisions at General Headquarters

later von Bartenwerffer. Political Section: Lieut.-Colonels von Fabeck, later von Tieschowitz—Personal Services and General Business—and Hentsch, later von Rauch—Information; and finally Major Nicolai—Intelligence Service.

In a wider circle there were the Quartermaster-General, Major-General von Voigts-Rhetz, later Major-General Wild von Hohenborn and Lieut.-General Freiherr von Freytag-Loringhoven, with Major-General Zoellner as Chief of Staff; the Intendant-General, Major-General von Schoeler; the Director of Munitions in the Field, Lieut.-General Sieger; the Chief of Staff of the Air Service, who at the same time filled the post of Commander, Major Thomsen; the Director of Field Railway Services, Colonel Groener; the General of the Foot Artillery, General Lauter; the General of the Engineers and Pioneer Corps, General von Claer; the Director of Medical Services, Surgeon-General Dr. von Schjerning, and some others.

CHAPTER II

GENERAL MILITARY SITUATION IN THE MIDDLE OF SEPTEMBER, 1914

THE SITUATION IN THE WEST
(See Map 1)

THE general situation of the Central Powers had become extremely difficult by the middle of September, 1914.

The retiring movements which were connected with the Battle of the Marne had, at any rate, come to an end. The German Western Army faced the enemy again. Yet the front between the Oise and Rheims was only maintained with difficulty against the assaults of the oncoming enemy. In the Champagne, too, the German lines were not yet consolidated.

In addition the danger of an effective outflanking movement threatened from beyond the Oise. The German right wing, which stood on this river without any reserves worth mentioning, was hanging in the air. There was definite information to hand that the enemy was continuing the movement of strong forces westwards. Whether the formations which had been drawn after September 5th and later from the German Armies in the Vosges and the Argonne, where the enemy's pressure was slighter, and which were either on the march or ready to start, would arrive in time could

Critical Decisions at General Headquarters

not be foretold, owing to the shortage of railways in working order, the long distances and the fluctuating state of things at the front behind which they had to march. Only one army corps could be safely reckoned upon, and that was coming from Belgium, and was marching upon Noyon from St. Quentin. Two other army corps, which had been disposable from the Vosges and from Maubeuge, had had to be thrown into the positions which were broken through for a time a little to the west of Rheims. Further reserves were not immediately available. The weakening of the Western front, which had taken place during the rearrangement of the command in the East before the Battle of Tannenberg, after General von Hindenburg had taken over the command of the Eighth Army in place of General von Prittwitz, still made itself gravely felt.* The numerical superiority of the enemy in the West, that had existed from the outset, was considerably increased thereby. The formations which had been withdrawn for the East were taken from the Western half of the army, therefore from the attacking wing. Consequently their absence was particularly felt during and after the decision on the Marne.

The great distance from General Headquarters in Luxemburg to the front occasioned serious difficulties in the transmission of information and orders. These had to be removed forthwith. It was therefore decided to bring G.H.Q. forward to Charleville—Mézières.

The new director of operations then took the shortest steps to prevent the continuance of the threatening

* To this end three army corps had been withdrawn from the battle-front. Only two of them, however, were transported. The third was sent back again to the Western front when the fateful consequences of the step were realized.

General Military Situation, September, 1914

movements of troops round the west flank. The transition to counter-attacks along the whole front was immediately ordered.

They did not produce the hoped-for advantages, in spite of the fact that the enemy was evidently suffering from the same internal difficulties as the Germans. The beginning of the attack on too broad a front, necessitated as it was by shortage of time, was just as much to blame for this as the condition of the troops.

Owing to the unexpectedly swift advance, the many fierce battles during it, and the severing of lines of communication, the fighting strengths had been greatly reduced. Reinforcements could not arrive quickly enough. There was everywhere a shortage of junior officers. The battles of the invasion had torn huge gaps in their ranks that could not be immediately filled. The supply of reinforcements was often blocked, because the rail-heads on the Western wing were five days' march behind the troops. *Matériel* was urgently in need of replenishment. The spectre of the shortage of munitions was already apparent. According to the views accepted hitherto the German Army had gone into the war well prepared. The Ministry of War had done everything possible during the last few years before the war, according to the views current at that time, to meet the demands of the General Staff. Consumption, however, exceeded peace-time estimates many times over, and was on the increase in spite of the strict measures taken to avoid wastage of ammunition. *A propos* of which it may be remarked that our enemies were undergoing exactly the same experiences in this matter.

As has been stated, the counter-attacks improvised by the Germans did not attain their real object. Both the

Critical Decisions at General Headquarters

French and the English were compelled to assume the defensive on the battle-fronts from the Moselle to the Oise. Their mistake in assuming the events after the Battle of the Marne to mean the collapse of Germany was hammered into them. The attempt to divert or put a stop to their movement of troops round the German right wing was unsuccessful. Any, even if only temporary, gain there on the part of the enemy, however, would be bound to lead to incalculable consequences.

The only line of supply of any use to the greater part of the western half of the German Army was the railway connection leading from Belgium into the St. Quentin district. This was almost wholly unprotected against enemy attacks. It is a puzzle why the French and English cavalry divisions did not avail themselves of this circumstance.

Even though the Belgian Army had been thrown back upon Antwerp, with its English supports, its strength and proximity to the most important German lines of communication necessitated a continuous and close watch on it. It was not possible to say when those troops which had been turned against it could be set free for other purposes. Their numbers were very considerably inferior to those of the enemy opposing them.

It only remained, therefore, to carry out with the greatest speed movements behind the German front corresponding to the enemy's movements, with the object of not only meeting the enemy's efforts at envelopment, but of countering them also, so far as the circumstances permitted, by means of an enveloping movement by the Germans. At the same time the threat to the rear from Antwerp had to be removed at all cost. General von Beseler, who was commanding

General Military Situation, September, 1914

in that area, received orders to push forward the attack upon the fortress by all means, without regard to the relative strengths of the forces engaged. The necessary artillery was sent to him with all haste.

The question as to whether it would be expedient by withdrawing the front to facilitate the German movements in the West, and render the enemy's attempts at envelopment more difficult, was negatived.

A withdrawal of the front could not affect the necessity of immediately parrying the threatening outflanking movement by counter-measures and of firmly establishing the right flank on the sea at any cost. The western territory of the Empire, with its sensitive as well as indispensable resources, had to be protected at all events. Any new front which came into consideration was exposed from the outset to a renewed enveloping movement, owing to the enemy's start and the good means of communication at his disposal. The maintenance of Holland's neutrality and the inviolability of her frontiers could not be included as definite quantities in the reckoning.

It still seemed possible, if the present German front held, to bring the northern coast of France, and therefore the control of the English Channel, into German hands. It was all the more inadvisable to abandon this possibility, since the Chief of the General Staff clung to the object which was at the root of the original plan of campaign—first of all to seek the decision in the West; at any rate to restrict the forces employed in the East to a minimum, so long as the front in the West was not securely established. There is no need to prove that this condition had not been approximately realized in September, 1914.

Often has the question been debated, whether a "two-

Critical Decisions at General Headquarters

front" war might not have been begun the other way round—in other words, whether it should have begun with a defensive in the West and an offensive in the East. The supporters of such a scheme refer among other things to a statement made by Field-Marshal Count von Moltke, which is reported in Bismarck's "Gedanken und Erinnerungen." Yet it is scarcely right to base such an assertion upon this weighty voice. The Field-Marshal certainly did not take into account England's participation in the war. With this reservation, the method of procedure mentioned in the conversation with Bismarck would have been applicable. The creator of the scheme carried out in 1914, General Count von Schlieffen, had on the contrary to take England's intervention very seriously into consideration. If this was done, then scarcely any other method of conducting the war was imaginable than that which was actually chosen. In view of the almost unlimited power of the Russians to evade a final decision by arms as long as they pleased, there was no hope of finishing with them before the enemies in the West had either won a decisive success or had so strengthened themselves with their almost unlimited resources as to leave little prospect of any German success over them. The fact that the Russians in 1914 acted contrary to the intentions here ascribed to them, probably being fully aware of the German scheme of concentration, is no proof to the contrary.

However that may be—once the deployment had been effected on the lines I have just mentioned and the enemy engaged in battle accordingly, and once the decision on the Marne had not secured the desired result, the Chief of the General Staff, who was responsible for the conduct of the whole war, could not hesitate. Every attempt to deal with the East before the Western

General Military Situation, September, 1914

front was thoroughly consolidated must necessarily lead to an intolerable situation in the West, whilst a smashing success was not to be hoped for in the East, if only on account of the advanced state of the year.

But to a German leader it was quite beyond doubt that the securing of the Western front had to be attempted by means of an offensive, so long as such a thing seemed at all possible.

At the moment it could certainly not be foreseen when a new blow could be struck in the West. One of the main stipulations, as was believed at the time, was to supplement those deficiencies among the troops that have been already mentioned. It seemed justifiable to assume that the Germans could do this better and swifter than the enemy, who was in a similar predicament. If this did not prove altogether true, the reason for it was that the support given by America and Italy to the enemy in the shape of supplies of material, from the outbreak of war, had not been reckoned with in the calculations and could not be.

Even the growing probability of having to help Germany's allies in their difficulties in Galicia could not upset this decision. It was assumed that, if the worst came to the worst, the new formations, which were training in the Empire at home, would suffice to hold the Eastern situation until the severe winter would have brought operations to a standstill there. No such restrictions owing to weather were expected in the West. The course of the war, however, has shown that the nature of the ground in Belgium and North-Eastern France imposes very considerable restrictions upon big military operations during the wet season.

If, however, the determination to force the decision in the west first was maintained, then there were further grave scruples against a withdrawal of the front. Quite apart from the fact that it would have given over to the enemy large tracts of territory, the exploitation of which was of the greatest value to Germany in the war, it would in any circumstances have placed the German Army in a much more unfavourable position than its present one for the resumption of the offensive. The enemy would have gained for a considerable time a free hand to do as he pleased ; at one stroke he would have been freed from the pressure which hampered him, in spite of the events on the Marne.

This had to be avoided all the more as the naval engagement off Heligoland, on August 29th, had plainly shown that an effective prevention of English sea traffic could not be demanded of the Navy for the time being. The naval command refused to risk a decision with the fleet by an offensive into enemy waters. In the event of an unfavourable issue, which was considered probable in view of the relative strengths of the fleets, the naval command did not believe that it would be able to ensure the safety of the German coasts. The important rôle which was later to fall to the lot of the submarine in this direction was not yet realized at that time, and moreover they were wholly insufficient as regards numbers. Attempts at landings by the enemy on German or neutral territory could not be left altogether out of consideration.

In addition to all this the psychological and political effects weighed heavily, and these, as had been sufficiently experienced after the Battle of the Marne, had to be eradicated in friend and foe, and particularly in the so-called neutrals, in the event of our giving ground again. These would have to have been borne, and could have been, if the beginning of the new offensive could have been foreseen. But it was not so.

General Military Situation, September, 1914

Fig. 1.—The situation in the East. Middle of September, 1914.

Critical Decisions at General Headquarters

THE SITUATION IN THE EAST
(See FIG. 1, PAGE 17)

In the East, in the German sector of the theatre of war, the Russians were retiring about the middle of September out of East Prussia, behind the middle Niemen and the upper Narew, before the 8th German Army, under General von Hindenburg, whose Chief of Staff was Major-General Ludendorff. It could be taken for granted that they would not attempt a decisive operation here, in the near future. On the other hand, it was known that fresh Russian forces were massing on the other side of the two rivers named. The continuation of the frontal pursuit of the enemy's Niemen Army, which had developed out of the Battle of the Masurian Lakes in the first half of September, and only a small part of which had been defeated, did not allow, therefore, any prospects of speedy, far-reaching results. The situation on the Polish Galician front forbade such action.

There the Austro-Hungarian Army was in retreat from the San sector. It had defended itself valiantly in the battles around Lemberg at the end of August and beginning of September, against the superior numbers of the Russians.* Its loose structure had not been equal, however, to such a test. About the middle of September the German G.H.Q. came to the conclusion that the decision as to whether and when this retiring movement would cease depended mainly upon the decisions of the enemy, owing to the weakness and the condition of the allied troops. If the enemy took

* See Appendix: Relative Strengths of the Forces on the Eastern Front, under 1 (c).

General Military Situation, September, 1914

advantage of this and pressed ruthlessly forward, a grave danger to the province of Silesia would necessarily arise. Even a temporary over-running of Upper Silesia by the Russians, however, was inadmissible. It would have robbed Germany of the rich resources of Silesia, and consequently would have made it impossible for her to continue the war beyond a limited time. Further, the dangers of the proximity of the Russians to Bohemia could not be underestimated. This would presumably have led to internal convulsions within the Dual Monarchy, which would have completely crippled the latter's military strength.

Last, but not least, it seemed at that time as though any further successes on the part of the Russians over the Austro-Hungarian forces would destroy the hope of inducing the Balkan nations, principally Turkey, to join the Central Powers. The Chief of the General Staff considered it indispensable that this alliance should materialize. If the Straits between the Mediterranean and the Black Sea were not permanently closed to Entente traffic, all hopes of a successful course of the war would be very considerably diminished. Russia would have been freed from her significant isolation. It was just this isolation, however, which offered a safer guarantee than military successes were able to do, that sooner or later a crippling of the forces of this Titan must take place, to a certain extent automatically. If such a strictly disciplined political organism as Germany, accustomed as she had been for centuries to conscientious work, and having at her disposal an inexhaustible wealth of skilled organizing forces in her own people, was only barely able to accomplish the mighty tasks imposed upon her by the war, it was certain that the Russian State, so much weaker internally, would not succeed in doing this. As far as human calculations went, Russia would not be able permanently to meet the demands of such a struggle, and at the same time to effect the reconstruction of her whole economic life, which was necessitated by her sudden isolation from the outer world, owing to the closing of the western frontiers and of the Dardanelles.

These reflections pointed to the necessity of an immediate, speedy and ample support of Germany's allies. The question how this was to be done was, to be sure, not easy to answer.

From what has already been said, any weakening of the Western Army was inexpedient. Moreover, it was not to be assumed that sufficient forces could be sent from there to the allies in time. Against any attempt to do this, there was a warning in the fact that the forces which were withdrawn in the West before the battles on the Marne and of Tannenberg were sorely missed on the Western front, and had produced no decisive advantage in the East at the time. This is mentioned here once again because its evil influence upon the course of this part of the war can scarcely be sufficiently emphasized.

Within the Empire there were, at all events, numerous divisions of infantry in training. Their formation had been ordered by the Minister of War in the first days of mobilization, as soon as he was convinced beyond doubt by England's attitude, together with the intelligence of the early appearance of Asiatic contingents in West Russia, that the peace-time calculations of the General Staff as to the numerical strengths of the opponents for the first months of the war would be far behind reality. The Ministry of War, under the guidance of the Deputy War Minister, Lieut.-General von Wandel,

General Military Situation, September, 1914

who found an indispensable assistant in the Director of the General War Department, Colonel von Wrisberg, had proceeded with these new formations to the utmost possible limits of the available officers and *matériel*, and had speeded them up as much as possible. Yet the young portions of the German Army could not be regarded as ready for use at the time in question.

The most natural, and, if it succeeded, the most effective operation, that of directly relieving our allies, had to be abandoned. It would have consisted in converting the offensive from East Prussia into a deep thrust into Russia or East Poland. A preliminary condition for such indirect assistance would have been the transferring of considerable other forces in addition, as direct supports of the allies on the latter's northern flank. Without this the consequences of a further Russian advance towards Silesia, as described above, would certainly materialize before the thrust from East Prussia would have become sufficiently menacing to the enemy to cause him to relieve his pressure upon the Austro-Hungarian Armies. It was further considered extremely questionable whether such a far-reaching operation could take effect before the beginning of the "roadless season," owing to the advanced time of the year. This was the period, often lasting many weeks, in which the autumn and spring rains render any traffic impossible, except on the few main roads. It is only the frost, in the first instance, and the sun getting higher in the sky in the other, that brings any relief from this. Moreover, the experiences of the winter of 1914–15, which were a revelation to every soldier concerning the capability of modern man under the most unfavourable climatic and atmospheric conditions, were not yet available. But even if they had been known it would

Critical Decisions at General Headquarters

not have been possible to have reckoned upon a well-timed success, owing to the gigantic distances which were involved.

Similar reasons opposed an operation on the Eastern bank of the Vistula against the swampy sector of the lower Narew, which was strong by nature and had been strongly fortified.

Consequently the Chief of the General Staff resolved to continue the pursuit from East Prussia only with the weaker forces of the 8th Army under General von Schubert. The main mass of the troops there was then moved as swiftly as possible to Upper Silesia and Southern Posen, as a newly-formed 9th Army under General von Hindenburg. From there it was to move to the attack in conjunction with the Austro-Hungarian Army. When the new offensive was contemplated, in spite of the blow which the army had already suffered, the justification of this step lay in the fact that numerous reinforcements had been sent to it in the meantime.

It was also believed that better achievements might be expected from the allied troops in the impetus of the advance than in a purely defensive action of long duration, which demands the strictest discipline.

The object of the offensive was to remove the main mass of the enemy as far as possible from the German frontier and to cause it to draw further reserves to this battle front. By this means other sectors of the Eastern front would be able to get considerable relief. Thus the Chief of the General Staff hoped to gain time for the development of plans in the West. The manner of carrying out this very difficult task was left to the discretion of the local commanders, the Commander-in-Chief of the 9th Army and the Chief of the Austro-Hungarian General Staff, General Conrad von Hötzendorf.

General Military Situation, September 1914

General von Falkenhayn left the political leaders in no doubt as to the seriousness of his view of the general military situation. He supplied both the Imperial Chancellor and the Foreign Secretary von Jagow with the necessary information.

In this he started from the assumption that there was no reason to despair of a satisfactory conclusion to the war, but that the issue of the war had been rendered altogether uncertain by the events on the Marne and in Galicia.

The intention of forcing a speedy decision which had hitherto been the foundation of the German plan of campaign had come to nought.

Even if it was assumed that the circumstances to which the reverse was to be ascribed would not repeat themselves in the future, it was impossible to make up for the irrecoverable time which had been lost, and difficult to efface the influence of the retreat on the Marne upon the strengthening of the enemy's *moral*. And it was certain that it would not be altogether possible to cure the evils which had revealed themselves, in isolated cases it is true, but still plainly, in the allied army.

One had, therefore, to familiarize oneself with the possibility of the success of England's plan, which was daily becoming clearer, of winning the war by starvation and attrition. According to the opinion of the Chief of the Naval Staff there was no prospect at present of frustrating this plan by any offensive action on the part of the navy. It was to be hoped that with careful economy of Germany's and her allies' means, this plan would not be successful. A very much longer duration of the war than was generally assumed was, however, certainly to be reckoned with. This meant that demands of quite extraordinary magnitude on the internal

Critical Decisions at General Headquarters

force of resistance on the part of the Central Powers would have to be made. It could not yet be seen how they would respond to these demands, but meanwhile any relief of the pressure bearing upon them from two sides was of the greatest importance. If the political leaders had at their disposal any practicable method for opening a way to an understanding with the enemy —whether in the East or in the West was all the same from a military point of view—it was advisable to employ it. If this was not the case, as was convincingly maintained by the political leaders in perfect agreement with the Chief of the General Staff's estimate of the situation, then no means should be left untried by which the capability and the will to hold out could be raised and strengthened in the German people and in the Dual Monarchy.

CHAPTER III

THE BATTLES OF THE YSER AND AROUND LODZ

THE offensive begun by the 9th German Army and the Austro-Hungarian Army at the end of September on both sides of the Upper Vistula did not attain its object.

The enemy forces which had pushed forward over the Vistula and the San, were indeed driven out of these sectors. But when the enemy brought his main body into action the situation was changed. Our allies were not able to hold the Russians in the San sector. The latter consequently moved very strong forces from Galicia to the north at the right moment. They also received reinforcements from the rear. By this means they succeeded not only in driving in the Austro-Hungarian northern flank on the left of the Vistula, but also in threatening to encircle the northern flank of the 9th Army from Warsaw. In order to escape this danger, the army had to begin the retirement upon Silesia towards the end of October, which then also caused the Austro-Hungarian Army to give ground.

Again and again urgent appeals for assistance came from the Eastern front to the West, from the middle of October onwards. Their justification could not be denied. In spite of this the Chief of the General Staff was not in a position, owing to developments in France,

Critical Decisions at General Headquarters

to comply with them to anything like the desired extent. In particular the demand made by the Austro-Hungarian General Headquarters, and supported by the Commander-in-Chief of the 9th Army, for about thirty divisions to be sent from the West to the East had to be refused. The sending of these would have made the position on the Western front untenable. Never could the advantages to be expected from such a transference of forces to the East stand comparison with this disadvantage in the West, even if it was not taken into account that the transport of those forces would be bound to take so much time that they could not have afforded any relief in the present emergency. Considering the military situation as a whole, there only remained a delaying action in the East to be carried out by turning to account the greater manœuvring ability of the allied armies. If the enemy could be taken successfully in the flank, there was a hope that the desired object would be attained. To this end it was necessary to give the 9th Army greater liberty of movement, *i.e.*, not to compel it to keep permanently in direct contact with the northern wing of the Austro-Hungarian front in South Poland. The German General Headquarters urgently recommended that this should be done, and at the same time did everything possible to create the fundamental conditions for such action, without, however, necessitating any abandonment of the Western plans.

The 9th Army was therefore supplemented by the assignment of almost the whole of the trained reserves at home, to make good its very serious losses. One of the newly-established army corps from home had already been sent to the East, as it was greatly feared that since the 9th Army had been transferred to Silesia the

The Battles of the Yser and Lodz

Russians might break through on the southern wing of the weakened 8th Army and occasion grave consequences. This army corps was now followed by two cavalry divisions from the West. The 8th Army was also subordinated to the former Commander-in-Chief of the 9th Army, General von Hindenburg, in order to give him a free hand over all German troops on the Eastern front for his own decisions, as Commander-in-Chief in the East, whilst the command of the 9th Army was taken over by General von Mackensen, with Major-General Grüner as his Chief of Staff. The despatch of further forces from the West could not, however, come into question until after the decision had been taken in the operations which were proceeding on the Franco-Belgian front.

THE DECISION TO USE THE NEW ARMY CORPS IN FLANDERS. END OF SEPTEMBER, 1914 (See MAP 2)

Here the enemy's attempts at envelopment were repulsed at the end of September and the beginning of October, but the German enveloping movement was not realized. This had been prevented by the superiority of the French network of railways. Although very considerable forces had been employed meanwhile, as, for instance, the bulk of the 2nd Army from the Rheims area, the 6th Army, which had hitherto been employed in Lorraine, and strong cavalry detachments, which were pushed forward in a wide circle round the northern wing, the German front did not progress beyond a line west of Roye, west of Bapaume, and west of Lille. The coast on which the right flank was to rest, and from which it was hoped to obstruct England's Channel traffic, effectively attack the Island itself, and turn the French flank, was not reached.

In order to compel this end, a new 4th Army was formed in Belgium towards the middle of October* out of three divisions of the besieging troops from Antwerp, who had been set free by the fall of the fortress on the 9th of the month after a siege of barely twelve days, and four army corps from Germany which had just become fit for service, under the command of General Duke Albrecht of Würtemberg, with Colonel Ilse as Chief of Staff. It was ordered to advance against the Yser sector with its right flank resting on the sea. At the same time from the 6th Army under General the Crown Prince Rupprecht of Bavaria, with Major-General Krafft von Dellmensingen as Chief of Staff, an attacking group concentrated north of Lille, the former right wing of the German front in Flanders, was to attack straight ahead west of Lille.

If the shortage of artillery had made itself seriously felt in the race to the sea which had been going on till then, it was thought that this could now be remedied by bringing up the siege guns from Antwerp. Unfortunately, lack of ammunition afterwards prevented this circumstance from being turned to account.

While exhausted troops had had to be brought into action in the previous enveloping movements, the majority of the formations which advanced to the new struggle were quite fresh.

The prize to be won was worth the stake. Strong French and English forces had already reached the Yser during the first ten days of October—the English had been withdrawn altogether from the old front near Rheims—and were trying to get into touch on the eastern

* See Appendix: Relative Strengths of the Forces on the Western Front.

The Battles of the Yser and Lodz

bank with the Belgian divisions which were retreating from Antwerp. Our forces had not been sufficient to prevent the withdrawal of these troops before the fall of the fortress. Although the Belgians were in an extremely miserable condition they would soon be able to attack again if supported by English or French formations. There was no doubt about the resolute offensive intentions of the English and the French. Not only had the danger that the Germans would be finally cut off from the Belgian coast again become acute, but also the danger of an effective encirclement of the right wing. They both had to be removed unconditionally. If this, at least, was not done, then the drastic action against England and her sea traffic with submarines, aeroplanes and airships, which was being prepared as a reply to England's war of starvation, was impossible in their present stage of development. It was also questionable in certain circumstances whether the occupied territory in Northern France and Western Belgium was to be held; the loss of it would necessarily have led to evil results.

If, on the other hand, the German Army succeeded in throwing the enemy back across the Yser sector and in following him, it could expect to force a favourable change in the whole situation on the Western front after the supplies of troops and ammunition had been meanwhile replenished. The same result could naturally have been expected from a big success in another part of the Western front. It was therefore examined whether an attempt to break through could be more expediently undertaken with the help of the new army either in Artois or Picardy or Champagne. A consideration of the transport and other requirements of concentration showed that it would no longer be possible

Critical Decisions at General Headquarters

to forestall in this way the enemy who was pressing strongly forward in the Yser area. Other forces would, therefore, have been required to hold him up. These did not exist. The same calculations showed that there was no longer time to exchange the young troops for tried formations.

Under these conditions the Chief of the General Staff was still firmly convinced of the necessity of carrying out the attack in Flanders when symptoms became evident that the objective which had been set in the East would, perhaps, not be attained. It seemed as if the numerical superiority of the enemy and the diminished driving power of a portion of the attacking troops would prevent the Russians from being brought to a standstill on the Vistula and the San.

THE FIGHTING ON THE VISTULA AND THE SAN IN OCTOBER, 1914 (See FIG. 2, PAGE 32)

This did not, in fact, happen. While the German attacking columns in the West were moving against the Yser sector from October 17th onwards, it became evident almost at the same time that the allies could not maintain themselves on the Vistula and on the San. Soon afterwards the retiring movements had to be begun there before the counter-thrusts of the superior forces of the enemy. The only prospect of our front being formed for any length of time was in the Carpathians behind the Dunaczek, the Nida and the Upper Pilitza. Moreover, it could certainly be taken for granted from the outset that the army would also be further outflanked in the north. The intercepted wireless, which allowed us to follow accurately the movements of the

The Battles of the Yser and Lodz

enemy in the East from week to week and often from day to day since the beginning of the war till far into 1915, and to take corresponding measures, showed this beyond a doubt—by this means the war in the East assumed quite a different and a much simpler character for us than that in the West.

The new Commander-in-Chief of the German forces in the East resolved at the beginning of November to take advantage of this change in the situation to make a surprise flanking movement with the assistance of the efficient German railways; it was to be made from the north with all the forces at his disposal and supported by the left bank of the Vistula. He, therefore, arranged for the transference of considerable portions of the 8th Army from Lithuania and for the transport of the mass of the 9th Army, which was retreating from the Vistula above Warsaw, into the area of Thorn and Gnesen. The basis for the removal of this army was provided by the readiness of the Austro-Hungarian G.H.Q. (which was obtained by the strong representations of the German G.H.Q.) to fill the gap which would thereby be caused in the Polish front by the Austro-Hungarian army on the Austro-Hungarian southern wing in the Carpathians. This proof of solidarity in case of need was all the more highly to be valued because it deprived a portion of the Hungarian frontier of its protection. At any rate this front did not seem to be directly threatened at the moment.

During these happenings in the East until November 12th, on which day the offensive of the 9th Army, under the leadership of General von Mackensen, began from Thorn and Gnesen, the offensive which was begun in

Critical Decisions at General Headquarters

Fig. 2.—The situation in the East. Beginning of November, 1914.

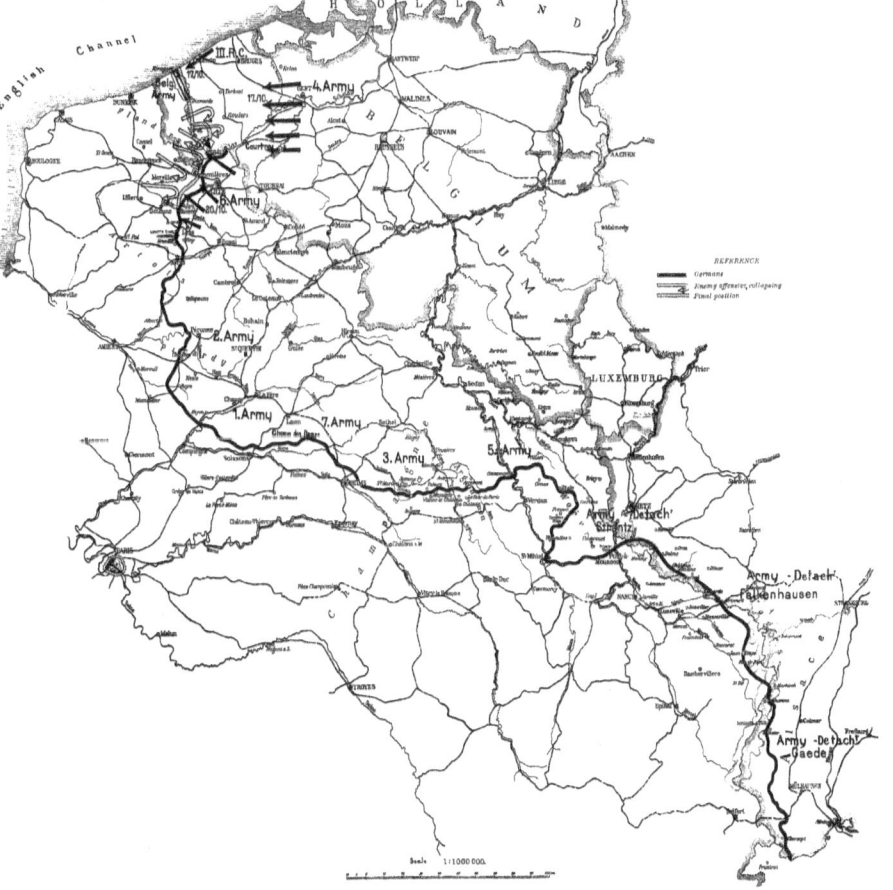

MAP II

The Situation in the Western Theatre. Middle of October, 1914.

The Battles of the Yser and Lodz

Flanders in the middle of October, and is popularly styled the Ypres Battle, was carried out.

The enemy's offensive was completely broken. He was thrown back almost everywhere either to, or across, the Yser, and a firm connection was established between the coast at Nieuport and the previous German right wing near Lille, thus forming a front from the Swiss frontier to the sea. That which had to be attained under any circumstances, if the war was to be carried on with any hopeful prospects, was attained. Several times it seemed as though it only needed perseverance in the offensive to obtain a complete success—how near we actually were to it has since been made sufficiently plain. At the time, however, our movement came to a standstill.

DECISION TO BREAK OFF THE FLANDERS OFFENSIVE

Inundations, skilfully managed by the Belgians, put an end to the attack of the German right wing, which was making good progress and bore the main pressure. The young army corps further south fought with incomparable enthusiasm and unexcelled heroism. The disadvantages of their urgent and hasty formation and training, and the fact that they were led by older and for the most part retired officers, as others were not to be had, naturally made themselves felt. In particular there were deficiencies in the new field-artillery formations, a fact that was emphasized all the more strongly by the shortage of ammunition. Nor was the leadership entirely satisfactory. At the beginning of November, G.H.Q. could not conceal from itself that a further thorough-going success was no longer to be obtained here, particularly in the inundated area, in the face of an opponent who was continually growing stronger. It was now debated whether by suddenly shifting the pressure a break-through should be attempted against a portion of the enemy's front on which he had weakened himself for the sake of the defence of Flanders. The district of Artois and Picardy, in the area of the 2nd Army commanded by General von Bülow, with Lieutenant-General Lauenstein as Chief of Staff, again came under consideration for this purpose. The idea, however, soon had to be dropped. After the East had been provided with all the reserves at hand, both of men and ammunition, the forces in the West were no longer sufficient for its realization.

It was just as strongly opposed by the prospects which opened for us in Poland. The Russians evidently had no knowledge of the storm that was brewing for them on the left bank of the Vistula. They continued their advance westwards slowly, *i.e.*, as well as the communications permitted, these having been thoroughly destroyed by the 9th Army on its retreat from the Vistula above Warsaw to Silesia and Southern Posnania. Their right (northern wing), which was advancing approximately along the line Warsaw–Kalisz, was not echelonned deeply enough. On the other hand they had left strong forces on the right bank of the Vistula north-east of Warsaw. Apparently they were led to do this by the fear lest the 8th Army might be suddenly thrown on to the Vistula from East Prussia, to attack the Russian lines of communication there on the right of the Vistula. The half voluntary retirement of the army, when it had to be weakened for the Mackensen offensive, was no secret to them, and may have

The Battles of the Yser and Lodz

caused them to dispose their flank-protection in such deep order of echelon. Demonstrations by the main reserves from Thorn and Graudenz across the line Lipsno–Mlawa may have had the same result.

Thus the operations entrusted to the 9th Army offered favourable prospects. There was no doubt at G.H.Q. that all forces that could be spared even from the West must be used to make it a success, after it was realized that the hoped-for decision in the West could not now be forced. In contradistinction to the view represented by the Commander-in-Chief in the East it was, to be sure, quite clear to G.H.Q. that the advanced season of the year and the numerical superiority of the Russians would not allow matters to come to a really decisive success in the East. The Chief of the General Staff trusted, however, that the success would be big enough to check the enemy for a long time. Even this was a gain which justified the attempt. About seven infantry divisions and one cavalry division were withdrawn from the West and dispatched as speedily as possible to the East to be at the disposal of the Commander-in-Chief. This was only rendered possible, however, by the decision to act purely on the defensive in France, with the most careful application of every imaginable technical device. Trench warfare in the real sense, with all its horrors, began.

BEGINNING OF TRENCH WARFARE ON THE WHOLE WESTERN FRONT

In the regulations issued to this end, G.H.Q. broke with the hitherto accepted German principle that only one line of defence was to be constructed. A defence system consisting of several lines connected with one another was everywhere to be instituted, with two or several positions one behind the other. It was intended to provide by this means a security against the front lines, or even the positions, being broken through, for this was unavoidable, owing to the immense superiority of the enemy even if the troops acted in the bravest possible manner. In spite of this innovation the second German principle that the line apportioned to troops for defence was to be maintained at all costs, and if lost to be retaken, was rigidly preserved. The garrisons in the front line were indeed to be kept as small as possible in order to avoid losses by artillery fire. But they had to hold out at all costs until the reinforcements stationed in the rear-lines could come up to give what support they could.

These regulations were often challenged and were even altered at times later in the war. They were believed to be to blame for the high losses that occurred now and again. It was hoped to avoid these by allowing the men holding the front line to retire in case of need to a comparatively distant line where the main resistance was to be offered. Reinforcements were only to be brought so far and not into the front lines. Experience, as a whole, will scarcely support the assertion that this regulation proved its value in general. It did not sufficiently take into account the psychology of the average soldier. It also compelled the artillery to be kept so far behind the main line of resistance, if one did not want to run the danger continually of losing one's artillery, that it was scarcely possible to support the front line effectively. If selected, well-trained troops, under perfectly safe leaders, applied this precept, it may have fulfilled its purpose as a rule. Very often

The Battles of the Yser and Lodz

it has not done so, but has rather caused heavier losses both of men, in the gravest of all forms, namely voluntary surrender, as also of positions. It has been proved that it is a great danger in trench warfare for a man to be placed at a post where he feels himself abandoned because he knows that he cannot hope for assistance. If, in addition, he is left a possibility of interpreting regulations concerning retirement, then the ordinary mortal is readily inclined in the hell of a modern battle to interpret them in a way which may indeed promise him salvation, but which is ruinous for the whole front. It gives rise to voluntary surrender or premature retirement, which it is also impossible to stop at the main line of resistance.

In order to enable mobile reserves to be held in readiness and to secure their timely concentration in threatened sectors, the armies on the Western front were first arranged in three, and later four, army groups. This arrangement was, however, annulled again in March as the desired objects could not be fully attained. Just as in the East it became difficult for the Army Group Commands, obviously as a result of deficient peace-time training, to agree to exercise great self-denial for the sake of the general good in certain circumstances. They inclined very often to regard their own work as the most important and the troops allotted to them as a kind of private possession. Instead, as was hoped, of promoting the preparation of reserves for the purposes of G.H.Q., they were the more ready to support their armies in resisting the surrender of forces which had once been allotted to them. Such tendencies, thoroughly in keeping as they are with human nature, have existed as long as there have been commands. But they have never been less justified than in this war, in which the

Critical Decisions at General Headquarters

great tension, resulting from the numerical disproportion of forces, constantly compelled the German G.H.Q. to count on every single battalion. Cases of friction arose which often had a very unpleasant influence upon the course of affairs.

THE FIGHTING AROUND LODZ IN NOVEMBER, 1914

The boldly conceived, admirably prepared and forcefully executed operations on the left of the Vistula, in which the foremost columns of the formations coming from the West were soon able to take part, won brilliant initial successes. Even such experienced leaders as were on the Staff of the Commander-in-Chief in the East allowed themselves to be temporarily misled by them. In reply to a question from the Chief of the General Staff it was reported that if further reinforcements could be liberated in the West for the East, these should not be employed in the battle-area west of the Vistula, but in East Prussia, where the Russians had taken advantage of the weakening of the 8th Army, in favour of the 9th Army, to push forward over the frontier again, and were advancing towards the Masurian chain of lakes. The enemy leadership, however, soon showed in Poland how much it had learnt since the days of August. Very swiftly it swung the flanking corps northwards, brought up other corps from the Austro-Hungarian front, and hurled the troops which had hitherto been guarding its flanks across the Vistula against the German flank on the left of that river. The German attack became paralysed and threatened to change into a retiring movement, when the other forces arriving from the West instilled fresh life into it. Lodz was now

The Battles of the Yser and Lodz

captured from the Russians; then they were driven back behind the Bszura, the Ravka and the Pilitza. They even stopped their pressure on the Austro-Hungarian front east of Cracow, after the forces there, in conjunction with von Besser's German infantry division, succeeded in the Battle of Limanova on December 12th in throwing back again those Russian troops which had pushed over the Dunaczek. The blows administered to the enemy had accomplished all that they could do. The force of the German offensive was exhausted. The influence of the Eastern winter made itself acutely felt. It also compelled the Russians in East Prussia to stop at the chain of lakes.

TRENCH WARFARE IN THE EAST

The trench war began in the East, where, like the war of movement, it took different and far lighter forms than in the West. Only in a few sectors and at intervals was it carried on here with that grim bitterness which was always characteristic of it on the other side. The climate, the temperament of the enemy, and his military stolidity, moderated it.

CHAPTER IV

THE PERIOD FROM THE BEGINNING OF TRENCH WARFARE IN NOVEMBER–DECEMBER, 1914, UNTIL THE RESUMPTION OF THE WAR OF MOVEMENT IN 1915.

G.H.Q. was fully conscious of the disadvantages involved by the transition to trench war. It was chosen purely and simply as being the lesser evil.

No progress was made because of the shortage of troops and material. A retirement was not desired because, as the German lines were very thinly held, the gain which might have been obtained by economizing troops through a shortening of the front, bore no relation to the certain disadvantages of such a step. They have already been dealt with in another place. Added to this, no positions and dug-outs had been constructed behind the army at that time. It was doubtful whether it would be possible to build them in time in the winter. It was to be assumed that the increase of the front line garrisons necessitated thereby would use up almost all the troops that were thus economized. In no case would the troops obtain the rest which they needed for the welding of their formations, for training and for re-equipment.

The transition to trench warfare was not effected by the independent decision of the Chief of the General Staff, but under the stern pressure of necessity.

November, 1914, to the Spring of 1915

It was very soon realized, however, that this kind of warfare, alternating with hard, well-prepared blows directed against sections of the enemy, was the only means by which it could be hoped to bring the war to a favourable end in view of the change made in the Central Powers' position by the events on the Marne and in Galicia. It was only by its adoption that Germany was able permanently to hold her frontiers. But the frontiers had to be held, not because G.H.Q. lacked the courage to abandon German soil temporarily to the enemy if the common good had demanded this, but because the loss of the frontier territories would have rendered the continuation of the war impossible after a comparatively short time. The industrial and agricultural districts of the East were quite as important as the industrial districts on both banks of the Rhine. Neither the exclusion of the one nor the other was practicable for Germany or her allies.

But the transition to trench warfare once more allowed full advantage to be taken of the interior lines, and so restored the freedom of action to strike with sufficient forces wherever a decision was necessary.

It was the systematic application of trench warfare which first rendered possible such an increase in the capacity of the railways that they became in effect the equivalent of a reduplication of the reserves.

It was this which first gave time to exploit science and engineering to their full extent in the interests of the war. Thereby it supplied a basis on which brave and well-trained men, inferior in numbers, could hold out indefinitely against a manifold superiority.

The first premise, at all events for the successful application of this form of warfare, was the intrinsic superiority of one's own troops over the enemy. That

Critical Decisions at General Headquarters

this existed with regard to the Russians was certain. After a short observation, however, the question whether a similar comparison existed with regard to the enemies in the West, who were to be rated more highly, could also be answered with a definite affirmative. Although the German Army, in contrast to the French, for example, had not had a really thorough peace-time training in trench fighting, the troops succeeded in mastering it far more quickly and better than any one of the enemies. Contrary to all expectations, the French, in particular, did not distinguish themselves at all in this. The old truth that the soldier who is well-disciplined and has his heart in the business, and in addition has learnt to attack, is equal to any situation in war, was once more fully confirmed.

Nowhere have the admirable warlike qualities of the German, supplemented by his strict training, celebrated greater triumphs than in the trench war; that is, of the German as he was before the accursed revolution, which was just as unnecessary as it was unfruitful.

When G.H.Q. decided to adopt trench warfare in the two last months of 1914, the answering of the further questions as to the sector in which the next offensive was to be made was not an urgent matter, as the required forces were not available. The first that could be reckoned upon were a new army of nine divisions. Their mobilization had been ordered by the Minister of War immediately the new formations which were used at Ypres and Lodz later, were ready, and training personnel and equipment had been set free. These divisions, however, could not be ready for use before the end of February, unless they were to be sent prematurely to the front. Experiences with the first new formations

November, 1914, to the Spring of 1915

had shown that it was absolutely essential to avoid this. The eagerness, therefore, of one leader or another, and the impatience of the allied G.H.Q., had to be curbed. This reticence was repaid in excellent fashion. The new divisions responded brilliantly to the expectations placed in them by the result of the winter battle in Masuria. The fact that they were ultimately rendered unfit for further fighting for a long time by these short operations, was due to the very high demands which had to be made upon them under particularly unfavourable weather and road conditions, in order to attain any result at all from the undertaking.

The further mobilization of troops at home was out of the question for the time being, owing to the shortage of junior officers and equipment. Another obstacle was the necessity of practising economy with the reserves of men, owing to the long duration of the war which was now inevitable. The biggest successes at the front were fruitless if the situation at home was rendered impossible by a scarcity of labour, or if the swiftly increasing requirements of the army in the field could not be satisfied for the same reason.

On the other hand G.H.Q. entertained no doubts that the mere addition of the nine divisions in training, even if they were most carefully prepared, would not be sufficient to effect a real decision either in the West or in the East. The moral and technical superiority of the German soldier over his opponents which was daily becoming more evident, also offered a way out of this difficulty. It turned out to be so great that it was possible to entertain the suggestion of the Director of the General War Department, Colonel von Wrisberg, to reduce by about 25 per cent. the strength of the fighting units, the divisions, without doing any harm to their effectiveness, to correspond to that of the enemy units in their original strength. This created the possibility of forming new fighting units out of the surplus of the old formations that were already trained, equipped and provided with leaders. This plan was adopted with great success after the artillery, machine-guns and other war material, which was needed to supplement the arrangement, could be supplied. The advantages gained in the Eastern campaign in the summer of 1915 were largely due to the adoption of this plan.

Just as the course of the war hitherto had given every soldier new conceptions of human powers of endurance, so it had also established totally new standards for the requirements of *matériel* and its efficiency. Only those who held responsible posts in the German G.H.Q. in the winter of 1914–15, during which almost every single shot had to be counted in the Western Army, and the failure of one single ammunition train, the breaking of a rail or any other stupid accident, threatened to render whole sections of the front defenceless, can form any estimate of the difficulties that had to be overcome at that time. The requirements of the Eastern Army were always given the preference on account of its being composed of many units in which the process of consolidation was incomplete. Only those who had to listen to the moving complaints of our wonderful troops about these conditions, and the incessant appeals of our allies for assistance in the shape of war supplies of all kinds, can understand the ardent efforts with which some relief was sought. Thanks to the co-operation of the widest and best sections of the people it was found more quickly than could have been expected. The adjustment of science and engineering,

November, 1914, to the Spring of 1915

the re-construction of the whole of industry in the interests of the war, with due regard for their usual indispensable work, took place almost noiselessly, so that they were accomplished before the enemy quite knew what was happening. Indispensable assistance was afforded by the regulation of the raw materials question which was effected by the Minister of War with the advice of Dr. Walter Rathenau; for this question had become of decisive importance now that Germany was cut off from the outer world.

Particular stress was laid upon the promotion of the production of munitions and the manufacture of long-range guns, the elaboration of the trench mortar into a serviceable weapon, the increase of the machine-gun supply and of the air-services, as well as the development of gas as a means of warfare.

The most urgent was the supplementing and increase of artillery ammunition. It is not possible within the limits of this book to give sufficient praise to the admirable achievements in this matter, which were all the more admirable as the most careful attention was always paid to home requirements. It is to be hoped that a more famous pen will take this task in hand. It shall only be mentioned here that as early as spring, 1915, G.H.Q. was relieved of any serious anxiety with regard to the munitions supply. This welcome state of things continued until midsummer, 1916, although the Entente was able gradually to avail itself of the munitions supply of the whole world, excluding the Central Powers, whilst Germany was not only thrown back upon her own resources but was also forced to guarantee her allies ample assistance in this matter as well as in every other province of war material. It was only the requirements during the simultaneous battles

Critical Decisions at General Headquarters

on the Meuse, on the Somme, in Galicia, and in Italy in August, 1916, that, exceeding as they did all anticipations, brought about a critical period in the supply of ammunition for a time. However, the programme of production which had been drawn up continued to supply such increasingly enormous quantities of munitions that it was very quickly possible to remove the deficiency which had occurred. This programme then held good till far into 1917 at least. Its conception and execution was primarily due to the expert knowledge and indefatigable work of Major-General Coupette, Majors Wurtzbacher and Koeth in the Ministry of War, and also Major Bauer, who belonged to the General Staff, as Artillery adviser.

Although the high-angle fire of all calibres was very effective, particularly of the light and heavy field howitzers, against which the enemy produced nothing approaching them in value during the first years of the war, yet the troops felt very acutely the inferiority in range and effect of our field-guns against the French. In order to remove this deficiency steps were taken to construct a new field-gun and more effective ammunition. The manufacture of this, it is true, as is always the case with new productions in war time, was bound to take considerable time; the issue of the new guns to the troops could not be begun before the end of 1916. In the meantime an attempt was made to meet the deficiency by extensive adaptation of the *matériel* at hand in the fortresses at home, in the navy and in captured stocks. As always where patriotic interests were involved, the Krupp works in Essen took the lead in this. The long-range artillery which was thus obtained has done excellent service. Its most brilliant technical feats were the bombardment of the English landing-

November, 1914, to the Spring of 1915

place at Dunkirk and the arsenals near Nancy and at Belfort. Still more important was the fact that it made it possible to compel the enemy continually to keep his batteries, stores and other establishments of importance, as well as his concentrations, far back from the front line. Yet its powers were just as insufficient as those of the high-angle artillery to prepare for assault those positions which were constructed with all the modern methods of the art of fortification, owing to the still restricted number of guns and ammunition. Where one party had gained time, by the adoption of trench warfare, to apply these means methodically, the ordinary weapons of attack often failed completely. A weapon had, therefore, to be found which was superior to them but which would not excessively tax the limited capacity of German war industry in its production. Such a weapon existed in gas. The use of this in fights for fortified positions is known from times of old. The use of it by the French in the form of gas-shells with asphyxiating effect and of so-called stink-pots, frequent announcements in the French press that a gas of annihilating effect discovered by a famous physicist would shortly be used, the serious wounds caused by the French incendiary shells filled with phosphorus, as well as the poisonous effect of the English picrin shells, had directed attention again and again to this weapon. German chemistry soon succeeded in solving the problem which was thus put to it. But these inventions too were not spared the shortcomings of new productions in time of war. It was years before it was possible to control gas with any certainty as a weapon.

During the first months of the war the German airservices had shown themselves to be fully equal to the enemys', if not in numbers at least in value, although

Critical Decisions at General Headquarters

the chief merit, to be sure, was not due to the technical perfection of the *matériel*, but to the self-sacrificing spirit of the personnel. It was also evident, however, that the peace-time doubts of the Ministry of War as to the utility of the dirigible airship in war were justified. Quite apart from many other obvious difficulties, so long as it was not possible to discover a less dangerous gas wherewith to fill the balloon, the great hopes placed in Count von Zeppelin's productions could not be fulfilled. The dirigible airship had a limited importance for a few special purposes. In general the duties assigned to it had to be taken over by the aviators. As a result of this, and also of the palpable efforts of the enemy to lay the greatest stress on the war in the air, a speedy expansion of the German air-service became necessary, although it was in fact equivalent to a new construction enlarged many times over. Major Thomsen, as he was then, was entrusted by the Chief of the General Staff with the elaboration of this question; in his work he has erected an abiding monument to himself. He not only understood the right paths to indicate for aeroplane construction at home, but also the true spirit to be maintained among the flying men, and without which all technical perfections would have meant nothing at all. As could not be otherwise in the case of so young a service which was dependent upon the spasmodic progress of engineering, the superiority in the air was many a time in the balance. Again and again, however, the German air forces triumphed, thanks to the sound foundations upon which their development was henceforward based, over the disproportion in the resources of the belligerents.

Side by side with the organizing activities of G.H.Q.,

November, 1914, to the Spring of 1915

which have only been suggested in outline, and in spite of the trench war and the advanced season, it was faced by other important problems during the weeks about the New Year 1914–15.

TURKEY JOINS THE CENTRAL POWERS

At the end of October Turkey had declared for the Central Powers. The great services rendered by the German Ambassador, Freiherr von Wangenheim, in this matter, and by the German naval attaché Humann, as a result of special circumstances, ought not to be left unmentioned. The decisive importance of Turkey joining in the struggle against Russia has already been touched upon. Turkey was absolutely indispensable in this context and was to be valued all the more highly at the given moment because she provided at the same time a certain counterpoise to Bulgaria's attitude, which had become rather doubtful. Conversations with the latter regarding the conclusion of an alliance had not been continued after the events upon the Marne, upon the San, and upon the Vistula, although Bulgaria had on the other hand steadily resisted all the Entente's temptations to get her to join them.

The Turkish Command resolved forthwith to forestall the danger which threatened from an invasion, in process of preparation, of the politically unreliable province of Armenia by the Russians, by a surprise move into Georgia. She achieved this object also. The operations, however, had soon to be stopped as a result of heavy losses incurred by the unusually early coming of winter in the frontier mountains. The same circumstances, however, also removed the Russian danger, at least until the late spring. This provided an opportunity of moving Turkish forces against Egypt. Even if the Chief of the General Staff did not expect any decisive influence upon the war from such operations, he yet hoped to cut the Suez Canal, one of Great Britain's most important arteries, for a time, or at least to keep strong English forces away from the main theatre of war, whilst Germany's resources were not involved to any harmful extent by enterprises in Asia.

At the same time a propaganda on a grand scale was instituted in the Caucasus and Persia, as well as being sent over Afghanistan into India. Among other things this was aided by the proclamation of a " Holy War " by the Sultan of Turkey in his capacity of Caliph. It was evident that these steps could have but a limited success owing to the weakness of Turkey and the difficulty of sending German help to those remote regions. Yet it was considered absolutely necessary to start and to further it, if only to forestall the dangers created by the activities of England, which were following similar lines but in a contrary direction. The latter had in her favour the fear, deeply rooted in the East, of England's power, superior resources and greater liberty of movement. Yet the boldness and tenacity of the work of men like Niedermayer, Hentig and others made it possible to sow a seed which would have borne fruit a hundred-fold in the event of a satisfactory conclusion of the war.

In criticizing Turkey's achievements in the war, the fact must not be lost sight of that she came into the world-war deeply exhausted by six years of almost uninterrupted war and was altogether dependent on Germany's support in all technical matters and questions

November, 1914, to the Spring of 1915

of equipment. This could not really be given until the Balkan corridor had been opened through Serbia and Bulgaria in the winter of 1915-16, and even then it could only take effect very gradually. The difficulties of communication with Constantinople were not altogether overcome right up to the end of the war. Germany's own needs and the necessity of having to help Austria-Hungary also in this province prevented it.

Still less were the difficulties of the further connection with Asia Minor overcome. In peace time, traffic between Constantinople and the coast of Asia Minor as well as the Syrian and Armenian coasts had been for the greater part by way of the sea. This was now closed. Recourse had therefore to be had to the land routes. There was no through railway connection, however. In the promotion of the building of the Bagdad Railway economic and financial considerations had played a decisive part, and the military considerations had been neglected. The Anatolian line, which led across the highlands of Asia Minor to the south-east, ended at the western foot of the mighty Taurus range. From thence to the front in Armenia the traffic had to pass along 450 or 500 miles of country roads running through wild and barren mountain districts. Communication with the fronts in the south-east was indeed facilitated by the fact that different sections of the railway could be used to this end. Thus one railway was working in the plain of Adana from the eastern foot of the Taurus as far as the western slope of the Amanus. Another bridged the distance from Aleppo to Jerusalem. A third was being constructed from the eastern foot of the Amanus to Aleppo, and in a north-easterly direction from thence to the Euphrates, where the river could be used to Bagdad during the short period of high water.

Critical Decisions at General Headquarters

All these railway sections, however, suffered most painfully from a shortage of rolling-stock, building-materials, fuel, and both workmen and personnel. The efforts of German engineers and German railway troops to master these conditions probably constitute the greatest achievements ever performed in this province. The construction of the line over the mountain range of the Taurus and across the chain of the Amanus, the building of a viaduct north-west of Aleppo and the bridge over the Euphrates, are technical achievements of the highest rank. In the circumstances, however, even the self-sacrificing devotion of these men was not able to effect more than a limited improvement.

THE FIGHTING IN THE WEST, DECEMBER–JANUARY, 1915

In the Western theatre of war it was possible to keep in every respect to the guiding principle which had been formed for the conduct of the war in Europe.

The French, indeed, attempted more serious attacks in December in Alsace against the army of General Gaede, Chief of Staff Lieutenant-Colonel Bronsart von Schellendorff; in the Woevre against the army of General von Strantz, Chief of Staff Lieutenant-Colonel Fischer, and soon afterwards in Champagne against the 3rd Army under General von Einem, Chief of Staff Major-General von Hoeppner. In spite of the heavy transfers of troops to the East they were roundly repulsed everywhere. And after some painful blows had been successfully inflicted upon the enemy in January by throwing in at several places swiftly concentrated front reserves—with the 5th Army under Lieutenant-General the Crown Prince Wilhelm, Chief of Staff Major-General Schmidt

November, 1914, to the Spring of 1915

von Knobelsdorf, in the Argonne, and with the 7th Army under General von Heeringen, Chief of Staff Lieutenant-General von Hänisch, north of Soissons, a welcome if only short pause set in. The hope was justified that time would be gained in order to concentrate really sufficient forces of troops and material for a decisive blow.

Developments in the East did not permit such plans to mature.

DECISION TO USE THE NEW FORMATIONS IN THE EAST, JANUARY, 1915 (See MAP 3)

In order to relieve the Austro-Hungarian front, including the hard-pressed fortress of Przemysl, the last bulwark in Central Galicia remaining in Austrian hands, by holding Russian forces in Northern Poland, the 9th Army, after a short breathing space, resumed its attacks on the Bszura and Ravka in the direction of Warsaw at the end of December. The attempt had no results worth mentioning. Under the influence of this impression, and also of unfavourable intelligence which had reached it regarding the attitude of Italy and Rumania, the Austro-Hungarian G.H.Q. proposed in January, 1915, an offensive through the Carpathians supported by German forces. In this the intention permanently to secure Hungary's frontiers and to relieve Przemysl was probably the chief consideration. In addition to this the Austro-Hungarian G.H.Q. believed that it could promise a decisive success against Russia from a military point of view, if the new army corps training in Germany were used simultaneously for a thrust from East Prussia against the Russian right flank.

Critical Decisions at General Headquarters

The Commander-in-Chief in the East, Field-Marshal von Hindenburg, gave his most pressing support to this proposal. He, too, opined that the final decision in the East might be expected from such operations against both Russian flanks.

It was not to be denied, indeed, that four quite fresh German army groups, formed and trained with particular care, would presumably win considerable successes at any point in the East where they might go into action. It remained doubtful, however, in the highest degree whether an advantage to the whole would, or even could, be attained thereby, which would be in just proportion to the value of the stake. And yet in the present position of the Central Powers the satisfactory answering of this question was the most important premise for any decision on the part of G.H.Q. Before it was answered in the affirmative without any ambiguity, not one drop of German blood should have been shed, much less should almost the only German military reserves have been risked.

No pressing emergency from which Austria-Hungary had to be relieved existed at the moment. A relief of Przemysl would certainly have been valuable. But no such great importance with regard to the general conduct of the war could be attached to it as to make it repay the expenditure of the German reserves. In addition it was most improbable that an attempt at relief would be successful in the depth of the Carpathian winter. The Austro-Hungarian front on the Hungarian frontier stood fast at the time. Even if the enemy was continually reinforcing himself there, the relative strength of the forces was not such, that in view of the natural strength of the defence in mountains, a brave army could not have looked confidently into the

November, 1914, to the Spring of 1915

future.* In spite of this it would have been very desirable to relieve the front permanently of the Russian pressure. In a sober estimate of all the circumstances, however, it was to be feared that the proposed operations had little prospect of achieving this. The Chief of the General Staff was altogether sceptical of the possibility of conducting two enterprises, separated from one another by a weakly-held space of more than 375 miles, so as to take effect simultaneously, when there were only comparatively limited forces at his disposal. The Russians had the advantage of the inner lines. As not one German division more could be withdrawn from the West at the time, there were, apart from the formations which would be offered by Austria-Hungary, and which were certainly not particularly good storm troops, and the few troops which might be drawn from the German Eastern front, only the four young corps ready for the suggested operations. With these it was, perhaps, possible to win large local successes in the two proposed sectors of attack, if we were ready at the same time to run the danger of completely exhausting the troops participating in the operations by the hardships of the winter campaign. It was scarcely to be hoped that this effort would be sufficient to win from the enemy an advantage which was really important for the general situation, and especially as it was improbable that the natural difficulties occasioned by the wintry weather, particularly in the mountains, would allow initial successes to be turned to full advantage.

The assumption that a final decision in the East could be obtained was, of course, still more unfounded.

* See Appendix: Relative Strength of the Forces on the Eastern Front, under 2 (c).

Critical Decisions at General Headquarters

Moreover, this belief was based on sophisms. As a result of the unfortunately widespread catchword " the war must be won in the East " even people in high leading circles inclined to the opinion that it would be possible for the Central Powers actually " to force Russia to her knees " by force of arms, and by this success to induce the Western Powers to change their mind. This argument paid no heed either to the true character of the struggle for existence, in the most exact sense of the word, in which our enemies were engaged no less than we, nor to their strength of will. It was a grave mistake to believe that our Western enemies would give way, if and because Russia was beaten. No decision in the East, even though it were as thorough as was possible to imagine, could spare us from fighting to a conclusion in the West. For this Germany had to be prepared at all costs. This would not be the case if forces which were indispensable in France, either for keeping the enemy at bay until the decision, or for the decision itself, were tied up in the immeasurable spaces of Russia. The employment of such forces would have been required, however, even to attempt the desired final decision against the Eastern colossus. Even then it was still very uncertain whether the object would be attained. Napoleon's experiences did not invite an imitation of his example, and he had been able to undertake the march to the East under far more favourable conditions than was the case at present.

The Chief of the General Staff, therefore, adhered to his decision to use the new corps in the West. In order, however, to put a stop to the movement of Russian forces, which was taking place against the Austro-Hungarian front, he called upon the Commander-in-Chief in the East to make a further relief thrust with

November, 1914, to the Spring of 1915

front reserves against the Russian front west of the Vistula—this time in the more favourable terrain on the Pilitza, and with the heaviest concentration of the available forces of troops and artillery. It was suggested to the Austro-Hungarian G.H.Q. that an attempt should be made to crush Serbia with the forces which were intended for the operations in the Carpathians, and which could be reinforced by some Germans on the Eastern front. As far as could be seen, it would not be difficult to deal such a blow at the Serbian Army, which was very much weakened by fighting, disease and privation, and was suffering from a shortage of *matériel*. It was considered opportune by the German G.H.Q., because Austria-Hungary's reputation among the Balkan peoples and in Rumania and Italy was urgently in need of heightening, if serious developments were not to ensue. The particular cause of this was the fate of an expedition which had been undertaken in Serbia by the Austro-Hungarian Army there, under Lieut. Field-Marshal Potiorek, in November and December, 1914, without the co-operation of G.H.Q. After a short initial success, these troops had been thrown back across the Save in dire confusion and with the heaviest losses. The simplest means of toning down] the impression of this misfortune would have been a counter-stroke against Serbia. By opening up the communications with the South-East, such an action held more promise than did any local successes in the Carpathians or on the East Prussian frontier.

It soon appeared, however, that this attitude could not be maintained. Under the increasing Russian pressure, it proved to be impracticable to send any Austro-Hungarian forces from the Carpathian front to

Critical Decisions at General Headquarters

Serbia.* On the contrary, formations which were already on the Danube had to be sent to support the Carpathian front. Moreover, the condition of the allied troops gave rise to well-founded doubts as to whether that front could be maintained at all without strong German assistance. The collapse of it would have been insupportable, for it would have cut out Hungary, the strongest pillar of the war-spirit in the Dual Monarchy. Steps had immediately to be taken to give direct support to the Carpathian front. This swallowed up the available German forces for the undertaking that had been planned on the Pilitza, which was also hindered by weather conditions. It soon became clear, however, that even this immediate stiffening of the front would not be of any permanent use, especially as terrain and winter in the mountains, as well as the bad communications to and on the Carpathian front, only allowed a scanty measure of troops to be sent there by the Central Powers. An end had to be put to the uninterrupted stream of Russians arriving there, if the fall of Przemysl was not to be followed within a conceivable time by an irremediable break-through in Hungary. The need for some relief by means of an attack in another spot, therefore, became imperative. With a heavy heart, therefore the Chief of the General Staff had to make up his mind to employ in the East the young corps who were the only available military reserves at the time. This decision meant the further abandonment of any active campaign on a large scale in the West for a long time. It could not have been hoped to shake seriously the solid Anglo-French front with the new formations which were contemplated. It was, on the

* See Appendix: Relative Strengths of the Forces on the Eastern Front, under 3 (c).

November, 1914, to the Spring of 1915

other hand, not at all out of the question that it might be possible, by using them later in the East, to get rid of the Russian danger for an appreciable period, if the enemy was successfully driven to the same enormous consumption of men and *matériel* as hitherto.

The proposals of the Austro-Hungarian G.H.Q. were agreed to. Although the Chief of the General Staff reserved to himself the use elsewhere of those excellent troops which were now going to the East, as soon as the object was achieved on that front, he did not entertain any illusions as to the uncertainty of these calculations. His consent could only be obtained on condition that the operations in the East were directed with constant regard to all the requirements of the whole situation. To this end the presence of G.H.Q. was necessary. The Chief of the General Staff therefore began to familiarize himself with the idea of taking the conduct of operations in the East into his own hands. The translation of this idea into fact was prevented at the moment by gigantic preparations on the part of the enemy for an offensive in the West. Consequently one reason alone actually justified the new decision: the conviction that Austria-Hungary must otherwise collapse in a short time under the burdens of the war.

From the middle of January, 1915, Field-Marshal von Hindenburg was given four corps of the army reserve*—including the best that Germany possessed in the war—to carry out the offensive from East Prussia, according to his proposal and that of the Austro-Hungarian G.H.Q. They formed a new 10th Army, under General von Eichhorn, Chief of Staff Colonel Hell.

* There were three fresh corps among these; the fourth a corps that had been kept in reserve on the Western Front, and was replaced there by a fresh one.

Critical Decisions at General Headquarters

The Austro-Hungarian offensive in the Carpathians, for which, in addition to the Austro-Hungarian Armies participating, the so-called Southern Army, under General von Linsingen, Chief of Staff General von Stolzmann,* had been formed out of three German and some Austro-Hungarian divisions, came to a standstill after making very little progress. As had been feared, the mountain winter proved to be stronger than human powers of endurance. It did not even succeed in quite clearing Hungarian soil of the enemy. Soon the allied troops once more had difficulty in beating off the Russian counter-attacks. The German troops of the Southern Army did, indeed, continue the offensive and performed individual feats. Progress was also made in the Bukovina, where German cavalry, under Lieut.-General Freiherr Marschall, was fighting in conjunction with the Austro-Hungarian Army under General Pflanzer. It was soon apparent, however, that the relief of Przemysl or any other decisive success was not to be counted upon.

A little later the offensive in East Prussia set the winter battle in Masuria ablaze on February 8th. Besides the 10th Army, the left wing of the 8th under General von Below, Chief of Staff Major-General Böckmann, also took part in it. As the enemy was taken by surprise and the fresh German troops readily responded to the most gigantic demands, it succeeded in liberating German territory once more from the Russians. The greater part of their wing army, the 10th, met with its destruction in the Forests of Augustow. But the German forces were also at the end of their endurance.

* For the preparation of these operations General Ludendorff, who had given his particular support to the undertaking, was lent to Genera l von Linsingen temporarily.

November, 1914, to the Spring of 1915

Weakened as they were by weather conditions and difficulties of commissariat, they were no longer able to break the resistance of the Russian reinforcements, which were once more thrown against them swiftly and skilfully.

In order to prevent further sacrifices, which in his opinion could scarcely be of any more use, the Chief of the General Staff pointed out to the Commander-in-Chief in the East that the general situation imposed certain limits upon the endeavour to complete the victory in the winter battle by trying the powers of the troops to the utmost.

The Commander-in-Chief, however, adhered to his resolve to continue the offensive. He hoped by means of this further pressure to compel the Russians to withdraw their front from the left of the Vistula behind the river. To this end another attacking group of front reserves, gathered together under the command of General von Gallwitz, was thrown against the lower Narew front. This had practically no result, neither was any further progress made in the north. On the contrary the Russians gained advantages at several points in their counter-attacks. The forces used in these were partly brought up out of Poland, west of the Vistula, but the Russian front there was kept in its old position. Attempts by the Germans to take advantage of this by offensive action in this sector came to nothing. Towards the middle of March the allies were once more thrown on to the defensive along the whole Eastern front. This was effected without any particular trouble where there were German formations, but it was only with great exertion that the Austro-Hungarian troops, against whom the Russians directed their main pressure, succeeded in maintaining their front generally.

Critical Decisions at General Headquarters

This made itself particularly felt after the fall of Przemysl, on March 22nd, which set at liberty the Russian besieging army.

The operations against both wings of the Russian front had not come up to the far-reaching expectations which had been placed upon them in the East. The reports which came in regarding the situation and the condition of the troops showed this. As early as the first days of March, the Chief of the General Staff had to refrain from carrying out his intention of again withdrawing the forces which had lately been sent to the Russian theatre of war on the conclusion of the operations. Luckily, he was in a position to do this at the moment without getting into any awkward dilemma. The favourable issue for us of the relief offensives attempted by the enemy on the Western front to help the Russians could already be foreseen, and Italy was still keeping quiet, although relations with this former ally had become dangerously acute.

On the other hand, these operations had done their duty, inasmuch as they had inflicted losses upon the Russians which must be described as quite extraordinary, even when it was considered that our allies also had to lament very severe losses. G.H.Q. took occasion from this to hope for the coming of at least a temporary lull in the crisis on the Carpathian front. It therefore returned once more to its old idea. The Austro-Hungarian G.H.Q. was called upon to profit by the occasion, while maintaining the strictest defensive in the Carpathians, to strike a surprise blow at Serbia. This undertaking was just as desirable for the securing of the flank and rear of a front which might have to be formed in the near future against Italy, as for the opening of the corridor by which help could be sent to Turkey, which

November, 1914, to the Spring of 1915

was just then being hard pressed in the Dardanelles. Meanwhile, the premise upon which this proposal was based proved to be incorrect. According to reports from the Carpathian front, the Russians were not slackening their attack, and the allies were not faring any better than they had done before. There could be no thought of transferring any forces from there. On the contrary, German support had to be sent along again at the end of March at the instigation of the Austro-Hungarian G.H.Q. The Beskides Corps, under Lieut.-General von der Marwitz, composed of three divisions from the German section of the Eastern front, was pushed forward into the mountain sector of the same name, in order to counteract a serious reverse which had happened to the Austro-Hungarians there. The corps succeeded in doing this, as regards the enemy, very much more easily than was expected. Symptoms appeared among the Russians which could not be interpreted otherwise than as a considerable diminution of their fighting strength. Together with other observations made upon the Eastern front during this time, they furnished G.H.Q. with important bases for conclusive decisions soon to be arrived at.

Similar signs, though of a negative nature, had been obtained by the Chief of the General Staff from the general course of the operations. In his opinion, a fact had become clearly evident therein which had already proclaimed its existence in the fighting on the Vistula in October, and still more in the struggle for Lodz in November. With the comparatively modest forces at Germany's disposal for offensive action, the continuation of the operations against flank or wing of the Russian front could no longer offer prospects of important successes. The enemy had long been watching for them

Critical Decisions at General Headquarters

with particular attention, and knew very well how to make the counter-strokes. He could not be prevented in this, because Germany was not in a position, with the existing proportion of forces, to tie him down sufficiently along the front, and he always had plenty of room in Russia into which to withdraw. No less valuable than this knowledge was the fact that a measure had been obtained of the performances which might generally be expected of the Austro-Hungarian troops. If, in future, they were to do useful service in big offensive actions, then care had previously to be taken to use them side by side with the Germans, and to let the latter do the real work of the attack. This method of procedure was accordingly adopted as the war went on, in so far as G.H.Q. could render it possible.

Where this was not done, owing to a shortage of available German forces or for other reasons, as in the Austro-Hungarian offensive in Volhynia, in the autumn of 1915, or in that from the Tyrol, in the spring of 1916, the deviation from the rule has bitterly avenged itself.

THE WINTER BATTLE IN CHAMPAGNE

Whilst all these events were taking place in the East, relief offensives for the Russians had been developed by strong forces of the English and the French in the Western theatre of the war.

In the middle of February immensely superior masses of the French attacked the German positions of the 3rd Army in Champagne, others, north of Arras (in the neighbourhood of the Loretto heights), the portions of the 6th Army there.

MAP III

Operations against the Wings of the Russian Front. January and February, 1915

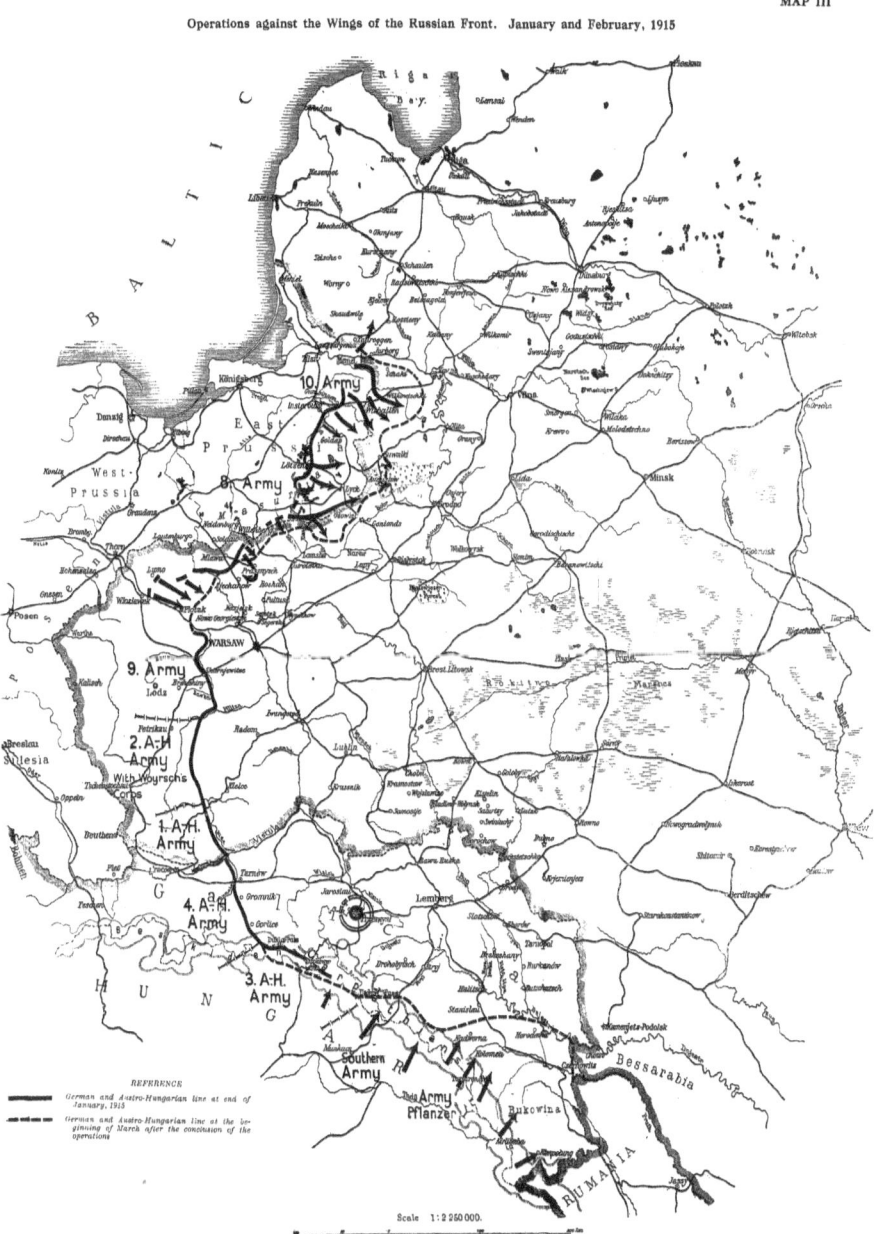

November, 1914, to the Spring of 1915

In the first half of March the English attempted in dense formations to over-run the very weak German forces of the 6th Army, which opposed them south-west of Lille, by a massed attack.

Almost at the same time the French attacked on the right bank of the Meuse, south-east of Verdun (Combres heights, then Bois du Prêtre, St. Mihiel), in the 5th Army sector.

No notable advantages were gained anywhere by the enemy. After unimportant initial successes the fighting developed everywhere into a monotonous fluctuating struggle. In it the Germans had a very hard time in consequence of their inferiority in numbers—during the winter battle in Champagne the proportion was no more than one to six, and around Lille one to sixteen. Everywhere, however, they held their lines in the main, and inflicted disproportionately heavy losses upon the attackers. At many points they were even able not only to wrench from the enemy the territory which he had taken at the first onset, but to proceed to counter-thrusts into the enemy's lines. The behaviour of the troops was sublime beyond praise. In just the same way did the German system of defence prove its own worth, and similarly the construction and garrisoning of the lines, as well as the measures for the swift transference of the reserves.

Towards the end of March the German G.H.Q. arrived at the firm conviction that it would not be possible for the enemies in the West to force a decision within a measurable time, even if further portions of the formations in process of reconstruction on the Western front had to be used in the East to annihilate the offensive power of the Russians for all time. This gave G.H.Q. an unusually free hand in its decisions, which was all

Critical Decisions at General Headquarters

the more valuable since the general situation in the East had begun to cloud again.

At the beginning of February the Turks had actually reached the Suez Canal, but were unable to maintain themselves upon it. Thereupon the English and French fleets immediately began a bombardment of the Dardanelles fortifications. At first they were pronounced to be merely a counter-stroke to the Suez expedition. It was soon proved, however, that they were seriously endeavouring to force the opening of the Dardanelles. The safeguarding of this claimed the whole of Turkey's limited resources of troops and *matériel*. The rapid dwindling of the latter in particular gave the German G.H.Q. the greatest anxiety. Turkey had no factories at her disposal for the production of serviceable weapons and ammunition. Communications with her were cut off progressively by Rumania, as Austria-Hungary's powers of resistance in the Carpathians threatened to go to pieces. This circumstance exercised a similar effect upon Italy's attitude.

THE NEGOTIATIONS WITH ITALY, 1915

How far, before the outbreak of war, the German General Staff had hoped that Italy would, in a case of necessity, fulfil her obligations as a member and co-partner of the Triple Alliance for more than thirty years, may be set on one side. If any assumption of this kind had been made, it would have been based, in the main, on the promises of Pollio, the Italian Chief of the General Staff at the time, and of the Staff Officers whom

November, 1914, to the Spring of 1915

he had sent to Germany. Unhappily, Pollio died suddenly a few days before the war began. For the rest the hopes placed by the General Staff in him and Italy were not generally shared in Germany. Italy's open coasts, with their populous towns, and her dependence on sea-traffic for her food and coal supplies, made it almost impossible for her to take part in a war against England. Indeed, it was generally evident in the very first days of the war that there was no question of this. Italy declared herself neutral. The immediate entry of England into the war had achieved one of its most important ends. On the other hand, the secession of Italy to Germany's enemies still seemed to be outside the bounds of possibility in those days. It was not until the defeat of Austria-Hungary in Serbia, in December, 1914, and the crucial developments in the Carpathians, that this question caused serious anxiety. In order to prevent its materialization, the German political leaders suggested to Austria-Hungary that she should satisfy Italy's demands without delay. When this proposal met with strong resistance, G.H.Q. was requested to support it. The latter did so, with all the means at its disposal, and ultimately succeeded, after tedious and painful negotiations, which lasted from January to March, 1915, in inducing the Dual Monarchy to take the necessary steps. Whether these concessions were made too late is not yet known for certain. In any case, Austria-Hungary's resistance to the proposed cession of territory to Italy was quite intelligible. She pointed out, with justification, that experience had taught her of old that it is impossible to silence a blackmailer by giving way, and further, that any acquiescence in the blackmail, in view of the loose structure of the Dual Monarchy and the attitude of

Critical Decisions at General Headquarters

Rumania, would bring in its train two-fold danger in the future. Yet neither the German political leaders nor G.H.Q. could withdraw their proposal. From all that was known, there still existed a possibility of preventing Italy by this means from going over to the enemy. If it became fact, it was not inconceivable that a more amicable change in Italy's attitude could be brought about later. Even if this did not succeed, however, any delay in Italy's joining the opposite party was of the greatest importance. Considering the tension which continued unabated on all fronts after the battles on the Marne and in Galicia, and the abortive offensive against Serbia, it would have been scarcely possible for the Central Powers in the winter of 1914–15 to hold another enemy at bay. Forces would not be available for this purpose until Russia's offensive powers had been crippled. Moreover, our communications with the outer world through Italy, which provided us with extremely important raw materials, could not be dispensed with except under the most compelling necessity. It is often enough maintained that a firmer attitude towards Italy would have borne better results than complaisance. The supporters of this view overlooked the real facts of the situation in which the Central Powers were placed at that time, and Italy's close knowledge of them. G.H.Q. could not run the risk of prematurely breaking-off relations by using methods of intimidation. It was fully aware of this at the time, and during the whole period that can be discussed here, never lost sight of the fact that this war was a life-and-death struggle for Germany, and that any overstraining of her powers, even though they might lead to initial successes, must in the long run unquestionably end in collapse from exhaustion, owing to the superiority of the enemy.

November, 1914, to the Spring of 1915

BEGINNING OF THE UNRESTRICTED SUBMARINE CAMPAIGN
IN FEBRUARY, 1915

The period under discussion included the first appearance of one of the most important questions which occupied G.H.Q. during the war. At the beginning of February, 1915, Vice-Admiral von Pohl, the Chief of the Naval Staff, informed the Chief of the General Staff that the Navy now believed itself in a position to take up the war with submarines against England, with a prospect of overwhelming success, if it could be conducted in the only way befitting the nature of this weapon, namely, without restriction in its application. In the case of neutral vessels, acts of violence would be refrained from only when they were recognizable. To be sure, complications with the Neutral Powers, particularly with America, were not unlikely. But their movements in the waters round England would be prohibited altogether, *i.e.*, still further restricted than was permissible on the basis of international agreements after a blockade had been declared. A declaration of blockade, however, could not be made, because the premises for such were entirely lacking. On the other hand the submarine weapon had not been taken into consideration at all in these agreements. Moreover, there was no doubt that according to the law of self-preservation it was just as incumbent upon Germany as it was justifiable to take counter-measures against the blatant violations of international law by England. These violations consisted of the war of starvation which had been initiated against the non-combatant population of Germany, including old men, women and children, by the declaration of the North Sea as a war area ; a method of warfare that was being maintained with ruthless severity and utter disregard for the rights of neutrals; by England's interpretations of the regulations concerning contraband, which were contrary to all the precepts of international law, and by her action against all German nationals whom she could lay hands on, outraging not only every written law, but the very dictates of humanity.

The Chief of the General Staff was naturally not deaf to these persuasive representations. He agreed with them all the more readily, since they opened up a possibility of turning to account the valuable portion of Germany's forces, contained in the Navy, for the war on land, by preventing England from bringing her forces into play. However valuable might have been the protection of Germany's coast, which the Navy had accomplished so thoroughly, it had not fulfilled the hopes entertained for this arm in the event of war. Unfortunately they have remained unfulfilled for the whole of the war. The naval leaders, during the first two years of the war, adopted the standpoint that an offensive was only advisable under extraordinarily favourable circumstances, owing to the very great risk entailed by bringing out the German fleet for a decisive action against the infinitely superior naval forces of the enemy, particularly for the protection of our coasts. These circumstances were not forthcoming. The infection of the North Sea with mines, the comprehensive bases of operations for the enemy's fleet, their unenterprising caution, prevented them from coming to pass. An offensive with a view to forcing a decision had therefore to be abandoned.

As for the United States of America, G.H.Q.'s decision was mainly determined by the answer given to

November, 1914, to the Spring of 1915

the question, whether the advantage which might accrue to the general conduct of the war from the unrestricted submarine campaign could be balanced by the attitude by that predominating neutral, or not.

In the opinion of the naval staff, the result of the submarines was to render England incapable, within a period to be reckoned in months, of continuing the war on the Continent, in anything approaching the same manner as hitherto. If this proved correct, then an advantage of inestimable value would certainly be obtained. There was no better means than the failure of England for breaking the fighting spirit of all other members of the Entente. Even the danger of serious complications with America could not justify an abstention from the use of it.

If matters came to a breach, it was not to be assumed that America would make her influence felt in the war before the submarine campaign had taken effect. It was, however, not yet certain that matters would come to a breach. In face of the grave violations of international law by the Entente, the Government in Washington had restricted itself to protests, and, indeed, had said nothing when these protests remained unanswered. As things stood, it was not evident why it should adopt a different attitude to Germany's action, which, as a counter-measure, was incomparably more justifiable.

Public opinion in America, it is true, was for the greater part on the side of the Anglo-Saxons. The ever-growing association of America's economic interests with the welfare of the Entente threatened to gain a fateful importance. The heart-rending fact was already well-known that the Americans of German blood were exerting only a small and ever diminishing influence in favour of their old fatherland.

Critical Decisions at General Headquarters

Further, people were still convinced at the time that the Government of the United States seriously intended to remain neutral, and it was also credited with the strength of carrying out its intentions, all the more so as it was not expected that this Government, too, which could not be a stranger to the real whys and wherefores of the war, would fall a victim to the hypnotic power of the lying propaganda of the Entente.

The opening of the submarine campaign in the form mentioned above was accordingly decided upon.

CHAPTER V

THE BREAK-THROUGH AT GORLICE-TARNOW AND ITS CONSEQUENCES

THE DECISION TO ATTEMPT TO BREAK-THROUGH (SEE MAP 4)

THE general military situation, at the beginning of April, 1915, was summed-up as follows :
The serious attacks of the French and the English during recent weeks had left the German front in the West completely unshaken, in spite of their superior equipment in artillery and ammunition, which they owed to America's assistance, and in spite of their superiority in infantry, to the extent of 600 battalions. True, the French were obstinately continuing their offensive between the Meuse and the Moselle. Nor was the outcome definitely ascertainable as yet. But there was little reason to fear that the result would be of any more than local importance.

In the long struggle on the Western front, the French had proved themselves to be the more dangerous enemy, compared with the English. Yet it was known that their resources in men in their depots at home would not permit them to strengthen their formations at the front to any appreciable extent within the next few

Critical Decisions at General Headquarters

months. The reserves would probably at most suffice to replace the heavy losses they had suffered.

Conditions were much the same in this respect with the English, particularly when the fact was taken into account that they had evidently despatched strong forces to the Mediterranean. They certainly did not suffer from a shortage of men. On the other hand, however, they had difficulties with their recruiting, and still greater with the training of their men, owing to their lack of suitable officers and N.C.O.'s. On the assurance of the Navy, it was also permissible to hope that the submarine war would embarrass the English supply of men and *matériel*.

In any case, the English troops, in spite of undeniable bravery and endurance on the part of individuals, had proved to be so clumsy in action, that they could offer no prospect of accomplishing anything decisive against German troops for the immediate future.

The latter stood at a higher degree of efficiency in the West. Firmly confident in their leaders and in their positions, which were being strengthened from day to day, and supported by the consciousness of their moral superiority over the enemy, they looked forward to further attempts at a break-through with a feeling of security and self-confidence, undisturbed by the relative strengths of the armies. The greater part of fourteen new divisions, which, to be sure, represented no numerical increase, since they were composed of sections of formations already existing, had almost completed their concentration behind the front. The training of those which remained to be brought up was nearing completion.

Conditions on the German portion of the Eastern front, between the Baltic and the Pilitza, were not so favourable. This front, too, stood firm. But it had not been possible

The Break-through at Gorlice-Tarnow

to prepare army reserves, although the superiority of the enemy was not so great as in the West, and the Russians, as far as military value is concerned, were not even to be compared with either the English or the French. The new formation of five divisions desired by G.H.Q., on the lines of the method applied in the West, had not yet begun here. This was due to the fact that in many cases the troops in the East were composed of older categories, and that good fighting units were continually being detailed to our allies. Notwithstanding all this, it was assumed that the German front would be equal to any attack that might be made upon it by the Russians. Unfortunately, from the reports, it seemed to be equally certain that it would not be capable of proceeding on its own to any big undertaking, even within its limits, or of giving further support to its allies should necessity arise.

On the other hand the imminence of the latter eventuality had to be reckoned with, although the Austro-Hungarian front was already strongly reinforced with German contingents.*

On the Nida, in the region between the Pilitza and the Upper Vistula, General von Woyrsch's detachment, with Colonel Heye as his faithful Chief of Staff, was keeping watch with the 1st Austro-Hungarian Army. Between the Upper Vistula and the foot of the mountains, von Besser's division was inserted in the front occupied by the 4th Austro-Hungarian Army. In the Beskiden, the strong corps under von der Marwitz had just stiffened the wavering lines of the 3rd Austro-Hungarian Army. General von Linsingen's Southern Army was working slowly forward through the Car-

* See Appendix: Relative Strength of Forces on the Eastern Front, under 4 (c).

Critical Decisions at General Headquarters

pathians, east of Munkacs. The cavalry of Lieutenant-General Freiherr Marschall was taking an ample share in the burden of the fighting in the Bukovina.

However, the equilibrium, which was aimed at, had not only not been effected, but further Russian attempts to break through into Hungary were to be feared. The appeals of the allies for assistance, in constantly new forms, never ceased. To be sure the attentive observer was able to notice on the Russian side symptoms favourable to the Central Powers. The persistence of the enemy's offensives diminished from week to week. Even where successes were obtained, the attacker was no longer in a position to exploit them fully. The enormous losses which the Russians had suffered in their reckless attacks during the winter in the Carpathian mountains, could only be made good by bringing up ill-trained troops. Signs of an incipient shortage of arms and ammunition among them were reported in many cases. But even in this state they threatened the Austro-Hungarian front in a way which could not be borne for any length of time on account of the decreasing *moral* of certain sections of the allied troops. Symptoms of disintegration became more and more evident in formations of Czech and Southern Slav recruits. In these circumstances, there could be no question of concentrating reserves for special eventualities. The Austro-Hungarian G.H.Q., however, considered the concentration to be absolutely necessary, because it had arrived at the conviction that Italy and Rumania could not be prevented by any negotiations from entering the war at an early date, and that even Serbia was contemplating a new offensive action. In order to take precautionary measures against this, the Austro-Hungarian G.H.Q. demanded from the German more assistance

The Break-through at Gorlice-Tarnow

in the shape of ten additional German divisions. These were to be used in the Carpathians to relieve an equal number of Austro-Hungarian divisions. Of these latter, it was intended to concentrate seven on the Italian, and three on the Rumanian frontier. In addition the Austro-Hungarian G.H.Q. promised itself the advantage of the enemy front being shattered by an attack from East Prussia against the Russian right wing.

In Turkey, the exertions of the French and the English against the Dardanelles were constantly on the increase. The Turkish command defied them with admirable tenacity. Loyally supported by the personnel of the former German warships lying in Constantinople and General Liman von Sanders, the commander at the Dardanelles, it did all that was possible to supplement the weaknesses of Turkey's equipment. Of course the German G.H.Q. helped wherever and in any way it could. Everything that could be provided was sent by means of the very limited communications through Rumania, by the most various other ways, by the air and under the water. Unfortunately it was not much. It was not enough to cover Turkey's needs. It was to be assumed that a serious attempt at landing, such as was being prepared according to definite information, would be bound to succeed forthwith under the protection of the superior enemy artillery. What would happen then was shrouded in darkness. Upon one thing it was possible to depend absolutely: on the firm determination of the leading men in Turkey to defend every inch of Turkish soil and to continue the war even if Constantinople was to be lost. During the whole length of the war Enver Pasha never wavered for a moment in this heroic fidelity to the alliance. The fact that the basis for this was the unshakable conviction that this was the only way to maintain the Ottoman rule against the greed of Russia, England, France, Italy and Arabia, did not diminish its value for us.

It was impossible to prevent the situation in the Dardanelles making itself felt on the other Turkish fronts. At times the necessary reserves could not be sent thither. After the failure of the expedition against the Suez Canal, the Turkish troops had retired behind the Turkish frontier on the Sinai Peninsula. Even if the time of the year had permitted a repetition of this advance, which would have been urgently desired for the purpose of holding English troops, it would have been out of the question for the reasons given above.

Things were no better on the Mesopotamian front. The English were pressing forward along the rivers, and slowly but surely gaining ground towards Bagdad.

In Armenia there was a lull in the fighting. The Russians had not turned to account the advantage obtained by them during the winter. If they had attempted to do so, the Turkish troops which still remained there would not have been able to hold them in check. In short, a review of the military situation in Turkey presented no more satisfactory aspect than that of Austria-Hungary.

The moment had come when the decisive action in the East which had been contemplated for a whole month by G.H.Q. as an emergency measure, could be delayed no longer. But it was thought that a solution of the question was to be found by other means than those recommended by the leaders in the East and once more by the Austro-Hungarian G.H.Q.

The Break-through at Gorlice-Tarnow

The mere relieving of Austro-Hungarian forces in the Carpathians by Germans would have established those formations in process of development in a region that was highly unfavourable for a military advance, without offering any security that the Austro-Hungarian front would not be pierced by the enemy at some other rotten spot. It would have led once again to the consumption of German troops in the form of auxiliaries in Austro-Hungarian formations, which previous experience had proved to be altogether undesirable. The concentration meanwhile of the liberated Austro-Hungarian troops against Italy, Rumania, or Serbia, before any more definite conclusions were possible regarding the intentions and measures of the latter, meant a holding up of forces which the Central Powers could not afford—and still less since G.H.Q., according to information which had been received, did not believe that Rumania would soon come into the war, nor that Serbia was meditating an offensive, and could take it for granted that Italy would not proceed to open acts of hostility before the end of May. Even then, so clumsy was the mobilization in Italy that weeks must necessarily pass before her army would be capable of undertaking serious operations.

It was a question of turning to account for a decisive blow the time that would thus probably be gained in between. This could only consist in delivering a powerful offensive with all the means that could be made available to that end. An offensive in the form of a new edition of the operations against the Russian right wing facing East Prussia, offered no prospects of success. If the German forces which were just ready, were put against this wing of the enemy, then they would be missed in the Carpathians. Nor was there any prospect of any successes which would be gained on the frontier of East Prussia, making themselves really felt on the frontiers of Galicia and Hungary. And if these forces were put into the Carpathians, then there would not be sufficient resources left for operations from East Prussia. The object now desired by G.H.Q. could only be attained if the intended blow was so dealt, that it had in view the permanent crippling of Russia's offensive powers as its ultimate aim, but in the first place the freeing of the allies' front from the pressure upon it.

This could only be expected from a break-through, and not from operations against the Russian wings. Operations against the Russian right wing were prohibited by the reasons just mentioned, and they could not even be considered against the left wing, owing to the technical difficulties in their way—mountains, bad communication.

Thus the choice of the place of break-through was from the beginning limited to a few sections of the front. It could only fall either on the sector between the Pilitza and the Upper Vistula, or on that between the Upper Vistula and the foot of the Beskiden. The Chief of the General Staff decided in favour of the latter.

This allowed of a sharper concentration of the break-through troops. Their flanks were here exposed to considerably less danger of encirclement—in consequence of the restrictions imposed upon the movements of the Russian troops by the valley of the Vistula in the north, and the ridge of the Beskiden in the south—than is usually the case with break-throughs, and as would have been the case between the Pilitza and the Upper Vistula from the direction of Warsaw. The difficulties caused by the natural obstacles which had to be met in the event of any further progress of the operations in Western Galicia, the water-courses of the Wislok and the San—

The Break-through at Gorlice-Tarnow

were not to be compared with those of the passage of the Vistula. The Russians had just withdrawn such strong forces from Western Galicia for their Carpathian offensive that they were no longer able to replenish this front in time, even if they did perceive the danger which threatened it. We could hope with some certainty to appear at the decisive spot with undoubted superiority. There was even a probability that this favourable proportion could be preserved for some length of time, if the operations were conducted with energy. For swift lateral movements of the Russians from their attacking fronts, either in the Carpathians or the bend of the Vistula, were, as stated, not possible. They would always have to be preceded by inconvenient and extensive movements to the rear, which wasted time. Even if the break-through was only conditionally successful, it could be assumed that it would render the northern portion of the Russian Carpathian front untenable, and thereby give the allies the most valuable relief. In just the same way a serious shaking of the front at the bend of the Vistula lay, even in such an event, thoroughly within the bounds of possibility.

The good prospects of the operations as planned were still further improved by securing for the Germans the advantage of surprise and by delivering the thrust with great force.

THE DECISION IS CARRIED OUT : PREPARATIONS

Specially seasoned troops were therefore selected for the undertaking. They were provided as abundantly as was possible with artillery, even with the heaviest calibre, which had scarcely been used at all in the open

Critical Decisions at General Headquarters

field till then, with ammunition and trench-mortar batteries. Numerous officers who were intimately acquainted with the incisive modern methods of war on the Western front were detailed to them.

The work on the preparations proceeded with particular caution, in order to keep them secret. The consequent proposals were not even made known to the Austro-Hungarian G.H.Q. till about the middle of April, when the troops were already entrained at the stations and ammunition trains were moving towards Galicia. It was possible to proceed in this way, because the consent of the allies was certain, for they had just begun again to send repeated requests for German assistance on the front of the 4th Austro-Hungarian Army in Western Galicia and of the 2nd and 3rd Austro-Hungarian Armies in the mountain region south-east of Gorlice. The Austro-Hungarian G.H.Q. either intended to put these supports straightway into the positions of the 2nd Army, or use them for a relief offensive in the flank and rear of the Russian forces which were pressing the army in the mountains. These proposals could not be accepted as they would not have meant an effective piece of work. It was now pointed out to the Austro-Hungarian G.H.Q. that the break-through itself would be facilitated and its "harvest prospects" improved, the more the Russians entangled themselves previously in the mountains south of the front of attack. In this respect it was suggested that it would be an important advantage if the Austro-Hungarian lines in the sector in question could be withdrawn a short time before our offensive began, in order to induce the enemy to follow in as deeply as possible.

This suggestion was not acted upon. It was probably determined by the hesitation, intelligible in itself, to abandon voluntarily Hungarian soil. Further, the

The Break-through at Gorlice-Tarnow

notorious difficulty of getting troops who have once began a retiring movement to form front again, may have influenced matters. All the same, it is regrettable that this step was not taken. As circumstances developed later it might have led to quite an astounding success.*

The German transport was taken to Galicia by wide détours. Nobody knew his destination till shortly before arrival at the detraining station. Strict postal censorship was instituted.

In spite of all these arrangements the experience of the whole war confirmed itself in this instance, that preparations for big undertakings can never be wholly concealed from the enemy. It can only be hoped to

* The telegrams exchanged before the operations ran as follows:

"Mézières,
"April 13th, 1915.

"To GENERAL VON CONRAD, Teschen.

"Your Excellency knows that I do not consider advisable a repetition of the attempt to surround the Russian extreme (right) wing. It seems to me just as ill-advised to distribute any more German troops on the Carpathian front for the sole purpose of supporting it. On the other hand, I should like to submit the following plan of operations for your consideration, but I may add that, in view of its urgently necessary secrecy, I have not yet had it worked out by my own Staff.

"An army of at least eight German divisions will be got ready with strong artillery here in the West, and entrained for Muczyn–Grybow–Bochnia, to advance from about the line Gorlice–Gromnik in the general direction of Sanok. This army must be joined by Von Besser's division, which must be relieved in its position by Austro-Hungarian troops at the proper moment, and by one Austro-Hungarian cavalry division. This army and the 4th Austro-Hungarian Army would also be united in one command, and naturally a German one in this instance. If, during the concentration of the attacking forces, the 2nd and 3rd Austro-Hungarian Armies could give way step by step, drawing the enemy after them, to about the line Uczock–Perecseny–Homonna–Varanno–Zboro, such a movement would considerably increase and facilitate the success of the operations.

"I ask your Excellency to let me know as soon as possible your general attitude towards this scheme and the following questions:

"Is the area of operations perfectly accessible to troops with German

Critical Decisions at General Headquarters

delay their discovery for some time by means of suitable arrangements, and this in itself means such a big gain as to justify the severest measures against conscious treachery as well as unintentional disclosure. The Russians received intelligence of the concentration soon after the middle of April, but they did not realize its importance in time. It is possible that the movements arranged in other sectors of the front played some part in diverting attention.

Lively activity in the positions along the whole Western front, combined with attacks, in so far as the modest numbers remaining there permitted, were to cloak the transportation of the troops to Galicia. One such under-

means of transport? Would the Austro-Hungarian G.H.Q. be in a position to detail the usual waggon-trains to the German Army? What is the capacity of the railways from Rutka–Eperyes–Muczin and Rutka–Nowytarg and Sucha–Neusandec–Grybow, and, lastly, Cracow–Bochnia? Further arrangements would have to be made in a personal interview, for which purpose I might meet your Excellency in Berlin to-morrow afternoon, April 14th.

"Apart from the strictest secrecy there remains a further preliminary condition for the execution of the operations, and that is, that Italy is kept quiet by meeting her as far as possible, at least, until we have dealt the blow. It is indeed well known to your Excellency that no sacrifice seems to me too great if it keeps Italy out of the present war, etc.

"Von Falkenhayn."

"Teschen,
"April 13th, 1915.

"Excellency, General von Falkenhayn, Mézières.

"The operations proposed by your Excellency coincide with those that I have so long desired, but which were hitherto impossible, owing to a lack of sufficient forces. The use of the largest possible forces is necessary to ensure success. I shall arrive in Berlin to-morrow, April 14th, about 5 p.m., to discuss matters with you, and shall come to the War Ministry at 6.

"In reply to your questions, etc.

"General Conrad."

The Break-through at Gorlice-Tarnow

taking in the area of the 4th Army before Ypres developed into a serious attack because the gas weapon, which was used for the first time on a large scale, supplied the opportunity. Its surprise effect was very great. Unfortunately we were not in a position to exploit it to the full. The necessary reserves were not ready. The success achieved, however, was considerable. The English suffered heavy losses. The fact that the English relief offensive after the break-through at Gorlice–Tarnow did not last, was in some measure due to this.

A similar course of action was also prescribed for the German portion of the Eastern front. The Commander-in-Chief obeyed this by pushing forward against the enemy's right wing an army corps from his left wing on the northern frontier of East Prussia. It was the duty of the corps at the same time to act as a support for a larger, far-reaching cavalry sweep behind the Russian front. Such an operation around the Russian right wing near Kovno in a south-easterly direction, with the sole purpose of interrupting the enemy's lines of communication, had been suggested by G.H.Q., and the cavalry had been got ready, when the Russians concentrated their reserves in the Grodno district as a result of the winter battle in Masuria. The sweep was not then carried out, probably because the condition of the roads was against it. Its failure in the present instance was due to the fact that the enemy had changed his position in the meantime. He had once more disposed serviceable forces in order of echelon behind his flank. Partly to blame may also have been the fact that the cavalry did not advance in mass, but distributed itself over the space between the Niemen and the Baltic Coast. The German thrust reached Shavli, and cavalry patrols even swept up to the Aa ; with the help of the fleet Libau was occu-

Critical Decisions at General Headquarters

pied. Soon, however, a reaction set in. Shavli had to be evacuated again. It was only with difficulty, after reinforcements had been brought up, that the Dubissa sector was maintained and the cavalry kept on the Windau. Yet the main purpose—the distraction of Russia's attention from Galicia and the pinning down of the forces on the Russian right wing, was achieved. It is true that in return for this the disadvantage of tying up considerable German forces in a new direction had to be accepted into the bargain. And a resumption of relations with the Baltic populations of German origin subsequently caused strategic considerations in this locality to be influenced to an undesirable extent by sentimental values. Both circumstances proved to be most disadvantageous later on.

THE BREAK-THROUGH

The Galician operations for the break-through began on May 2nd, under the leadership of General von Mackensen, with Colonel von Seeckt as his Chief of Staff. Under him were placed the 11th German Army, consisting of eight German and two Austro-Hungarian divisions of infantry, as well as one Austro-Hungarian division of cavalry, and the 4th Austro-Hungarian Army, composed of five Austro-Hungarian divisions of infantry, one Austro-Hungarian division of cavalry, and one German infantry division. Its first objective was to break through the Russian front on a general line from Gorlice to Gromnik in order to make the enemy's position untenable as far as the Lupkow Pass. This limitation was considered advisable in the first place. It was to prevent any possibility of the Austro-Hungarian G.H.Q.

The Break-through at Gorlice-Tarnow

deducing from the agreement permanent claims for the maintenance of such strong German forces on its front.

The break-through succeeded along the whole line of the 11th Army, and along a part of the front of the 4th Austro-Hungarian Army. The Russians showed themselves unequal to the heavy fire which was severely concentrated on the points to be breached. The troops, freed from the fetters of trench warfare, swept the unwieldy enemy before them in the exuberant joy of the attack.

As early as May 4th there was no longer any doubt in the German G.H.Q., which had removed to Pless on the Eastern front, that the enemy could not succeed within an appreciable time in bringing the offensive to a standstill, if we were able to keep up the impetus of the forward movement. So that nothing would be neglected in this direction the transference of another division from the West was arranged, although symptoms of a relief offensive on a grand scale were becoming evident there.

It was begun on May 9th by the English at Loos, south-west of Lille, and by the French on the Loretto Heights, north-east of Arras, mainly in the sector of the 6th Army, therefore. The powers of resistance of the Germans were put to a hard test by this offensive, and still more the strength of nerve of the leaders, as always in big defensive battles, the local commanders no less than G.H.Q. Nevertheless, all previous calculations proved to be correct. After the situation had hung gravely in the balance for one day, owing to the numerical superiority of the enemy, it was completely restored by throwing in the German reserves, which were naturally very scanty. Then the old, hopeless struggle for positions set in once more. It was dragged out by the enemy with heavy losses until the middle of June. Of course there were losses to be lamented on the German side also. In proportion to far greater damage inflicted upon the enemy, however, they were bearable, and indeed all the more since the repeated successful repulse of enormously superior numbers gave the troops a very welcome increase of proud self-confidence.

Similarly with the idea of not depriving the breakthrough in Galicia of any of its force, requests from the Austro-Hungarian G.H.Q. for the employment of German forces elsewhere were refused in the middle of May. These requests were actuated by the desire to support the Austro-Hungarian Army in the Bukovina, which was being strongly attacked by the Russians, or to crush the Russian front in the bend of the Vistula. But German G.H.Q. adhered to its opinion that every available man must be employed to extend and deepen the breach once it was made. As regards Russia it seemed of less consequence than usual merely to gain ground. The essential thing was to smash the enemy's fighting machine. This could be done nowhere better and more swiftly than in the breach where the enemy was forced to give battle on unprepared terrain, if he did not want to run the danger of upsetting his system of defence along the whole front. In addition to this, the creation of new places at which to exert pressure would cost time, none of which, however, could be lost.

As had been feared, the English set foot on the Gallipoli Peninsula on April 25th. Italy's entry into the ranks of the enemy became daily more probable. Nobody could foresee how the situation would develop, as a result of these events, and whether it would not force us very soon to adopt special measures. As the forces required for these could only be taken in the bulk from the Galician attacking group, if the fronts which were already at full tension were not to be too over-strained

The Break-through at Gorlice-Tarnow

at some other place, the movement of this group would certainly come to a standstill. In any case it was doubtful whether any timely advantage would be gained at any of the places of attack which were now proposed. It was not to be forgotten that the Russians had almost everywhere far better communications at their service than the Central Powers. In short, any relaxation of the main operations was the equivalent of the action of the man who lets go the bird in his hand to catch the two in the bush.

The question has been discussed here in some detail, because it often cropped up again in the most varied forms during the long war. Again and again there were local commanders who maintained that they had discovered a sure way of striking a more or less serious, indeed decisive blow—if only the necessary means were placed at their disposal. Now it was four, now twenty or more divisions, of course with the corresponding heavy artillery and ammunition, which were to suffice. But unfortunately the advisers usually forgot two very important facts. These escaped them because they were only perceptible from the centre and not from the circumference.

In the first place, they, as sectional commanders, did not feel the enormous pressure under which German power had permanently to labour. They therefore over-estimated the forces which were at the disposal of G.H.Q. for special purposes.

Then they overlooked the fact that the Central Powers were in many respects in a far more perilous situation than even the defender of a fortress besieged by a superior force. No sortie, however brilliantly accomplished, could save them from ultimate ruin if the enemy forced his way into the inner works through a place where the defence had been weakened in order to strengthen the sortie. For then the enemy would be able to strike them in their vital parts before they could win a decision in the outer lines. They could not leave the citadel in the lurch, like the defender of the fortress in a case of extreme necessity, to save the garrison by breaking through the enemy's lines.

THE CONSEQUENCES OF THE BREAK-THROUGH

The operation of the break-through in Galicia produced astonishingly big results. The enemy suffered the most serious and bloody losses. The amount of the booty speedily rose to improbable heights.

On May 6th the Russians were already in full retreat, which frequently degenerated into a rout, along the whole front of the 3rd Austro-Hungarian, the 11th and the 4th Austro-Hungarian Armies, *i.e.*, on a front more than one hundred miles wide between the ridge of the Beskiden and the Upper Vistula. A few days later their neighbouring sectors also gave way : in the south as far as the left wing of the Southern Army astride the Munkacs–Stryj road, in the north on the front of the first Austro-Hungarian Army as well as of Woyrsch's detachment as far as the Pilitza.

The allied G.H.Q.'s therefore felt themselves called upon to set new and further objectives for the " spearhead " group and the adjoining armies. They were ordered to keep in close touch with the enemy north of the Upper Vistula, and south of the Vistula to reach the line of the San, Wisznia and Dniester as swiftly as possible. Further orders would not be issued until a firm hold was obtained upon these strong sectors. The

The Break-through at Gorlice-Tarnow

reason for this advance by stages was the consideration due to Italy's attitude.

These intentions were adhered to, however, when it became evident in the middle of May that only a few days remained before our former ally would formally secede to the enemy. The armies on the wings, which were unfortunately still hanging back, were urged to do their utmost to reach their objectives as speedily as possible. The 11th Army, which had reached its goal, was ordered to assist its neighbours.

DECISIONS ON ITALY COMING INTO THE WAR*

Although there was complete unanimity on these points between the two G.H.Q.'s, there were differences of opinion between them as to the measures to be taken with regard to Italy.

The Austro-Hungarian G.H.Q. cherished the intelligible desire to punish with a firm hand and as speedily as possible the renegade ally, whose action was bound to make itself felt first on the body of the Dual Monarchy. It saw, at any rate, that this would be by no means possible on the frontier, although it considered that a blow there was most to be desired. This was excluded by the nature of the ground, just as much as by the shortness of time and the lack of available forces. The Austro-Hungarian G.H.Q. therefore proposed to concentrate forces in the valleys of Villach–Klagenfurt, and of Laibach, with the object of taking the enemy, who were pushing forward along the narrow mountain roads, by surprise, as he debouched into these valleys.

This would have been conditional on the Italians stepping into the trap which had been laid for them.

* See Fig. 3.

Critical Decisions at General Headquarters

If they had not done so, but had merely turned the tables on the Central Powers, the latter would have had to step into a trap, and probably without regard to time and circumstances. For they were not in a

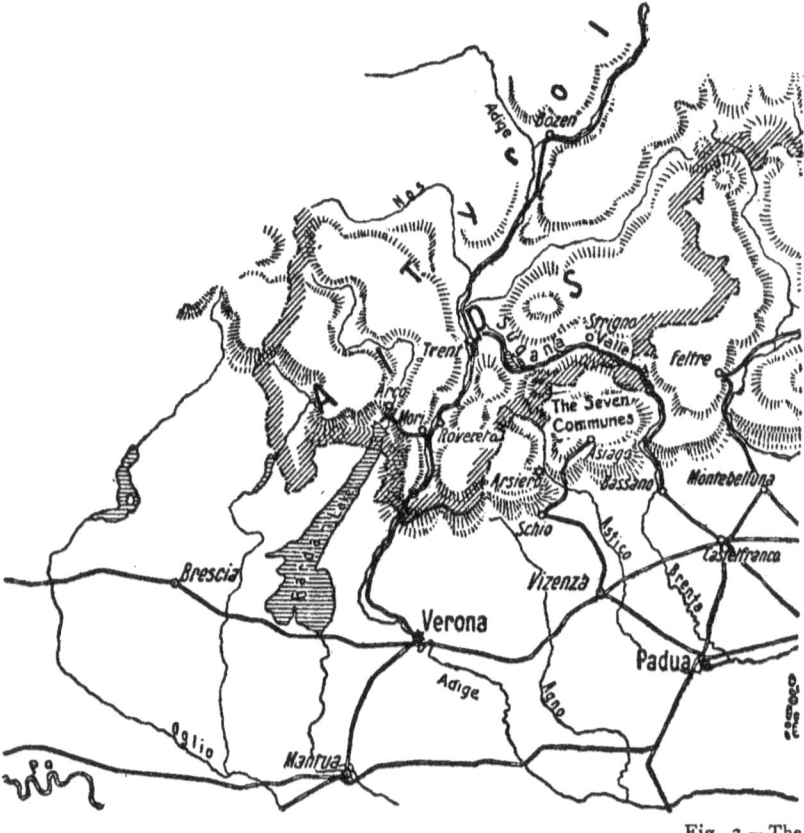

Fig. 3.—The

position to allow the formations which had once been concentrated to stand about waiting for an unlimited time. These reasons induced the Chief of the General Staff to reject the proposal of the allies. It was just as impossible owing to the fact that if it had been accepted, the continuation of the operations against the Russians

The Break-through at Gorlice-Tarnow

would have had to have been abandoned. It would have too seriously weakened the forces required for this campaign. It would have been more acceptable if it had been possible to use those troops intended for

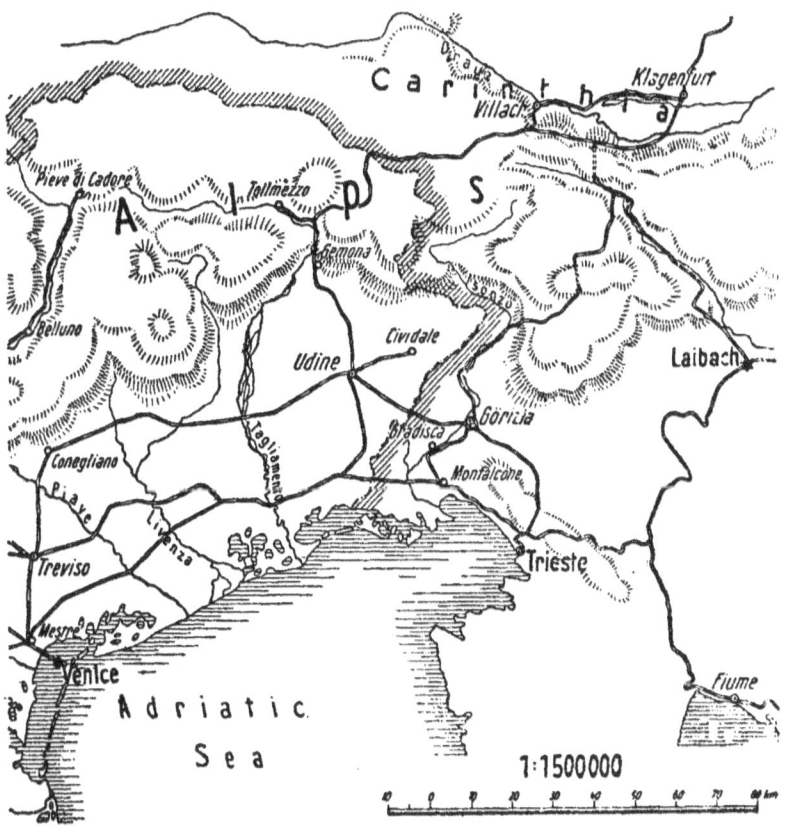

Italian Theatre.

operations against Italy for a swift blow at Serbia first, in order at least to open the way to the East before entering upon new undertakings. As a matter of fact, this question was also seriously examined. It had to be dropped, however, because Bulgaria resolutely refused to join in at this moment. In view of the fact

Critical Decisions at General Headquarters

that the Galician operations had begun to drag at that time, and in view of Italy's secession and the complications with America on the question of the submarine campaign, she could scarcely be blamed for doing so. But without her co-operation there was too much danger that the thrust into Serbia might only result in tying up valuable forces which perhaps were indispensable elsewhere, without achieving its desired purpose quickly enough. The adoption of a watching attitude in the mountain valleys would probably have resulted in nothing decisive being done against Russia, Serbia and Italy, whilst waiting to see what the enemy would do next. Such a development did not correspond to the intentions which determined the break-through at Gorlice-Tarnow.

On the peremptory advice of Germany it was therefore decided to carry on a purely defensive war against Italy for the present. Whatever the Italians might do, the operations against the Russians were to be continued with all energy until the offensive powers of Russia were crippled for an appreciable time. Mindful of the difficulties which had been encountered in the Carpathians and the Vosges, the Central Powers proposed to win back from their new enemy the mountain districts which had fallen into his hands, and not to abandon voluntarily any territory belonging to the Dual Monarchy, but to advance the line of defence as far as the Isonzo. Owing to the nature of the ground in this area, those considerable Austro-Hungarian forces which were already stationed near the Italian frontier, together with five divisions on the way from Syrmia and the two Austro-Hungarian divisions to be taken from Galicia, appeared to be enough for the defence. These latter were ultimately to spare after the losses of the German forces in Galicia had been repaired.

The Break-through at Gorlice-Tarnow

From Germany a division of troops specially trained for mountain warfare, the so-called Alpine Corps, was sent to the Tyrol, and a number of heavy batteries were detailed for the Isonzo. Three of the German divisions which had just been formed on the Eastern front went to Syrmia to relieve the five Austro-Hungarian divisions taken from there. They were to complete their establishment on the Save and the Danube, and fulfil at the same time the duty of a protection for the flank and the rear of the Isonzo front against Serbia, as well as that of a reserve for any eventuality, chiefly with an eye on Rumania. Their presence also served the important purpose of keeping down the agitation which was to be expected among the Southern Slavs on Italy's declaration of war. This, too, succeeded completely.

On May 24th Italy declared war, but only on Austria-Hungary, not on Germany. Both the political as well as the military leaders of the Central Powers had erred in their hopes of preventing this occurrence, the former by meeting Italy's demands, and the latter by victories over the Russians. This supports the fact that there was no other means at all of keeping Italy from coming into the war on the side of the Entente, apart from a totally different Austro-Hungarian policy during many years before the war, or an uninterrupted series of victories by the Central Powers. The really authoritative Italian circles, although they did not come into power until the war, had indeed been ready to break off in 1902, and had definitely decided to do so after the Austrian misfortunes against the Russians and the Serbs. The fact that Italy hesitated, however, until May, 1915, was influenced by the necessity of making this decision palatable to the masses of the people and

Critical Decisions at General Headquarters

to the army. The chivalrous sentiments existing in the hearts of Italians rebelled against the secession. But German diplomacy, under the leadership of the former Chancellor von Bülow, also deserves great credit. Every day by which its activities delayed Italy's change of front was, as has already been pointed out, of inestimable value. This cannot be denied by anybody who has visualized the situation which would have supervened if Italy had struck before the Galician breakthrough, or at the time of the heavy battles of the Carpathians, or at the moment when German reserves were exhausted after the Masurian battle, or during the serious defeat of the Austro-Hungarians in Serbia in December, 1914.

Germany's first response to the challenge levelled by Italy at Austria-Hungary would have been a declaration of war. Yet the Chief of the General Staff considered that this was not immediately advisable. He also clung firmly to his standpoint, which for the rest coincided with that of the political leaders, in spite of the urgent solicitations of the Austro-Hungarian G.H.Q. to the contrary.

It had formally been made known to Italy some time before, that wherever she might turn against Austria-Hungary, she would find the latter shoulder to shoulder with her German ally. In actual fact, Germany always acted in accordance with this. If this state of things had been supplemented by a solemn declaration of war, it was certain that the charge of being the aggressor would once more have been raised against Germany. This did happen at the beginning of the war as a result of the justifiable, but over-hasty and unnecessary, declarations of war on Russia and France. It was not desirable to repeat that process, still less in this instance,

The Break-through at Gorlice-Tarnow

since certain apparently well-founded information had it that Rumania was to be kept to the fulfilment of the obligations of her alliance with Italy, immediately the latter was attacked by Germany. Moreover, there were political and economic reasons for avoiding as long as possible the legitimate consequences of a declaration of war. It would have been very ill-advised to break off voluntarily the communications with the outside world, which were maintained through the medium of Italy. It could not be denied that this procedure might give the appearance of a lack of harmony in the actions of the Central Powers. As far as is known, it did not give rise to evil consequences. The situation was so transparent that it found sympathy in the Dual Monarchy also.

Italy's entry into the circle of our enemies was received with astonishing indifference by public opinion in the Central Powers, far more than Rumania's secession, for example. Yet there is no doubt that the latter event created incomparably less danger than the former.

Public opinion was excellently prepared by the Press for Italy's secession. Nobody was really surprised. Rumania's was handled less skilfully. The Italian declaration of war happened at a time when feeling was running high, both in Germany and in Austria-Hungary, as a result of the course of the campaign in Galicia, as well as the almost more brilliant defensive battles in the West. Rumania's took place during a period of depression which was explained, even if it was not fully justified, by the lack of any tangible results on the French battlefields and the wholly unexpected successes of Brussiloff's offensive. The powers of the Italian Army were put at a low estimate. It was generally assumed that the successors of Radetzky

Critical Decisions at General Headquarters

would cope with any number of such enemies. This optimistic verdict proved to be correct in many respects. It is not maligning the Italians to describe their achievements, from the purely military standpoint, as extraordinarily small. Yet their intervention was of great importance in the issue of the war.

The political structure of the Dual Monarchy proved unequal to the demands of a serious war on two fronts. This led to Austria-Hungary making increased demands upon Germany, which it was uncommonly difficult for the latter to fulfil, and considerably weakened her staying powers.

There was the almost greater danger that the Austro-Hungarian G.H.Q. could not take up the necessary impartial attitude towards events on the two fronts. The long-smouldering indignation regarding the renegade ally burst into fierce flames all over the Danubian Empire. This had one advantage in that this just anger increased considerably the powers of resistance of the Austro-Hungarian troops employed on the Italian front. It had its great dangers, however, because it caused the Austro-Hungarian Command to give the requirements of this front a certain precedence over those of the others. This tendency may have been influenced, though more unconsciously, by the conviction that Germany would be compelled to counteract with her own forces reverses on the other fronts before those on the Italian.

The hopes placed in the defensive strength of the mountainous territory on the Austro-Hungarian and Italian frontier were altogether fulfilled. Anticipating events, it may be stated in this context that the attacker was unable to gain any notable advantages, in spite of his great numerical superiority both in personnel and

The Break-through at Gorlice-Tarnow

matériel, until well after the winter of 1915–16. After what has been said, there is no need to explain any further that the fighting on this front made itself acutely felt in the other theatres of war where Austro-Hungarian troops were engaged. Its effects on the development of the situation, which was now and again unfavourable, on the Galician and South Polish front at the end of May, 1915, must be left undetermined.

DECISION TO CONTINUE THE OPERATIONS IN GALICIA ACROSS THE SAN SECTOR

The Russians had not continued their retreat across the river in front of Woyrsch's Detachment and the 1st Austro-Hungarian Army in the bend of the Vistula, south of the Pilitza, but had established a front again on the left bank. The weak forces of the allies there were not sufficient to eject them from their positions.

On the right of the Upper Vistula, in Galicia, new circumstances had arisen owing to the arrival of very considerable Russian forces. The reinforcements consisted for the greater part of the formations of the Odessa group, which had originally been concentrated for a move against Turkey. The lesser part of them was taken from the fronts north of the Narew and in front of Warsaw. The 4th Austro-Hungarian Army had only reached the Lower San with its right wing, where it was supported by the 11th Army, but it was only just holding its own against Russian counter-attacks. Symptoms of disintegration in some of its units could not be overlooked.

Assistance had also to be given by the 11th Army to its southern neighbour, the 3rd Austro-Hungarian

Critical Decisions at General Headquarters

Army, which was attacking Przemysl. Consequently it did not look as if the 11th Army would be able to continue the offensive on its own initiative. It is true that the Russian attacks directed against it broke down everywhere with the heaviest losses for the attackers.

In spite of the assistance given to it, the 3rd Austro-Hungarian Army made just as little satisfactory progress as the adjoining 2nd Austro-Hungarian Army, the Austro-Hungarian Detachment under Szurmay and the Southern Army.

In the Bukovina the 7th Austro-Hungarian Army was engaged in heavy fighting, in which the Russians mostly had the advantage.

Along the whole front of attack, therefore, the operations threatened to come to a standstill. The certain deduction would have been either that almost the whole of the German forces engaged would have to be left there, or heavy reverses reckoned with. The first event would have meant the crippling of the German plan of campaign, and the second would have offered the prospect with great probability of a collapse of Austria-Hungary at no distant date.

The only effective weapon against such dangers seemed to G.H.Q. to consist in bringing up sufficient fresh German forces to Galicia. It accordingly arranged for this to be done to the largest extent that was still possible, after it had once more ascertained whether they could have been used to a greater advantage at any other part of the Eastern front. This idea proved to be impracticable at that moment. A speedier and greater success was nowhere to be expected than by continuing the offensive on the present front of attack with all energy. No speedier, because preparations at any other point would have caused a very considerable

The Break-through at Gorlice-Tarnow

loss of time; and no greater, because the strategic envelopment of the Russian armies effected in Galicia by the advance of the former Carpathian front of the allies offered prospects which existed nowhere else. This was particularly the case on the German northern wing. In response to inquiries, the Commander-in-Chief in the East reported that even if two army corps were brought from the West, it would only be possible to achieve big tactical successes in his area. This number of reinforcements could not, however, be spared in the West. In addition to this, G.H.Q. could not regard tactical successes as an end in themselves. Only those were of any value which brought us nearer to the final end, the securing of a good peace. Added to all this, there was the decisive factor that success seemed nearer in Galicia than anywhere else.

The enemy had gradually brought up very great masses of troops there. But they were not put into the front in mass, but in relays, and were so scattered, that the superiority was not very much greater than on other sections of the front. The value of the Russian troops in Galicia had certainly sunk below their ordinary level. Moreover, their movements were extraordinarily restricted by the disposition of the masses, and by the great confusion which prevailed along the rear lines of communication. Apart from the works around the fortress of Przemysl, they had no properly constructed positions at their disposal.

Finally, when it was remembered that the capture of Lemberg, of which there was an immediate likelihood if the offensive in Galicia was continued, would create a disastrous impression for the Russians throughout the whole East as things stood, the decision was made.

The offensive in Galicia was to be continued. Every

battalion that could be spared by any means on the German fronts was again brought up. Austria-Hungary was unfortunately not able to contribute any.

Two and a half divisions were transferred from the Western front. This reduced the army reserves there to a scarcely bearable minimum. It was thought that the danger might be borne for some time, since the relief offensives had hitherto been broken so brilliantly by the admirable behaviour of the troops. The actual German front in the East had to supply two divisions, one from the 9th Army, which stood before Warsaw, and the other from the new formations. The transference was possible without any particular difficulty. Although the Russians had withdrawn forces from this sector for Galicia, they still had a numerical superiority there. But they had been obliged to send such large quantities of *matériel* and ammunition to the broken part of the front, that an offensive of any promise on their part in the north was no longer to be feared.

Lastly, preparations were made for the transport of two of the German divisions which had completed their establishment in Syrmia. They could be spared from there. The danger which threatened from Serbia, Rumania, and a possible Southern Slav movement, could be regarded as past after the blow which had been dealt at Russia, and so long as Italy did not make any dangerous progress, which was not probable in the near future. The other German divisions were left on the Save and the Danube, so that a reliable fighting force would be available in that district for any emergency. It was also necessary for the purpose of giving assistance in the reconnaissances and general preliminaries for a passage of these rivers, that had now been in progress for some time.

The Break-through at Gorlice-Tarnow

The success attempted by bringing up these fresh forces was achieved, although the encircling movement did not take place owing to the failure of a portion of the Carpathian wing. After the Russians had previously evacuated Przemysl, as soon as some of its forts were stormed by German troops, they were thrown back by the help of these reinforcements from position to position in quick succession with the heaviest losses. The southern portion in Eastern Galicia of the whole Russian front broke away completely from the northern. For a time there was a broad empty space in Volhynia. The break-through was accomplished. On June 22nd Lemberg fell.

CHAPTER VI

OPERATIONS AGAINST RUSSIA IN THE SUMMER AND AUTUMN OF 1915. BEGINNING OF THE UNRESTRICTED SUBMARINE CAMPAIGN

THE DIRECTION OF ATTACK CHANGED FROM EAST TO NORTH (SEE MAP 4)

THE events which were crowned by the reoccupation of Lemberg on June 22nd, 1915, meant a great deal to the cause of the Central Powers. The threat to Hungary had been completely removed; Austria-Hungary was given the possibility of sending sufficient forces to the Italian front; Turkey was relieved from the danger of an attack upon the Bosphorus by the Russian Odessa Army; these and the pacification of Rumania and the resumption of connections with Bulgaria were the immediate and highly valuable consequences. But enough had not yet been achieved.

The enemy was able almost to repair his losses, which were fixed at far more than half a million, from his practically inexhaustible human resources. The value of the troops had, it is true, sunk still further. It was not possible really to replace the losses by half or wholly untrained troops, or by officers who lacked the first conditions for the fulfilment of their duties. Even

Operations against Russia in 1915

if the Russian supply of war material had improved, it was still evidently far from being satisfactory.

As later events proved, the assumption that German troops would not have much to fear from this opponent for an appreciable time, was correct.

Unfortunately the same could not be said with regard to those Austro-Hungarian troops who were not of German or of Hungarian origin. Their value had sunk in a similar degree to that of the Russians, but for quite different reasons. Whether many sections of them would be able to weather an attack by the enemy without German assistance seemed particularly doubtful in view of the fact that they were not occupying constructed positions. This fact was all the more dangerous, as the Russians, who knew our weakness very well, kept in contact with the allies along the whole front from the Rumanian frontier to the Pilitza, and had brought up to this front considerable reinforcements from formations which were still unbroken, partly, as already stated, from Odessa, and partly from the Warsaw and Narew sectors. The main body of the Russians was disposed between the Vistula and the Bug in front of the 4th Austro-Hungarian Army, whose composition has already been discussed, and in front of those sections of the German 11th Army which had wheeled northwards.

In these circumstances it was clear that any breaking off of the operations in the East was out of the question.

On the other hand, there were important reasons for not continuing them in a way which would have favoured their unlimited expansion, quite apart from the fact that such a proceeding would have been in sharp contrast to G.H.Q.'s views on the conduct of the war in general.

Critical Decisions at General Headquarters

Thanks to the tenacity of the Turks, the enemy had not yet made any important progress at the Dardanelles, where the appearance of German submarines in the Mediterranean had exercised a beneficent influence. Yet the English had procured for themselves a firm footing on Gallipoli from which a further advance seemed comparatively easy. It was considered certain that they were planning a forward movement. It was reported that considerable reinforcements were being transported to the Mediterranean. Meanwhile the situation in Turkey as regards *matériel* was getting visibly worse, in spite of all efforts to improve it. Not only was it a necessity for the plan of campaign, but we were also in honour bound to open the way to the East as swiftly as was possible, in order to bring succour to this brave ally.

One possibility of doing this appeared in consequence of the resumption of communications with Bulgaria. Although a swift and thorough success against Serbia would be uncertain with a one-sided frontal attack by the Central Powers, it could be confidently expected with the co-operation of the Bulgarians on the flank. But at the time it could not be foreseen with any definiteness if and when matters would come to mutual operations with them. Owing to the rather wavering attitude of the leading politicians in Sofia, care had to be taken not to station on some other front the forces required for co-operation with Bulgaria, lest any opportunity should be missed of turning to account any favourable change in their feelings. It was believed, at any rate, that things should be kept in readiness for September at the latest. The probability was that the Bulgarians, who were mostly engaged in agriculture, would not consent to any military undertaking before the end of the harvest,

Operations against Russia in 1915

which fell in this month. Against this there was the necessity of beginning operations without any longer delay, because the bad weather which usually sets in about November in Serbia—Danubian storms, rain, which renders the few unmetalled roads impassable—threatened to offer serious hindrances otherwise.

On this occasion it was considered whether it would be advisable to seek the way to the East through Rumania instead of through Serbia. The idea had to be rejected, although its advantages were obvious: the liberation of Austria-Hungary from anxiety concerning Rumania, and the gain of a rich corn country. But the disadvantages were greater. According to the opinion of the German political leaders there was no hope of inducing Rumania to join the Central Powers in any way. Like Serbia, therefore, she had to be conquered, if the road to the East was to be made free. This fact alone did not put the undertaking in a desirable light. It was not advisable to give Germany another open enemy, except under the stress of necessity, still less since Rumania's attitude towards the Central Powers had become much more favourable after Gorlice-Tarnow.

The situation on the Western front also influenced the decision which had to be made. After the relief-offensive had died down in the first half of June, there had been no big actions there. The shortage of reserves on the German side had made the tension become so acute that the restoration of four divisions from Galicia to the Western front was deemed necessary. Any withdrawal of troops from another part of the Eastern front would not have been feasible, partly because the various formations could not now be spared from their respective sectors, and partly because experience had

Critical Decisions at General Headquarters

proved that troops which had hitherto fought only in the East were not equal to the far more serious effects of Western fighting until after a lengthy period of acclimatization. However, some speedy relief seemed to be necessary.

In addition to this, it could already be foreseen that further very considerable reinforcements would have to be sent from the East to the West in the first half of September at the latest. There was definite intelligence of extensive preparations on the part of the French for a new offensive which was to force a decision. This was to be expected in Champagne. Although photographic observations showed that the preliminaries had only just been begun, the certain conclusion was that it would start not later than September. Only thus could the enemy hope to obtain any result before the beginning of the bad season of the year.

All these reflections determined G.H.Q. to continue the operations on the Eastern front with a limited objective.

This required, at all events, a distinct change of direction. Hitherto the main pressure of the offensive had consisted in an advance from west to east. If this was persisted in, then it was possible to capture further ground from the enemy, but it was scarcely possible to inflict any real damage upon him in the broad plains of Volhynia and Podolia in the short time which was still available. He had withdrawn thither, *i.e.*, into the front stretching from Khotin on the Dniester through Halicsz up to Sokal on the Bug, comparatively weak forces not much greater in numbers than those sections of the Allied armies opposing them, but they possessed unlimited possibilities for retirement. His strong forces, on the other hand, stood in the area between the Bug

Operations against Russia in 1915

and the Vistula, behind the Solokiya and Tanev depressions. From thence they flanked most effectively any advance eastwards. This would have possessed all the disadvantages of an excentric movement. It was therefore decided to exert the main pressure from now onwards in a northerly direction in the area between the Bug and the Vistula. The hopes placed in such a movement are explained by a glance at the accompanying map.

The 4th Austro-Hungarian and the 11th Armies received orders to hold themselves ready until the middle of July, fronting northwards. Before then the 11th Army was to be reinforced by the German division which was still in Syrmia, the three divisions of the German Beskiden Corps, which had been fighting hitherto on the left wing of the 2nd Austro-Hungarian Army, and a German cavalry division from Belgium. In addition, two of the divisions which had been withdrawn in order to be sent back to France were transferred to this army a few days later. A temporary lull which had set in on the Western front made this feasible. As these reinforcements had made the 11th Army too big for a single command, the Bug Army was formed from it and placed on its right wing, under General von Linsingen. His command of the Southern Army was taken over by General Count von Bothmer, Lieut.-Colonel Hemmer becoming Chief of Staff.

In order to protect the right flank of this powerful attacking group against strong concentrations of Russian troops in the neighbourhood of Vladimir Volynsk, it was decided to transfer the three divisions of the first Austro-Hungarian Army from the district north of the Upper Vistula to the right wing of the Bug Army near Sokal, from whence it was to advance on Vladimir Volynsk. The Germans did not assume, it is true, that these divisions would make much progress there. As the army could not be given more than two German divisions from the right wing of the Bug Army for this undertaking, it lacked the attacking force required for a far-reaching success, which did not, however, lie within the scope of its task. Moreover, from all that was known of the nature of the terrain on the other side of the Bug, it was to be feared that the further course of the operations would meet with insurmountable obstacles.

This fact had also influenced the choice of the direction in which it was intended to place the centre of gravity of our attack. The existing maps and descriptions of the Pripet Marshes and their southern ramifications made them appear unsuited for the movement of large parties of troops. As a matter of fact this fear was confirmed, in so far as the operations of the 1st Austro-Hungarian Army was concerned. Later we discovered that the maps and descriptions, as well as recent reconnaissances, were either out of date or had exaggerated the difficulties. The great works which had been carried out during the years before the war for the improvement of conditions in the swamp area before the coming of the floods, had lowered the water-level so much that in such dry summers as that of 1915, the only real obstacles in this district were the watercourses. It would even have been quite possible to operate with large formations of troops, if the difficulties of transport could have been overcome. These existed in abundance owing to the total lack of railways and metalled roads.

Whilst the storming group was preparing for the advance, it was important to prevent the enemy from bringing up reinforcements against it from other sectors of the front.

This was comparatively simple in the south. It was

Operations against Russia in 1915

to be expected that the execution of the order given for this purpose to the 2nd Austro-Hungarian and the Southern Armies, to work their way forward against the Zlota Lipa in the area bounded by the Dniester, would be sufficient. The proportion of the forces on this front was so favourable to the allies, that the Russians dare not venture to withdraw any forces of any note in the face of such pressure. The 7th Austro-Hungarian Army was not to take part in the forward movement of its neighbours for the moment, as it had to reorganize. It received orders to station itself on the Dniester on the enemy's flank.

The problem was more difficult in the bend of the Vistula south of the Pilitza. The proposed transference of the 1st Austro-Hungarian Army was bound to lead to a considerable weakening there. An enterprising opponent would have been able to turn this to account. But the Russians were not credited with the necessary strength of determination to decide on a counter-stroke this side of the river, with the big offensive beginning on the right of the Vistula, nor did a sober estimate of time and place promise such a move any great prospect of success. It could make matters uncomfortable for the Germans, but not dangerous. Yet it seemed advisable to conceal as far as possible the removal of the 1st Austro-Hungarian Army. It was therefore ordered to break through the Russian positions south of the Kamienna in the direction of Tarlow with a swift thrust just before its removal. Woyrsch's Detachment was to take over the vacated sector, and by concentrating its main forces against one section of the Russian front, and leaving only scattered outposts in front of the others, to attempt to do the enemy some harm and to prevent him from withdrawing unscathed.

Critical Decisions at General Headquarters

The solution of the problem of binding the enemy offered still greater difficulties to the really German portion of the Eastern front, that from the Pilitza to the Baltic, under the command of the Commander-in-Chief in the East.

FORMATION OF THE NAREW ATTACKING GROUP, GALLWITZ' ARMY DETACHMENT, FIRST HALF OF JULY, 1915 (SEE MAP 4)

This portion of the front had not been idle during the month of June. Only the 8th Army—General Otto von Below; Chief of Staff, Major-General von Böckmann—whose area extended from the Schkwa to the Lyck, had not been able to take part, owing to the unfavourable terrain in front of it. On the other hand, the 9th Army —Field-Marshal Prince Leopold of Bavaria; Chief of Staff, Major-General Grünert—between the Pilitza and the Vistula, below Novo-Georgievsk, as well as Gallwitz' Army, extending on the right of the Vistula to the Schkwa, had tried to hold the enemy by means of lively demonstrations. Operations of any importance, however, had only been undertaken by the 10th Army, which stood on the left of the 8th Army as far as the Niemen below Kovno, and by the Niemen Army. These were to assist the operations begun by the Commander-in-Chief in the East against Courland, through Northern Lithuania, under the command of General von Scholtz, Chief of Staff, Colonel Count von Schwerin, with newly-established and continually reinforced formations which had been taken from the other armies of the same Command.

The 10th Army had not been able to overcome with its attacks south-west of Kovno the Russian reinforcements which were brought up in time. The Niemen

Operations against Russia in 1915

Army had fared no better north of Kovno. Their forces got lost in the big areas in which they had to operate. It is true that more had been hoped for, after an advantage had been gained at Rossieny on the Dubissa at the beginning of June. The Commander-in-Chief in the East promised at that time that if only two more divisions were employed north of the Vistula, a success would be obtainable that would contribute very considerably to the " annihilation " of the Russian Army. Yet the situation changed within the next few days. The army was brought completely to a standstill by the arrival of enemy reserves. We had to be satisfied that the arrival of those two divisions enabled the German front to hold north of the Niemen and near Libau. These divisions were taken away from the 9th Army with the consent of G.H.Q., as such forces could not be withdrawn from other fronts at that time.

These events on the German portion of the front had no perceptible effects on the situation in Galicia during June. The Russians transferred very strong forces from the north to the Galician theatre of war. It may be left undetermined whether the capacity of their means of transport would have allowed them to include any more troops in this movement. At any rate, more could hardly have been employed in the south.

For the rest the enemy still possessed, on the whole, a numerical superiority of more than one-fifth over the German forces in the north, which amounted to $39\frac{1}{2}$ divisions of infantry and $8\frac{1}{2}$ of cavalry. The previous victories over the Russians had certainly not been fought with any more favourable proportion of forces; but it could not be denied that the proportion was an uncomfortable one, if the Northern front was to assist in the operations planned in the south.

Critical Decisions at General Headquarters

This was pointed out by the Commander-in-Chief in the East with particular energy when he was called upon at the end of June to effect this support by concentrating forces in a determined attack at a point in the Polish front—the place in view being the Narew sector below Osowiec or in the Pilitza sector. He laid stress on the fact that he could only spare two divisions for this purpose, apart from the troops already belonging to the sector concerned, whether the offensive was begun in the region of the 9th Army or of Gallwitz' Army, or of the 8th or the 10th Armies. Nothing much could be done with those, he added, and the offensive would soon come to a dead stop everywhere. In his opinion freedom for operations existed only on the northern wing with the Niemen Army, and the employment of further forces there, if possible with a simultaneous attack on Kovno, would lead to a complete tactical success. "Although far removed from the main decision, this latter will be influenced more by the employment of these forces north of the Niemen than by directly feeding the main front with them. Therefore the reinforcement of, and an offensive by the Niemen Army, with a simultaneous attack upon Kovno, remain the most effective contribution of the army in the East to the whole operations."

These arguments did not appear convincing to the Chief of the General Staff.

The experiences of the Niemen Army a few weeks before showed that with a reinforcement of only two divisions in the long sector north of the Niemen nothing really effective could be done which would help the main operation. It was obvious that the Commander-in-Chief had in mind the bringing up of additional forces from other theatres of war. Unfortunately this was

Operations against Russia in 1915

impossible at the time. In the West not a single man could be spared from our exiguous reserves for the moment. Any weakening of our attacking groups in Poland and Galicia, in view of the strength of the enemy facing them and the condition of part of the Austro-Hungarian Army, involved the danger of serious defeats which had to be avoided, if only for their effect on public opinion in Rumania, Bulgaria, and not less in Austria-Hungary.

Apart from that the transfer of troops from there to Lithuania demanded so much time and could be concealed from the Russians so little that the latter would certainly have taken counter-measures in time. So it is probable that nothing would have been attained beyond creating insecurity on the Galician front, where absolute security was necessary, and, possibly, winning a tactical success of local importance in Lithuania. We could not have expected more. The Russians had long realized the dangers of strategic envelopment, as was pointed out in an earlier chapter of this record, and learned how to take measures against it. This was made easier for them by their superiority in numbers, the higher capacity of the railways, and the indifference with which they could, and as experience showed, did, abandon stretches of country as soon as that course seemed advisable.

Moreover, G.H.Q. could not allow itself to depend on a local tactical victory, more especially when such a success, as in the case in point, involved the danger of our spreading ourselves out on diverging lines and simply lengthening our line. It was G.H.Q.'s business to work for a victory which would probably have its effect on the whole operations.

Accordingly, when the Commander-in-Chief in the East, at a conference on this question on July 2nd, was

Critical Decisions at General Headquarters

forced to admit that it was more a matter of sentiment whether we attacked on the Narew front or north of the Niemen, his proposal was turned down. He was given instructions that Gallwitz's Army Detachment (Chief of Staff, Colonel Marquard) was to break through the Russian positions on the lower Narew on both sides of Prassnysch on the 12th July, and take the weight off Mackensen's group by pressing forward to the Bug. It went without saying that in so doing they were to try to cut off the hostile masses on the Vistula and facing Mackensen. All available troops were to be drawn from the sector of the 9th Army, as the Chief of the General Staff considered that there was no harm in leaving only a screen of troops there, as had been done in the sector south of the Pilitza.

On this hypothesis, and in accordance with the later statement of the C.-in-C. in the East, three divisions could be made available from the 9th Army. To facilitate their release three Landsturm regiments, fit for the field, were placed at his disposal by G.H.Q., while Woyrsch's Army Detachment succeeded in solving the same problem without receiving any reinforcements. The right wing of the 8th Army was to join in the attack between the Schkwa and the Pissa, making for Lomsha, where all the heavy artillery we could still lay hands on was to be employed.

For the same occasion the attention of the C.-in-C. in the East was drawn to the fact that it would be necessary for the moment that all the troops on his front which were otherwise still available should co-operate in the operations of Gallwitz's Detachment. Until that had been done no enterprise must be undertaken, even in the north, which did not directly contribute to securing our positions. On the other hand, it was indicated

Operations against Russia in 1915

that arrangements must be put in hand which could facilitate a rapid transfer of troops from the Narew group to the north, for a subsequent thrust against the Russian communications. It would then probably be better to launch the attack over the middle Niemen in a south-easterly direction, rather than give it the great tracts of country north of the river for its objective.

The next few days showed how necessary the immediate co-operation on the Narew front—which I desired—was for the Galician front.

While the Austrian 4th, the 11th and Bug Armies were making preparations between the Bug and the Vistula, a Russian counter-attack south of Krassnik struck the Austrian 4th Army, which had gained ground at the outset, and won a full success. Its support by the 11th Army was necessary, though the latter itself had a very superior hostile force in front of it. It was only with considerable difficulty that the ensuing crisis could be overcome.

All the more welcome was the success of the attack of Gallwitz's Army Detachment, which began on July 13th. The C.-in-C. in the East had after all managed to strengthen Gallwitz with as many as four divisions of the 9th Army. The Russian positions were broken through on both sides of Prassnysch. The enemy suffered heavy losses. As early as the 18th the leading German troops were approaching the valley of the Narew on the whole front between the Vistula and the Pissa.

The first strategic effects of this thrust were manifested in the bend of the Vistula by the withdrawal of the Russians. In front of the 9th Army they retired as far as the outer works of Warsaw, whereupon the C.-in-C. in the East decided to send two more divisions from the army to Gallwitz's group. An attempt of Woyrsch's

Critical Decisions at General Headquarters

Army Detachment to break through at Sienno was successful. This detachment followed close on the heels of the retiring enemy and on July 21st threw him into the fortress of Ivangorod, which it invested on the left bank of the Vistula.

The effect of the Prassnysch victory on the main operations was not so noticeable at first.

Our troops between the Vistula and the Bug only worked their way northwards slowly, and it was a troublesome business. Progress was hindered as much by the difficulties of the ground and supply as by the stout resistance of the Russians. On July 21st the Bug Army had just about reached the Ustilug–Woislawize line while the 11th, in touch with it, had got as far as south of Piaski. The Austrian 4th Army was a good day's march behind.

The operations of the first Austro-Hungarian Armies against Vladimir–Volinsk had been abandoned when it was realized that the army would not get through. It received directions to protect the right flank of the main group by assuming the defensive on the Bug. The enemy also withdrew the greater part of the units concentrated in the neighbourhood of Vladimir–Volinsk to the left bank of the Bug again. He replaced with them, as appeared later, those forces which had retired to the Narew after the break-through at Prassnyscz. Moreover, strange to say, he also had scruples about going into the Pripet region with large bodies of troops.

On the other sectors of the Eastern front there were no great changes corresponding to the situation. In Eastern Galicia the 2nd Austro-Hungarian and the Southern Army had pushed forward to the Zlota–Lipa. But they got no further. A thrust to relieve them, attempted by the 7th Austro-Hungarian Army across

Operations against Russia in 1915

the Dniester in the region east of the Strypa had no success.

Conditions on the northern wing in Lithuania were taking a more favourable shape.

The 10th Army had again attacked south-west of Kovno. It was in the act of driving the Russians back behind the Iesya sector, but its offensive powers were exhausted for the moment. North of the Niemen, the left wing of the Niemen Army had reached the swampy sector south of Mitau. After some lively fighting the Russians had retired behind this region. Even though the nature of the ground forbade any further progress at this point for the moment, a second offensive which the army had begun east of Shavli, in the neighbourhood of Schadow, seemed to be developing happily.

In spite of the more pleasant prospects offered by these events, the Chief of the General Staff adhered to his view that every possible effort must be continually directed at furthering the main operations east of the middle Vistula, in other words, to procure immediate relief for the heavily engaged front of Mackensen's Army. The possibilities of this were very limited, it is true. They consisted in an advance across the Vistula between Ivangorod and Warsaw by Woyrsch's Detachment and the bringing up of two more divisions from the West.

The passage of the Vistula was to clear the air for the 4th Austro-Hungarian Army, which hung like a heavy weight on Mackensen's front, by striking a blow immediately in the rear of the Russian forces which were holding it in check.

The temporary transference of the two divisions from the French front was permissible because recent and reliable intelligence showed that the big offensive expected there was not to begin before the second

Critical Decisions at General Headquarters

half of the month of September. It seemed justified, therefore, to shift the last available battalion to the spot where the decision was to take place. The Chief of the General Staff was in no doubt as to this spot. In his opinion a consideration of the situation indicated the sector of the Narew group for this purpose. Meanwhile objections were raised to both the relief measures intended.

The idea of a passage of the Vistula by Woyrsch's Detachment *below* Ivangorod was opposed by the Austro-Hungarian G.H.Q., to whom this army, which was fighting within the Austro-Hungarian front, was subordinated as a matter of form. The Austro-Hungarian G.H.Q. regarded the position of the 4th Austro-Hungarian Army as so difficult, that it considered immediate assistance by a passage of the river *above* Ivangorod to be necessary, regardless of the evident arguments against such an action. Only when Mackensen's Army Group formally promised to see that nothing serious should happen to the 4th Austro-Hungarian Army before the result of the operation was felt below Ivangorod, did the Austro-Hungarian G.H.Q. agree to this.

An opposite standpoint with regard to the employment of the two divisions coming from the West was represented by the Commander-in-Chief in the East, when he suggested that they should not be used on the Narew, but as far east as possible, best of all with the Niemen Army in Lithuania. He had now decided to take two more divisions from the 9th Army for the Narew Group.* With these he thought it possible to strengthen the group sufficiently in order to give it the necessary energy to make its action felt as far away as Mackensen's Group. He promised more extensive

* See page 114.

Operations against Russia in 1915

advantages from the employment of these Western divisions north of the Niemen.

He was supported in this view when the very skilfully-led Niemen Army inflicted another heavy blow upon the Russians near Schadow within the next few days—on July 23rd—and drove them back speedily in the direction Jakobstadt–Friedrichstadt, and when the Narew Group succeeded—on July 24th—in crossing the river with strong forces in the neighbourhood of Pultusk and Roshan. Consequently the Commander-in-Chief in the East extended his proposal to the effect that the 10th and the Niemen Armies should be given, apart from the Western divisions, portions of Mackensen's Army Group, Woyrsch's Detachment, and the 9th Army, after these latter had carried out the attack on Warsaw.

As he considered that the offensive force of the Mackensen Group was exhausted, and believed himself right in assuming that a passage of the Vistula by Woyrsch's Detachment would be out of the question owing to the river being so high at the time, so long as the enemy held the other bank, he was really justified in deducing that Gallwitz's Army would at most succeed in driving the Russians back on to the line Brest–Litovsk–Bielostock. It was his opinion that the most damaging blow could be struck at them in the north by the capture of Kovno and an offensive by the 10th and Niemen Armies against their lines of communication.

Once again, however, the Chief of the General Staff was unable to accept this tempting suggestion. The assumptions on which the proposal was based, had proved themselves to be wholly incorrect meanwhile.

On July 29th, Woyrsch's Detachment drove away the enemy on the right bank of the Vistula opposite the mouth of the Radomka and got such a foothold on the

Critical Decisions at General Headquarters

other side of the river that bridge-building could be begun. On the same day Mackensen's Army Group broke through the Russian positions in a brilliant attack, whereupon the enemy began a retreat along the whole front between the Bug and the Narew. In its pursuit this Army Group crossed the Lublin Heights on the very same day. After this it was to be supposed with every certainty that the enemy had come to the conclusion that it was impossible for him to hold his own in the endangered area between Mackensen's Group and the Narew Group. But if this was the case, it was to be supposed that he would secure himself against any surprises on his northern wing. It was all the more easy for him to do so, if the Germans attempted to bring off any such surprises by shifting forces belonging to Mackensen's Group or Woyrsch's Detachment to the northern wing. The advantage of far shorter and better lines of communication was altogether on the side of the Russians. These forces, and probably those remaining with Mackensen and Woyrsch too, would certainly have been tied up in the East until far into the winter. G.H.Q. did not want to risk the danger inherent in this, nor was it advisable to do so. The stormcloud which was gathering on the Western front and the incontestable necessity of intervening in the Balkans at the right moment, absolutely forbade such a risk. It only remained to apply all energies to the completion of the operations as planned, *i.e.*, to annihilate, as far as it was still possible, the Russian masses crowded together east of the Vistula. To do this it was necessary to push forward the Narew Group by all means on the right bank of the Bug. An answer to this effect was sent to the proposal of the Commander-in-Chief in the East.

In the same context he was consulted shortly after-

Operations against Russia in 1915

wards as to whether it would not be advisable to throw two more divisions of the 9th Army on to the left wing of the Narew Group in order to intensify the pressure. It looked as if the army could spare these, because an attempt by the Russians to break through westwards from Warsaw was now out of the question, nor was the fall of the city, the forts of which had been blown up by the enemy several days before, to be expected from the steps taken by the 9th Army, but solely and certainly from the progress of the operations on the right bank of the Vistula. The Commander-in-Chief in the East, however, viewed the situation otherwise. He considered that any weakening of the 9th Army was not feasible at the moment because it was in the closest contact with the enemy along its whole front—these were the rear-guards of the Warsaw garrison. And if these divisions were to be detached from the rest, he would prefer to use them with the 10th Army against Kovno, against which town this army was about to begin an attack. Taking this opinion into consideration G.H.Q. refrained from putting its suggestion into execution. He did not consider it proper to interfere in the actions of the local Commander-in-Chief in the circumstances, although the latter's opinion did not seem to G.H.Q. to be fully justified. Moreover events on the Vistula developed so swiftly that it was actually questionable whether it would still pay to send the two divisions to the Narew Group. One could only regret that it had not been done earlier.

On August 4th the enemy evacuated Warsaw and Ivangorod. At the same time he continued his retreat between the Bug and the Narew and his withdrawal through Brest–Litovsk, frequently making a stand for a short time. The Narew Group could not prevent him

Critical Decisions at General Headquarters

from doing so, for owing to a lack of forces it was unable to put any real drive into its left wing, and its direction had gradually fallen into a line running east and west.

On August 13th it was advancing with the 12th Army, which had been formed out of Gallwitz' Army Detachment, across the line Ziechanoviecz–Szokei. The formations of the 8th Army fighting with it had reached the Slina sector through Rutki. The remaining portions of the 8th Army were on the other side of the Bobr, on both sides of the Wissa and in front of Osowiec. On the right of the 12th Army, the independent Army Group of Prince Leopold, which had been formed from the remains of the 9th Army and Woyrsch's Detachment, had reached Siedlez with its northern wing and had taken Lukow. When this Army Group had crossed the Vistula and it was realized that it had only comparatively weak forces opposing it, although these forces were still in numerical superiority, it received directions from G.H.Q. to push forward its advance ruthlessly. It responded to these orders with splendid performances.

The fact that it did not succeed, as intended, in slipping between the enemy forces, which were fighting against the Narew and Mackensen Groups, was due to the speedy withdrawal of the Russians as soon as they felt the danger that threatened.

On the last-named day Mackensen's Army Group stood on the Vlodava–Lukow line. The 1st Austro-Hungarian Army was guarding its right flank in the neighbourhood of Dubyenko on the Bug. In front of the Army Group, just as in front of the Narew Group, there were very superior Russian forces who were stoutly defending every inch of ground.

In Eastern Galicia the situation remained unchanged on the whole.

Operations against Russia in 1915

The attack on Novo-Georgievsk, which was begun on July 24th by three divisions of the Narew Group under General von Beseler, reinforced by another division from the 9th Army after the fall of Warsaw, was proceeding vigorously. At G.H.Q.'s direction, rapid methods were applied here by making the greatest use of the heaviest artillery.

The 10th Army's attack on Kovno had just as good prospects. It had pressed back the enemy above the fortress as far as the Niemen and across the Suwalki–Olita railway. The outer lines of Kovno had been captured. The storming of the permanent works was to begin within the next few days.

On the other hand, the operations north of the Niemen had come to a standstill. After the Niemen Army's victory at Schadow on July 23rd, it had occupied Mitau, which was evacuated by the enemy, and had pushed forward as far as a line south of Ponieviecs–Posvol. Here it met with a counter-attack which was only repulsed after heavy fighting. After pursuing the retreating attacker for a short distance the army came to a stop on the line Onikschty–Popel before superior forces of the enemy. It had to be satisfied with being able to retain the territory that it had gained, and prevent a break-through by the enemy on the northern wing.

It had still been possible on August 9th to retain the hope that the strong Russian forces crowded within the area between Narew–Vistula–Viepsch and Vlodava would be prevented from escaping eastwards and would be annihilated. Consequently the Austro-Hungarian G.H.Q. suggested on that day that Mackensen's right wing on and east of the Bug should be reinforced in order to secure the attainment of this object. It proved shortly afterwards, however, that this idea had to be abandoned.

Critical Decisions at General Headquarters

The necessary transference of troops would have given the withdrawing Russians too much time. As the situation developed up to August 13th this hope had to be given up once and for all. The enemy had obviously succeeded in drawing his main forces out of the danger zone in time. The freedom of action which he had retained in the district north-west and north of Brest–Litovsk had rendered this possible for him. If any sensible injury was to be inflicted upon him now, it could only be done by trying to drive him northwards by means of an energetic advance on the part of Mackensen's Army Group on both sides of Brest–Litovsk, and by pushing the 12th Army through Bielsk into the flank and rear of the forces thus driven back. There was no time available for shifting large bodies of troops or for the preparation of far-reaching operations. Orders were issued to this effect by both G.H.Q.'s on the 13th of August.

It was thereby admitted to a certain extent that the most recent operations had not completely achieved their purpose. On the basis of this fact an exchange of views took place between the Commander-in-Chief in the East and the Chief of the General Staff, and it is reproduced here because it is the simplest way of explaining the divergence of opinion.

On August 13th the Commander-in-Chief in the East reported to G.H.Q. as follows :

" In spite of the excellent results of the thrust on the Narew, the operations in the East have not led to the annihilation of the enemy. As was to be expected, the Russian has drawn out of the pincers and is allowing himself to be driven back frontally in the direction desired by himself. With the help of his good railways he can concentrate just as he wishes and lead strong

Operations against Russia in 1915

forces against my left wing which is threatening his communications. I consider this wing to be in danger. On the other hand a decisive blow is only possible now from the Kovno region, although a serious amount of time has unfortunately been lost for this. I therefore urgently propose once more a reinforcement of my left wing, so that after its arrival the offensive can be resumed; or at least the territory captured hitherto retained. I once more stress the fact that I regarded an offensive by my left wing against the enemy's communications and his rear, as the only possibility of annihilating him. This offensive is probably even now the only means of avoiding a new campaign unless it is already too late for it."

The Chief of the General Staff replied as follows:

" The annihilation of the enemy has never been hoped for from the current operations in the East, but purely and simply a decisive victory in accordance with the aims of G.H.Q. Nor should annihilation, on the whole, have been attempted in the present instance, for it is impossible to try to annihilate an enemy who is far superior in numbers, must be attacked frontally, and has excellent lines of communication, any amount of time and unlimited space at his disposal, whilst we should have been forced to operate, with a time-limit, in a district destitute of railways and roads.

" That the enemy has already been decisively defeated for our purposes cannot be doubted by anybody who visualizes the fact that the Russians have lost in three months about three-quarters of a million men in prisoners alone, endless *matériel*, and Galicia, the Kingdom of Poland, and the Duchy of Courland, besides the possibility of seriously threatening Austria-Hungary during the beginning of the Italian campaign, or at all for an appreciable period, and, finally, the other possibility of employing their Odessa Armies at the critical moment in the Balkans. There exists a further prospect that the results of the operations will be intensified further, as we have succeeded in driving no less than five thoroughly beaten enemy armies into the space between Bielostock and Brest-Litovsk.

" It is to be assumed that the operations would certainly have been more decisive if it had been possible to deliver a simultaneous blow across the Niemen. But G.H.Q. had no forces at its disposal for this purpose, and Your Excellency considered the employment of the Niemen Army in Courland to be more necessary. This is not intended as a criticism, but merely as a statement of the facts."

G.H.Q. did not share the opinion that the left wing of the Commander-in-Chief in the East was threatened, as the Russians were still engaged along the whole front, and thus would not be able to appear in such strong force on the Lower Dvina as to render the German forces at disposal there insufficient to repel them. Any reinforcement of the 10th, or the Niemen Army from the West, or from Mackensen's and Prince Leopold's Army Groups, was out of the question at the time, and would only have been possible from the Narew Group after the conclusion of the present operations.

" It will always be necessary, however, to take the resultant general military situation into consideration before any forces are transferred to the 10th or to the Niemen Army."

This correspondence contains everything that was to be said on this subject at that time. To-day, however, it needs supplementing. There can scarcely be any doubt that an " annihilation " of the Russian

Operations against Russia in 1915

Armies on the Vistula would have been actually nearer than was the case, and still greater damage would certainly have been inflicted on them, if it had been decided to transfer all the formations that could be spared to the German Narew Group at the beginning of its operations.

The matter at issue here concerned the four divisions from the 9th Army, which were actually brought up, or could have been, during the operations, and two divisions at least of the forces which were transferred to the Niemen Army. The possibility of such a proceeding did exist. An extensive weakening of the front of the 9th Army in front of Warsaw was as harmless as it was on the front south of the Pilitza. The reinforcement of the Niemen Army took place, however, for offensive purposes which exceeded the range of what was necessary for the advancement of the main operations. In Northern Lithuania the Russians were the "followers-up" throughout. Until the middle of August the idea of threatening the German northern wing was certainly remote from them.

If the Narew Group had conducted its offensive with twenty divisions instead of with fourteen, it is in a high degree probable that it would have been in a position to prevent strong forces of the enemy from escaping from the pincers.

Accordingly the omission of this reinforcement was a mistake. As is shown by this purposely detailed analysis of events, its cause is to be sought solely in the fact that it was not possible to establish a uniform conception of the situation between the directing and executive authorities. As the fundamental idea of the plan of campaign in the East first demanded the sharpest concentration of all available forces and means for the

Critical Decisions at General Headquarters

main operations, the holding back of one single man for any reason whatever should not have been allowed.

Whilst it was certainly the duty of the Army Commander to adapt himself to the operations as a whole, a part of the responsibility for this not being done also rests with the Chief of the General Staff. It was his duty to secure the unrestricted use of every portion in and for the whole, even where he was opposed by extraordinary personal difficulties, as in this case.

It soon appeared, a few days after August 13th, that the driving of the enemy to the north, which was intended in the Bug region, would not actually be accomplished to any very great extent. The slow advance of the 12th and the 8th Armies left the Russians still plenty of freedom of movement in the region north-west and north of Brest-Litovsk. They put up an obstinate defence in front of Prince Leopold's Army Group as well as of the 4th Austro-Hungarian and the 11th Armies around and west of Brest-Litovsk, although with heavy losses. The plan of driving them from the great roads and railways, which lead eastwards from Brest-Litovsk, by an enveloping movement round the east of this place did not succeed. The Bug Army was not able to capture the entrances to the swamp region above Brest-Litovsk around Vlodava, which were tenaciously defended by the enemy. The 1st Austro-Hungarian Army, which was once more moved on Vladimir-Volynsk from Grubeschow to Dubyenko made some progress, but it was improbable that it would be at all dangerous to the Russians, if the latter continued their retreat at the same pace as hitherto.

On the other hand, the conclusion of the negotiations with the Bulgarians was coming palpably nearer. It necessitated the beginning of transport to the Serbian

Operations against Russia in 1915

frontier before the end of August. The continuation of big combined operations in the East had, therefore, to be abandoned.

In these circumstances the Chief of the General Staff now agreed to the proposals of separate operations, which were made by the Austro-Hungarian G.H.Q. and the Commander-in-Chief in the East, naturally on condition that the execution of G.H.Q.'s plans in the West and in the Balkans would not be prejudiced by them.

AUSTRO-HUNGARIAN OFFENSIVE IN VOLHYNIA, 1915

The Austro-Hungarian G.H.Q. rightly considered that it was scarcely bearable for the Russian lines east and north-east of Lemberg to be only two days' march off this politically and strategically important railway centre. In order to drive the enemy further back, out of Galicia if possible, and in order to inflict upon him a severe blow at the same time, it planned a strong push through Kovel into the gap which actually existed between the Russian western and south-western fronts. In its later stages the north wing of the south-western front in the region of Lutsk was to be pressed in and surrounded. It was intended to use the 1st and the 4th Austro-Hungarian Armies for these operations. Simultaneously with them the inner wings of the 2nd Austro-Hungarian and the Southern Armies were to attack south of the railway line Krasne–Brody. The argument against these operations was, that they had to be executed in very difficult terrain without the co-operation of German troops. They were strongly supported by the fact that a partial success only would mean a very

Critical Decisions at General Headquarters

considerable increase of the self-confidence and the inner value of the Allied Army, and a strong impression upon the enemy. G.H.Q. considered this gain to be so great, that it felt compelled to put all other scruples in the background. It therefore declared its readiness to agree to the withdrawal of the 1st and 4th Austro-Hungarian Armies, as well as of an Austro-Hungarian Army Corps fighting in the 11th Army from the formation of Mackensen's Army Group. The 1st Army was to be at the disposal of the Austro-Hungarian G.H.Q. immediately, the 4th Army and the Army Corps after the fall of Brest-Litovsk. This took place on August 25th. On the 27th, the above-mentioned Austro-Hungarian troops began their march to the south-east. On the same day the first German division was taken from the Mackensen Group to be sent to Orsova on the Danube. It had an important part to play there, inasmuch as a favourable influence on the negotiations that were proceeding so well with Bulgaria might be expected from its appearance on Rumania's flank and not too far from the Bulgarian frontier.

The Austro-Hungarian G.H.Q. was aware of this purpose. Yet it proposed to transfer the division to the Army Group of the Commander-in-Chief in the East for a thrust through Vilna planned by him, and which will be discussed later. This could not be agreed to by Germany. The Chief of the General Staff gave it as his opinion that it would have been very desirable during July, if strong forces could have appeared on the middle Niemen simultaneously with the offensive between the Bug and the Vistula. The Commander-in-Chief in the East had not produced these forces, however, and they were not obtainable elsewhere. In France the enemy now had a superiority of more than

Operations against Russia in 1915

seven hundred battalions. Therefore, reinforcements for the operations in Northern Lithuania and Courland could only have been taken from the Polish front. But the armies there had only just been sufficient to shake the enemy to such an extent as was absolutely necessary, owing to the condition of the Austro-Hungarian troops. In addition to this, if any reinforcement from the armies in Poland had been intended, the thrust on the Niemen would not have taken effect until six weeks after the order for the formation of this attacking group had been issued. Such a delay could not possibly be accepted in view of the Balkan situation. The Russians would have been able, with the assistance of their railway network, to throw sufficient forces against the Niemen Group in time, as soon as the pressure in Poland slackened, so that the operations in the north would not have proceeded any more speedily than actually happened; but, on the other hand, it is probable that no success would have been achieved anywhere, if all the attacking groups had been thinned.

The Chief of the General Staff concluded the report, in which he represented this point of view to the Austro-Hungarian G.H.Q., with the words:

"A reinforcement of the Kovno Group is certainly to be desired, but it is incomparably more important that the Dardanelles should be secured and, in addition, the iron in Bulgaria struck while it is hot. Consequently the forces which we are able to withdraw from the region of Brest-Litovsk, without slackening our hold on the enemy's throat, must go to the Danube."

Consequently the removal of the division continued. It was followed by eight more divisions from Mackensen's and Prince Leopold's Army Groups during the latter days of August and the early part of September,

Critical Decisions at General Headquarters

some under orders for Serbia and some for France, whilst the remaining portions of these Army Groups continued the pursuit of the Russians north of the Pripet. They were able to inflict considerable damage on them too. Field-Marshal von Mackensen then went to South Hungary, where he was to take command of the attacking group against Serbia. His former Army Group continued to operate under his name for some time, thereby successfully concealing the Field-Marshal's new mission.

THE VILNA OFFENSIVE, AUTUMN, 1915

In the area under the command of the Commander-in-Chief in the East, the fortress of Kovno was stormed by portions of the 10th Army on August 18th after a concentrated assault. The Commander-in-Chief desired to turn this success to account by continuing the offensive in his area. G.H.Q. readily consented to this, as there was no longer any question of co-operation between the Northern Army Group with the two southern ones for a common purpose, and any further damage to the enemy was most welcome. The reserves, which were once more asked for, could, however, only be promised in the event of portions of the army attacking Novo Georgievsk being liberated by the capture of that place. Happily this happened two days later. No less than eighty-five thousand prisoners and seven hundred guns fell into German hands. Of the four divisions of the besieging army, three could be sent to the Army Group in the north. The order for the offensive was given by the Commander-in-Chief in the East on August 28th. According to this, the 8th and the

Operations against Russia in 1915

12th Armies were to follow up the enemy closely, and the 8th was to take the fortress of Grodno. The 10th Army had to attack further in the direction Orany–Vilna, with its chief pressure directed towards and north of Vilna. The Niemen Army was to attack the enemy in front of Friedrichstadt and further cover the left wing of the 10th Army against the Dvina.

These plans were in agreement with the orders issued by G.H.Q. for the Northern Army Group on the very same day. The latter directed it to carry out the operations begun north of the upper Narew and east of the middle Niemen, and to do the enemy the greatest possible harm. The question as to whether the line to be held during the coming winter would rest on the sea in the Gulf of Riga or at Libau was to be left open.

The choice in detail and between a mobile defence and a consolidated position was likewise left to the Commander-in-Chief. It was only important, with regard to the general conduct of the war, that a defensive line should be found which could be held with a minimum expenditure of men and munitions.

A propos of this choice, it was repeatedly pointed out that it could not be considered possible to annihilate finally an enemy, " who is firmly resolved to give ground regardless of the sacrifice of territory and population, as soon as he is grappled with, and who, moreover, has the whole width of Russia at his disposal."

Before very long the necessity was bound to arise for ten or twelve divisions to be taken from the region of the Army Group in the north, for use in other theatres of war.

Similar warnings against the preparation of plans, which were now impossible to execute owing to the position of the Central Powers, and because they threatened to lead to an expenditure of irreplaceable force, had also to be sent to the Austro-Hungarian G.H.Q. in those days. It was informed that Germany, and in the opinion of G.H.Q., Austria-Hungary too, was not concerned with the occupation of Russian territory; but henceforward solely with the discovery of a line which guaranteed the permanent security of East Prussia and Hungary with the smallest expenditure of energy, whilst we sought to bring about the decision of the war on other fronts with as strong forces as possible. Moreover, the Chief of the General Staff did not conceal from the Austro-Hungarian G.H.Q. the fact that the hope, also expressed by the latter, that the intended thrust towards Vilna would lead to the final annihilation of the Russians, could scarcely be fulfilled. The enemy's advantage in better lines of communication, especially in the Vilna region, was so great that there was little probability of overcoming it altogether. This prophecy unhappily proved correct to its full extent.

THE VILNA OFFENSIVE OF THE HINDENBURG ARMY GROUP

On August 29th the Northern Army Group began its forward movement. On the same day the news arrived that the Russians were about to dispatch two and a half army corps to Vilna. These reinforcements were taken from the rear columns in the sectors in front of Prince Leopold's and Mackensen's Army Groups. The transference of these troops from these sectors northwards to the region of Dvinsk and east of Vilna continued. The army groups were not able to prevent these movements, because they were suffering from difficulties of transport, and were only advancing very slowly in the

Operations against Russia in 1915

difficult terrain against the obstinate resistance of the enemy. In the early days of September it was clear that the enemy was working with the same methods that he had used with success between the Vistula and the Bug. He strengthened himself on the wing, from the Pripet to the Upper Niemen on the one side, and in the Vilna region and north of it on the other, whilst he paid little attention to his centre. It would still have been possible then to have transferred the main pressure of the German attack against this centre, in the direction of Orany–Lida. By this means an important advantage would have been gained by driving the whole of the enemy's left wing on to the marshes of Slonim. The necessary forces could have been brought up in time, partly from the Niemen Army, whilst they also existed in part in four divisions which the Commander-in-Chief in the East was marching from the 8th and 12th Armies to the Niemen Army in front of Vilna. Of course, one condition for such a change in the operations was that the capture of Vilna and the offensive action in Northern Lithuania and in Courland would have to be abandoned. It is probable that the disinclination to abandon these operations caused the Commander-in-Chief on the spot, not only to cling to his old plan, but even to extend it.

On September 4th he reported that he intended to attack with the reinforced left wing of the 10th Army on the 8th or the 9th, according to the progress of the movement of troops, on and across the line Vilna–Vilkomir. Although the Chief of the General Staff had scruples against these operations, which were out of proportion to the means at hand, he did not press them, because local conditions could not be judged so reliably from a distance as from the army group itself,

Critical Decisions at General Headquarters

and because the freedom of decision which had just been granted to the Commander there ought not to be restricted by any interference at the eleventh hour. Experiences on the Narew during the summer led him to fear that such an interference would lead to half measures, and would therefore do more harm than good. The Commander-in-Chief in the East was aware how much the German plan of campaign in the East depended upon the considerations of the general situation. In order to emphasize this afresh, a reply was sent on the same day to the effect that the Northern Army Group would have to be decreased by two divisions in the middle of September, and that after this the other forces to be withdrawn from this area for other fronts would have to be taken after an interval of about three days.

The offensive begun by the Eastern Army Group on September 9th met with active resistance everywhere, which was weak only in the region of Orany. This could not be turned to account, however, owing to the lack of forces, because troops were drawn away from there for use further north after initial successes had been gained.

On September 12th the 12th Army was fighting for the Selvianka sector south of the Niemen on a level with the army groups of Prince Leopold and Mackensen. The 8th Army, which had just taken by storm on September 4th the last western bulwark of the Russians, Grodno, was about to force the opening of the lake sector east of this. These armies were opposed by immensely superior numbers of the enemy.

The right wing of the 10th Army had pressed back a weaker opponent in the direction of Orany. The centre was fighting on a level with Troki Nove against

Operations against Russia in 1915

strong Russian forces in front of Vilna, the left was north of the lower Viliya in an enveloping movement against the Viliya sector above the town, and its cavalry was approaching the Vilna–Dvinsk railway south of Novo Svenczyany.

The right wing of the Niemen Army had passed through Vilkomir in its eastward advance, its centre turned on Jakobstadt after taking Friedrichstadt, whilst its left wing stood unchanged north of Mitau.

In this situation the Commander-in-Chief in the East thought that he had urgent need of reinforcements for the left wing of the 10th Army, in the first place to give more weight to the intended thrust of this wing to the south-east, and, further, to have stronger reserves behind it for the event of an enemy advance against it from Dvinsk. He therefore requested, on September 11th and 12th, that the two divisions of the 10th Army Corps, which had been withdrawn from the Mackensen Army Group and were assembling at Bielostock for transport to the West, should be left with him for ten to fourteen days. The Commander-in-Chief wanted to concentrate the corps forthwith near Kovno.

His request could not be granted. Conditions at the front in France allowed of no delay in the transference of reinforcements thither. As a matter of fact, it was this corps that did the lion's share in the repulse of the great French attempt at a break-through in Champagne at the end of September. If it had not arrived in time, the situation would have been dangerous in a very high degree. The one or even two divisions of the 12th Army offered by the Commander-in-Chief in exchange for the corps did not constitute a sufficient reserve; nor could they begin to be transported across from Bielostock before some time had elapsed. Moreover, the time reckoning, "from ten to fourteen days," proved to be incorrect in another respect. Owing to the condition of the railways, the 10th Corps could not have been used as a unit in the region between Vilna and Dvinsk before the end of September or the beginning of October at the earliest, and would certainly not have been free again before the middle of October, probably much later. However, as G.H.Q. informed the Commander-in-Chief, it would unfortunately be impossible to continue the operations in the East with the forces hitherto available for so long as that.

A little later another exchange of views developed between the Chief of the General Staff and the Commander-in-Chief in the East. On September 19th the latter was informed that the removal of portions of the 12th and 8th Armies must be begun, and, indeed, a division standing in reserve (the 26th) behind the 12th Army was to be sent back at once. Six more divisions were to follow with all speed. The Commander-in-Chief complained about such an "interference" in his rights, as he had wanted to use those very troops for the taking of Riga.

He had to be informed in reply that the withdrawal of portions of his Army Group had been intimated to him on September 4th for the 15th of the month. The beginning of the transfer had been postponed until the 19th, in spite of the most pressing need, so as not to disturb the Vilna operations. But a delay of even one day more could not now be allowed, for the division was required on the Serbian front. Nor could the idea of any substitute for it be entertained owing to the loss of time that this would entail. For the rest, the withdrawal of the division could not do any harm to the current Vilna operations, because it had been intended

Operations against Russia in 1915

for use against Riga. But G.H.Q. had not been informed of any undertaking in this direction. Even if the left wing of the Niemen Army had to retire in consequence of the sudden withdrawal of the division, no particular disadvantage would be involved, for it would not matter essentially to the general course of the war, whether the German left wing stood on the Dvina, or further back behind the Niemen or the Aa. Every part had to submit to inconveniences for the sake of the whole.

The enveloping movements of the 10th Army northeast and, later, east of Vilna, made unusual demands on the endurance of the troops. They responded to them with great self-sacrifice, but these operations did not achieve their object. As had been feared, the Russians succeeded in taking counter-measures in time. But the continuance of the operations was hindered still more by the difficulties of transport, which speedily got worse and worse.

The Chief of the General Staff had already come to the conclusion on September 19th, when that exchange of views took place on the subject of the 26th Division, that no success of any great importance was to be obtained. However, the Commander-in-Chief was of a different opinion, as he reported on the 20th in reply to an inquiry. He still hoped for a favourable result, even if it might take several more days. This was not confirmed. On the 27th the Commander-in-Chief reported, in reply to a further inquiry, that he had to stop the attack and withdraw the left wing of the 10th Army, which had advanced to Vileika, back to the Lake Narotch sector. His Army Group would now establish itself in the consolidated positions stretching from the confluence of the Beresina and the Niemen—

Critical Decisions at General Headquarters

Lake Narotch—the region west of Dvinsk–Mitau–Schlok. The 8th and 10th Armies were to release forces for G.H.Q. as soon as possible. How many more divisions and within what periods they could be transferred the Commander-in-Chief was not yet able to say.

The last sentence of this reply created grave difficulties for the general situation. In the West, where the enemy's offensive had just begun, the forces, whose arrival had been depended upon for some time, were just as urgently required as on the Serbian frontier, where the Austro-Hungarian G.H.Q. had been unable to send troops of the strength promised for the combined operations. Yet an attempt was made to put up with the non-arrival of the forces from the Eastern front, because in the meantime an engagement had begun again in front of Smorgon which offered prospects, according to the information to hand, of removing a big salient in the German front which existed there and was a great inconvenience to our permanent lines. By the 3rd of October, however, it was plain from the reports, sent by request, that this hope would not be fulfilled. Consequently the Chief of the General Staff was able to demand the despatch of further portions of the Army Group, and was obliged to do so with regard to the situation on the other fronts.* In order to prepare these measures he again demanded from the Commander-in-Chief in the East the presentation of a statement of the position of the Army Group. This led to a correspondence, a reproduction of which will again explain the circumstances most simply. It provides at the same time clear information on the existing differences of opinion regarding the conduct of opera-

---

* See Appendix: Relative Strength of Forces on the Western Front.

Operations against Russia in 1915

tions during the summer. The Commander-in-Chief reported on October 6th :

" Russian 10th, 2nd and 1st Armies are attacking with all forces the 10th Army and the right wing of the Niemen Army, with the intention of breaking through to the Dvinsk-Vilna road or at least rendering the transference of further forces to the West impossible by their attack.*

" I expect that I shall succeed in preventing the enemy from breaking through. It is impossible, however, at the moment to send off any more troops. This can only be done when the attack has been beaten off and after the front has been shortened by the taking of Smorgon and the bridge-head of Dvinsk. For this purpose the sending of some heavy batteries is urgently required. This shortening of the front is all the more necessary since I am even compelled to withdraw reserves for myself from the centre, in order to strengthen the left wing of the troops under my command, as any breach of my front in the region of Mitau would have grave consequences."

The Chief of the General Staff replied :

" It would undoubtedly be of advantage if the present position of the Army Group could be permanently held and, in addition, pressure exerted in the direction of Dvinsk. But if it is asked, whether the retention of forces there to this end is permissible when their absence on the Western front can endanger the German positions here, this question must be emphatically negated. In

---

* It was improbable that the Russians could have pursued such aims. It was probably solely a matter of counter-attacks to relieve the pressure upon them. Moreover, they were repulsed so easily that a repetition of them could be regarded without anxiety.

Critical Decisions at General Headquarters

comparison with this danger, as Your Excellency has long known, it does not matter at all if the shortening of the front that you desire has to be effected by a withdrawal in consequence of the transference of the 58th and 115th Divisions.* For example, whether our line stretches from the Smorgon region through Dvinsk to Bausk, or goes in a more or less straight line from Smorgon direct to Bausk, is of no importance to the general course of the war. The loss of our positions in the West can mean an unfavourable conclusion of the war. Owing to the tension which prevails permanently in the West, and to the numerical superiority of the enemy in personnel and *matériel*, with which the superiority which likewise unfortunately exists on all the other fronts cannot be compared at all, owing to the military value of the Western enemies, every division counts on the Western front. The demand that Your Excellency should transfer the first of these two divisions to the West as soon as it is possible to entrain them from Vilna, must therefore be adhered to."

Meanwhile, the Commander-in-Chief refused to submit to this decision. On October 7th he took the following line :

" I cannot agree with the references to the position of my Army Group. The positions that are now being taken up are, with or without a shortening at Smorgon and Dvinsk, by far the most favourable that could be chosen. They can be held with a minimum of forces. Any position in the rear which is not covered by the Dwina,† would consume more troops than the present position as it stands, certainly not less.

---
* These were the two units in question.
† The river generally freezes from December to March.

Operations against Russia in 1915

"I have always taken the general situation into consideration by relinquishing as many troops as I could, as, for example, the ten divisions to the Austro-Hungarian front.* I have also sent off without delay any divisions that could be spared, and also despatched one belonging to the XIth Army Corps prematurely, an action which was described as a mistake at the time. The fact that the further relinquishment of divisions is now meeting with difficulties, is due to the plan of campaign favoured in the summer, which was unable to strike a deadly blow at the Russians, in spite of the favourable circumstances and my urgent entreaties. I am not blind to the difficulties of the general military situation which have ensued, and if the Russian attacks are beaten off really decisively, I shall relinquish further divisions as soon as it seems possible to me to do so—even before shortening the front at Smorgon and Dvinsk. But I cannot bind myself to a definite time. A premature relinquishment would give rise to a crisis, such as is now being experienced, to my regret, on the Western front, and in certain circumstances it would mean a catastrophe for the Army Group, as any retiring movement of my troops, which are but weak in comparison with the enemy, must lead to very great harm being done to the formations, owing to the unfavourable condition of the terrain. I request that my views should be represented to His Majesty."

With all the consideration due to the person of the Commander-in-Chief, whose name is associated by the German people with the victory of Tannenberg, and to the feelings which prevailed at his Headquarters, after the result of the operations around Vilna, it was impossible for the Chief of the General Staff to allow these remarks

* Refers to the period since the beginning of the war.

Critical Decisions at General Headquarters

to pass without a more determined reply. This ran as follows :

" Much as I regret that Your Excellency should without any cause consider the present moment* suited for explanations of events of the past, which are therefore unimportant at the moment, I should not trouble to refute your statements, if they concerned only me personally.

" But as it concerns a criticism of orders issued by G.H.Q., which, as is well known, have in all important cases met with the previous consent of His Majesty, I am unhappily compelled to do so.

" Whether Your Excellency agrees with the views of G.H.Q. does not matter, once a decision has been made by His Majesty. In this case every portion of our forces has to adapt itself unconditionally to G.H.Q.

" The despatch of forces from your area during the war to places where pressure was to be exerted, is no particular achievement, for it took place at the direction of G.H.Q., which can alone be responsible for such action.

" What Your Excellency says about the expression ' mistake ' used by me in the telegraphed correspondence concerning the transference of the 11th Army Corps is not correct. I considered it a mistake to march two divisions to a station at which only fifteen trains can be loaded daily, and made it clear that such an order had not proceeded from me.

" What operations Your Excellency had in mind in your effort to stigmatise ' the plan of campaign favoured in the summer,' is not clear to me.

" The attack by the Narew Group can scarcely come

---

* The French offensive in Champagne was at its height, and the offensive against Serbia had just begun. Both claimed the full attention of G.H.Q.

Operations against Russia in 1915

into question, for Your Excellency admitted personally in Posen that it was more a matter of sentiment, whether the Narew or the Niemen operations were decided upon. After the plentiful experiences of last winter, however, I am unable to rely on the feelings of other persons with regard to my proposals, but must depend solely on my own convictions, which considered the Narew operations to be more opportune.

"It could only refer to the rejection of your later proposal to strengthen the left wing of your Army Group with troops from Mackensen and Woyrsch. But this was based on two preliminary conditions which proved to be wholly unfounded.

"I do not hesitate to say to-day that the acceptance of your proposal would have been disastrous for us.

"Direct proof of this lies in the irrefutable fact that, if we had accepted the proposal, we should never have been in a position to transfer in time those forces which are urgently required for the support of the Western front. Any examination of the situation from the point of view of time and distance, with due regard to the condition of the railways and other transport systems, proves this beyond question.

"It is true that Your Excellency does not seem to have been informed of these conditions until very late. Otherwise the repeated and urgent requests for the despatch of the 10th Army Corps would have been quite incomprehensible.

"I can deduce indirect justification for my view from the course of the operations south-east of Vilna. Exactly what I feared and prophesied took place there. One cannot hope to strike a comprehensive and deadly blow, by means of an encircling movement, at an enemy who is numerically stronger, who will stick at no sacrifices of territory and population, and, in addition, has the expanse of Russia and good railways behind him; and particularly an encircling movement on the main front, in the course of which large sections of one's own troops are unavailable for action, whilst marching into position. The surprise required for success is, as this war has often shown, never successful enough to prevent the enemy from taking counter-measures in time.

"But it is indeed possible to inflict quite enough damage on such an enemy for our purposes by keeping up contact with him all along the front and thus preventing him from shifting his troops; then, to take him really by surprise in a well-chosen spot and with comparatively weak but strongly-concentrated forces to thrust deep into his lines. Examples of this are given by Mackensen's and Woyrsch's campaigns and also Gallwitz' tactics at Prassnyscz.

"A similar opportunity was, in my opinion, recently offered Your Excellency at Orany.

"If, in spite of my attitude to your operations, I did not propose to His Majesty to interfere, but even supported them in every way, the reason for this is to be found in my respect for the convictions of another person so long as they keep within the necessary limits, and so do not threaten to harm operations as a whole; and because it is impossible to gauge with mathematical precision the issue of any operations which are carried out with the energy usual in such cases.

"I will report to His Majesty the scruples which Your Excellency raises against the withdrawal of the two divisions. I must refuse to bring the remaining points of your telegram to the knowledge of the Emperor, because they do not concern authenticated considerations of past events, about which, therefore, I do not intend

Operations against Russia in 1915

in any case to approach the Supreme War Lord in these grave days."

The Emperor's decision was to the effect that the divisions were to be relinquished as ordered by the Chief of the General Staff. For the rest the latter's telegram fulfilled its purpose. The Commander-in-Chief in the East acquiesced in it. For several months there was a pause in these discussions, and the whole situation was helped thereby. It was not until the situation became acute in the summer of 1916, that the Eastern Command resumed its efforts to influence the conduct of the war.

The Army Group continued its endeavour to advance in the direction of Smorgon, Dvinsk and Riga until nearly the end of October, and inflicted upon the enemy, particularly in his counter-attacks, more damage than did the latter upon it. No particular gain was achieved.

PERMANENT POSITIONS IN THE EAST, WINTER, 1915–16
(SEE MAP 4)

A permanent position was taken up for the winter along the line: confluence of the Beresina and the Narew—east of Vilna—Lake Narotch—west of Dvinsk—Dvina on both sides of Friedrichstadt—Mitau—Schlok.

South of this stood Prince Leopold's Army Group behind the Servetch—the Schara—east of Baranovici—along Lake Vygonovskoye—the Oginski Canal—the Iasiolda as far as the Pripet.* It had been pushed thus

* In point of fact the right wing of Prince Leopold's Army Group stretched about twenty-five miles beyond the Pripet southwards, because the protection of the flank of the railway centre, Brest-Litovsk, as well as of the railways leading eastwards from thence, was to be kept in German hands. But this made no alteration in the agreement that the front south of this river was to be secured, as a matter of principle, by the Austro-Hungarian G.H.Q.

Critical Decisions at General Headquarters

far forward by continuous and often heavy fighting in order to afford relief to the operations of the Northern Army Group, and had reached its lines at the middle of September.

On the 25th, G.H.Q.'s orders were issued for the establishment of these consolidated positions on the German front from the Pripet to the coast.

THE AUSTRO-HUNGARIAN OFFENSIVE IN VOLHYNIA, END OF SEPTEMBER, 1915

A few days later this was begun in the Austro-Hungarian sector south of the Pripet.

The offensive measures begun by the Austro-Hungarian G.H.Q. at the end of August had not only produced no decided advantages but had even led to a serious reverse.

After initial successes in Eastern Galicia which facilitated a continued advance of the Austro-Hungarian front to the Strypa and past Brody, and assured material security for Lemberg, the left wing of the 7th Austro-Hungarian Army suffered a sensible defeat on the west bank of the Sereth during the first ten days of September. The situation could only be restored by G.H.Q. consenting to the employment of forces which were intended for the Serbian front, by promising to replace them with German troops there. This assistance was given on condition that the Volhynian offensive was abandoned, because no gains, but probably further losses, were to be expected from it, owing to the newly-apparent deficiency in the offensive powers of the Austro-Hungarian troops. But before the corresponding orders issued by the Austro-Hungarian G.H.Q. could take

Operations against Russia in 1915

effect, the position in Volhynia developed more unfavourably than that on the Dniester and the Sereth.

The 4th Austro-Hungarian Army, which was advancing from the Lutsk region upon Dubno–Rovno, collapsed so completely before a powerful Russian counter-attack east of the Styr sector towards the middle of September, that grave consequences were to be feared. In this case, too, G.H.Q. found itself compelled not to refuse the urgently requested assistance. Two divisions were immediately moved southwards from Prince Leopold's Army Group. Their intervention speedily brought the enemy to a standstill at the Styr sector. It is true that one more condition had to be attached to the sending of these troops. It had proved to be necessary to put the left wing of the Austro-Hungarian front under German command. The 4th Austro-Hungarian Army, which stood on the Styr in the neighbourhood of Lutsk, together with all the Austro-Hungarian and German troops north of it as far as the right wing of Prince Leopold's Army Group, were combined to form the Linsingen Army Group.

The winter positions of the Austro-Hungarian front stretched from Rumania along the Bessarabian frontier to the Dniester, then ran behind this river, behind the Strypa, east of Brody, behind the Styr, and sprang back below Rafalovka to the Stochod, following the course of the latter to 25 miles south of the Pripet.

The 1915 campaign against Russia fulfilled the intentions of G.H.Q. in view of the comparatively small forces available for it. It is true that the annihilation of the enemy had not been achieved. But it was not put forward as a goal, nor could it have been in the circumstances. On the other hand, a weakening and crippling of the enemy had taken place, from which he would be unable to recover properly if we succeeded in keeping him in his isolated state, and from which it was to be expected that his fighting spirit would be broken for an indefinite period. This was bound to take place the sooner, the less he was in a position to feed his people and army with hopes of a reversal of fortune by the successes which he had just obtained on the Austro-Hungarian front. In the German sectors there were scarcely any more reverses to be feared.

It was, therefore, of absolute importance to raise the fighting value of certain portions of the Austro-Hungarian troops. G.H.Q., therefore, turned its efforts in this direction. Attempts were made to achieve this object by the exchange of officers, by instruction in the building of positions, by influence—through the channel of the Prussian Ministry of War—on the Austro-Hungarian War Ministry making for a better use of the resources of the country, and many other measures besides. This had to be done very cautiously lest more harm than good should ensue. The very sensitive feelings of the Austro-Hungarian G.H.Q. and the Austro-Hungarian Government had not to be hurt, nor their reputation among the peoples of the Dual Monarchy diminished. A great deal of improvement was effected all the same.

In one matter, however, G.H.Q. was impotent. It had no possibility of exerting any influence upon the internal conditions of the Danubian Empire or of preventing the consequences of the existing ferment of feeling from affecting the Austro-Hungarian Army. The dangers inherent in that feeling were well known. Nothing was left undone in the way of warning and exhortation. But we never got to the roots of the evil.

The period under review, rich though it was in military

Operations against Russia in 1915

events, also witnessed great activity on the part of G.H.Q. in the military-political sphere. The negotiations with Austria-Hungary and Bulgaria have already been touched on above. I shall have occasion later on to deal with these and other questions in greater detail. But two matters of outstanding importance must be dealt with at this point. One is the efforts of the Chief of the General Staff to bring about an attempt to make peace with Russia, and the other the suspension, in its then form, of the submarine campaign in order not to jeopardize the conclusion of the negotiations with Bulgaria.

ATTEMPT TO BRING ABOUT A RAPPROCHEMENT WITH
RUSSIA, JULY, 1915

The consequences of the Gorlice-Tarnow battle for Russia and the (not, indeed, unexpected) failure of the Italian Army had strengthened our conviction that Germany would win the war if she succeeded, as she had hitherto done, in avoiding the overtaxing of her strength, either internally or externally. G.H.Q., accordingly, consistently refused to have anything to do with the pursuit of military successes of doubtful permanent value or any nebulous war aims.

Among such aims was the hope of inflicting on the enemies of the Central Powers so complete a defeat by force of arms that they would have to sue unconditionally for peace. The enemy's superiority of strength made this impossible. So far as the East is concerned, the reasons why this was impossible have already been stated several times. As for the West, to reckon, in the face of our very limited positive successes at sea, on achieving the objective in that theatre under all circumstances involved a fundamental misconception of the determination of our Western enemies, and of the power of resistance at any rate of England; it amounted, indeed, to risking far more than was justified on an uncertain hand. On the other hand, one could count, with as much certainty as can ever be present in war, on forcing the enemy in the West to abandon their intention of destroying us, if we deprived them of the prospect of defeating Germany and her allies in the long run by exhaustion, before they themselves had suffered irreparable losses. A peace, even on this basis, would really amount, in this war of defence, to a complete victory for the Central Powers, the fruits of which, while they would only ripen in the future, would for that very reason be the more secure. Accordingly, no stone should be left unturned which offered any prospect of lightening Germany's heavy task and of frustrating her Western enemies.

The position which developed in July, 1915, in the Eastern theatre of war presented a good opportunity for action in accordance with this line of thought. It seemed clear, on the one hand, that the Petrograd Government must by now realize that the Russian Armies could not recover in any calculable time from the blows they had received, and in particular that they could not prevent the loss of the capital of Poland if the German operations were continued. On the other hand, the stubborn resistance of the Russians in their hopeless position west of the Vistula betrayed the tremendous importance attached in Petrograd to the retention of Polish soil, and in particular of Warsaw. The Chief of the General Staff, thinking it necessary to make use

Operations against Russia in 1915

of these circumstances to our advantage, proposed to the Government that communication should be established with Russia with a view to an understanding, emphasizing that from the military point of view the advantages of a peace in the East were so great that the renunciation of territorial gains could not be counted against it. He was not shaken in this view by the consideration that it would probably involve an unhappy future for the population of German origin in the Baltic provinces, the future of the whole being of more importance than that of a small part.

Berlin raised no objections to the proposal, and the Chancellor approved the step suggested. It was undertaken, but unfortunately without any success. It resulted, indeed, in such an increase in hostility to Germany that we thought it better to break off entirely for the time all bridges with the East. This policy found emphatic expression in the well-known speech of the Chancellor in the Reichstag in the middle of August,* and the army had simply to accept the position.

* In this speech the Chancellor said :

" Our troops and those of Austria-Hungary have reached the Eastern frontiers of Congress Poland, and the two have now the task of administering the territory.

" The chances of politics and of geographical position have long forced Germans and Poles to fight against one another. The memory of these old enmities does not diminish our respect for the devotion, the patriotism, and the determination with which the Polish people have defended its old Western civilization and its love of freedom against the Russians, and retained them even through the misfortunes of this war. I do not imitate the hypocritical promises of our enemies, but I hope that the present occupation of Polish territory will be the beginning of a development which will put an end to the old antagonism between Germans and Poles, and will ensure to the country, freed from the Russian yoke, a happy future, in which it can plant and develop its special national characteristics."

Critical Decisions at General Headquarters

SUSPENSION OF UNRESTRICTED SUBMARINE WARFARE, SUMMER, 1915

It has been mentioned in an earlier chapter that since the month of February the submarine campaign had been carried on virtually without restrictions in the waters around England that had been declared as a war zone. Up to the end of the summer, however, it had only satisfied to a limited extent the hopes entertained as to its results. True, damage had been done to England, but there had so far been no perceptible influence on the enemy's warlike operations. In view of the conduct of the crews of the submarines, which was heroic and self-sacrificing beyond all praise, the reason for this could only be found in the fact that there were not enough boats available. Much time and work were required to make good this shortage. The navy, in spite of its well-known, often even excessive, optimism, did not expect that this could be done before the spring of 1916. This circumstance again constitutes one more earnest warning against the danger of the view so often held among civilians, who have no personal responsibility, that one can rely in war simply on new construction. It shows clearly what a disastrous mistake was made by Germany before the war, in preferring the construction of battleships to the sufficient development of the submarine, the real weapon of the weaker naval power.

But this was not the only direction in which the submarine campaign had brought us grave disappointment.

America had at first attempted to obtain the suspension of the campaign by proposing that Germany should give it up if England would undertake to permit in future the passage to Germany of foodstuffs destined exclu-

The Submarine Campaign, 1915

sively for the non-belligerent civil population of Germany, and accordingly not to be requisitioned for military purposes. America was willing to guarantee this by carrying out strict measures of supervision in Germany.

Although there were very serious objections to such an interference in the internal life of the country, our Government accepted the proposal immediately. They were quite right to do so, for its execution would have involved very close relations with America, from which great results might be hoped. England, on the other hand, refused, as indeed was inevitably to be expected from her standpoint. What the insistence of the English on this policy cost the German people, and what a tremendous influence it had on the result of the war, is now a matter of history. That it contradicted the first principles, both of international law and of humanity, caused no anxiety to the English, who have never been influenced by such considerations when their own advantage was in question.

England was, however, not content with the mere refusal. In March she published an Order outlawing everything of German origin at sea. This Order went far beyond the provisions of an " effective " blockade, although none had even been declared, and wholly disregarded the rights of neutrals.

America, however, took up a stronger attitude of objection, not to the English measures, but to those of Germany, which were merely measures of defence against openly admitted breaches of international law. England was thus able, not merely to disregard the protest, but even to leave it unanswered. The note, however, which America addressed to Germany concerning the torpedoing without warning of an American steamship (the *Lusitania*) amounted to a veiled declaration of war.

Critical Decisions at General Headquarters

After this note we could no longer cherish any hope that America would, even officially, preserve permanently the outward appearance of neutrality, and we had to reckon that she would proceed to open hostility if there were any repetition of such cases as the *Lusitania*. As such cases were bound to recur shortly if the campaign were continued in its existing form, Germany was faced with the choice between continuing the campaign at the price of bringing America into the ranks of her enemies on the one hand and the restriction of operations and the outward maintenance of peace with America on the other.

If America had joined the Entente at this stage of the war, it would have cost us at once the help of Bulgaria. The leaders in Sofia, with whom we had at this time just resumed negotiations, would never have made an agreement with us if America had ranged herself openly with our enemies. But, unless Germany gained the support of Bulgaria, it would be impossible permanently to keep the Dardanelles closed and Russia cut off.

The submarine campaign, with its relatively small actual results, was not worth this price, and we therefore had to suspend operations in the form hitherto employed until further developments. They could only be continued in the form of cruiser warfare, that is to say, that no commercial vessel could be sunk until it had been overhauled and examined.

CHAPTER VII

ATTEMPTS TO BREAK THROUGH IN THE WEST IN THE AUTUMN OF 1915, AND THE CAMPAIGN AGAINST SERBIA

AS has already been mentioned, since about the month of July, 1915, great weight had had to be given, in the decisions as to continuing operations in the East, to the question how we could ensure, without relaxing the pressure on Russia, that sufficient forces would be available to withstand the attack that was to be expected on the Western front and to open up communications though the Balkans. The question became more pressing as the year advanced, and we had to be ready to solve it at any moment in which it might suddenly become urgent. The Chief of the General Staff was convinced that it was more important than the question of bringing the Russians "to their knees" merely by military force.

If the German front did not hold in the West, or the Dardanelles were lost, no advantage that could still be gained against the Russians was of any value.

CONCLUSION OF THE CONVENTION WITH BULGARIA (SEE MAP 5)

Under pressure from G.H.Q. negotiations had again been under way in Sofia since July for Bulgaria to join

Critical Decisions at General Headquarters

the Central Powers. Ably conducted by Prince von Hohenlohe-Langenburg and by the new German military attaché, Major von Massow, they resulted in the attendance at G.H.Q. at the end of August of a Bulgarian representative, the then Lieutenant-Colonel Gantschew, to discuss the terms of a miltary convention. The real motive of the Bulgarians in joining us was presumably to be found in their realization that they could not expect from the Entente any support in their national aspirations for the acquisition of the territory inhabited by Bulgarians in Serbia and Rumania. Even in the matter of a possible extension of their territory at the expense of Turkey they could have little to hope for from the side on which Russia stood, while their adhesion to the Central Powers immediately brought them, thanks to the broad-mindedness of the Turkish statesmen, the Turkish territory to the west of the Maritza, for which they so earnestly longed. One need hardly mention that, apart from these considerations, confidence in the strength of the Central Powers and the ultimate victory of their good cause had great weight.

The convention was signed on the 6th September at Pless by Generals Conrad von Hötzendorf and von Falkenhayn and by Lieutenant-Colonel Gantschew. Full provision was made for Turkey's concurrence.

By the convention, Germany and Austria-Hungary, with six divisions each, were to be on the Serbian frontier ready for operations within 30 days, while Bulgaria had to reach the same stage with at least four divisions* within 35 days. Field-Marshal von Mackensen was to take supreme command of all these troops. Germany was ready, if the undertaking developed as was

* The Bulgarian divisions were almost double the German in infantry strength.

MAP IV

The Summer Campaign in the East, 1915

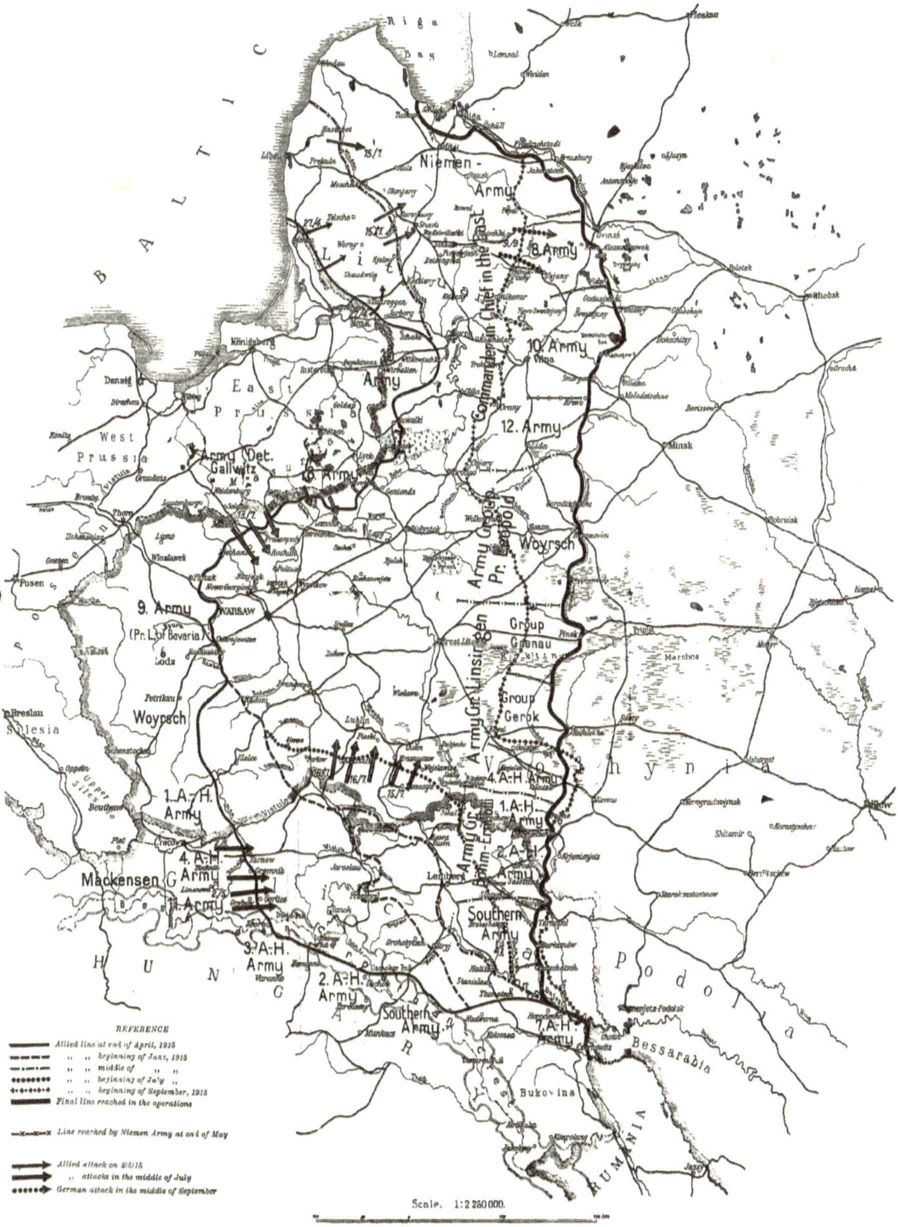

The West and the Serbian Campaign, 1915

hoped, to station one mixed infantry brigade at Varna and one at Burgas, and to ensure, as far as possible, the introduction of submarines into the Black Sea for the defence of the Bulgarian coast. In this way it was hoped to influence the attitude of certain circles of the Bulgarian population, which could otherwise not be relied upon against the Russians. Bulgaria further undertook to have the four above-mentioned divisions mobilized at the latest by the 21st September, and to move into Serbian Macedonia on the 11th October with at least one further division. Germany in return declared her readiness, in addition to granting substantial financial aid, to supply Bulgaria with munitions, so far as her own needs permitted. She also consented to induce the Turks, if Bulgaria desired, to defend the port of Dedeagatch against hostile landings, and to place the troops employed for this purpose under Bulgarian command. To avoid undesirable incidents, it was agreed that Bulgaria was to preserve unconditional neutrality towards Greece and Rumania until the completion of the operations against Serbia, subject to an assurance from these States that they would remain neutral and not occupy any Serbian territory. A further clause, by which Bulgaria was bound to allow absolutely unrestricted transport of troops and material to and from Turkey, so soon as the way through Serbia, the Danube route, or through communication via Rumania should be open, may seem superfluous, but was nevertheless advisable, having regard to conditions in the Balkans.

The agreement gave us the long yearned for opportunity to act energetically in clearing up the position in the South-East, where there was much to be gained. If we succeeded in eliminating Serbia as a serious factor in the war—and of that we had no doubt—the threat to the Austro-Hungarian flank, and with it the whole of the South Slav danger, would disappear.

The establishment of communications with Turkey would presumably ensure the safety of the Dardanelles and the final isolation of Russia from her Entente partners. It also gave prospects of new possibilities for the Turkish operations in Asia.

The adhesion of Bulgaria to the Central Powers, and the successes which were soon obtained in Serbia as a result, could not fail to have an effect on the attitude of Rumania.

Sources of supply for foodstuffs, and important raw materials, especially copper, were rendered available.

PREPARATIONS FOR THE CAMPAIGN AGAINST SERBIA

In view of the above facts, the Germans of necessity attached the greatest weight to the smooth and punctual carrying out of the agreement. Accordingly, when in the middle of September the Austro-Hungarian G.H.Q. stated that, as a consequence of the initially successful Russian counter-offensive in Volhynia and East Galicia, which is dealt with in the previous chapter, it was not in a position to fulfil the obligations it had undertaken, and when the German liaison officer in Southern Hungary reported that he did not think that the Austro-Hungarian troops that were already assembled there were capable of offensive fighting, we did not hesitate to send to the Serbian frontier, to replace the four Austro-Hungarian divisions* that thus fell out, an equal number of German troops beyond the divisions agreed on. To secure

* In fact, the Austro-Hungarians did later send more than just the two divisions; some of the troops, it is true, being of very limited value.

The West and the Serbian Campaign, 1915

their deployment at the proper time it became necessary to withdraw one division from the Western front, in spite of the anxious position there. It was only possible to take this risk because the 10th Army Corps and other troops following them were already on their way from the northern part of the Eastern front to reinforce our troops in the French theatre.

The hope that the campaign against Serbia could be carried through rapidly was based on the fact that both the relative strengths of the forces available and the strategical position favoured the allied forces.

The Serbian troops that were still fit for battle were estimated to number in all 190,000 to 200,000. Our troops available against them were some 330,000, who in the main must have been superior in military value to the Serbians. The latter could hardly be expected to withstand the effects of massed heavy artillery or of trench mortar batteries.

Our geographical position in relation to Serbia enabled us to undertake effective enveloping operations from the outset. We could not, it is true, take full advantage of this circumstance, as the Austro-Hungarian troops stationed in Bosnia and Herzegovina, weakened by drafts for the Isonzo front, were not really equal to undertaking an offensive movement into Serbia. We were content that they were strong enough for their other task of holding the Montenegrins in check by their presence, little as one believed in the offensive capacity of the sons of the Black Mountain. The poor condition of the communications rendered it impossible to assemble any German formations on the Bosnian-Serbian frontier, and according to our reports there was no possibility of their early improvement.

We had accordingly to abandon the scheme of attacking

Critical Decisions at General Headquarters

the western flank of Serbia also, confining ourselves to a simultaneous advance against the northern and eastern fronts. The prospects were still unusually favourable. On each of the two fronts we had forces available which were certainly superior to the whole of the Serbian forces in fighting value, if not in numbers. The enemy could thus not use the advantage he possessed in having interior lines, even apart altogether from the fact that his communications were insufficient for such purposes. It became the more difficult for him to follow this course, the more he decided to divert some of his forces to meet the troops which were to move, far to the south, from Bulgaria into Macedonia to cut the line to Salonica, the only railway link between Serbia and the outside world.

The orders for the deployment of the troops and the beginning of operations were drawn up in agreement with our allies, in the light of these considerations.

The 3rd Austro-Hungarian Army of four divisions, under General von Kövess, reinforced by a German army corps of three divisions, assembled on the Save and at the confluence of the Save and Danube. The main body of this army was to force the crossing at Belgrade, and the remainder at Kupinovo, and then, after taking precautionary measures against danger from the Kolubara region, to advance via Topola in the direction of Kragujevac.

A new 11th German Army, under General von Gallwitz, who was succeeded in the command of the 12th Army by Infantry General von Fabeck, marched, seven German divisions strong, along the Danube to the east of the mouth of the Temes, facing the bridging points that had been reconnoitred there. Their main forces were to cross at Ram, and the rest at Semendria. A

The West and the Serbian Campaign, 1915

feint crossing was to be arranged at Orsova. The army was then to advance up the Morava.

Of the 1st Bulgarian Army, under General Bojadieff, the 6th division was assembled at Kula, the 5th and 8th round Bielogradchik, and the 1st at Zaribrod, while the 7th division and the Macedonian Legion, consisting of volunteers, assembled at Kostendil. This 7th division and the Legion were later formed into the 2nd Bulgarian Army, under General Todorow. The 6th division was to move on Zajecar, sending a detachment to Negotin to open the Danube, the 5th and 8th were to move on Nish via Kniazhevac, and the 1st via Pirot to the same point. The 7th division and the Macedonian legion were to be moved into the Vardar valley, to cut the Nish-Salonica railway as soon as possible.

The 6th October was fixed for the opening of the operations of the 3rd Austro-Hungarian Army and of our 11th, and the 11th October for the Bulgarians. It was possible to fix so early a date, as the preparations for the deployment and the river crossing had been absolutely completed. As early as the spring German General Staff officers had reconnoitred the whole position in minutest detail, and every measure of preparation then possible had been taken. Every battery position, every possible bridging point, the billeting of the troops on assembly, and their supplies, were settled, and bridges and other crossing material, ammunition and commissariat, were all in readiness. The troops had virtually nothing to do but to march up and proceed instantly with the crossing. The far-sighted officer in charge of these preparations, Lieut.-Colonel Hentsch, of the Saxon General Staff, joined the staff of the Mackensen army group as Quartermaster-General. It was mainly due to his work that we were able to achieve the effect of surprise by not bringing the troops up until the last moment, and, indeed, that the whole tremendous military undertaking of the crossing of the Save and Danube was carried smoothly through without a hitch.

In the South-Eastern theatre the programme only suffered one modification, and that through the Bulgarians. It soon became clear that, owing to difficulties of administration, they would only be able to mobilize by the 23rd September, instead of the 21st, and that their main body would not be ready to move on the 11th October, and in all probability not until the 15th. As, however, they asserted positively that they would cross the Macedonian frontier on the 11th October, in spite of this delay, no alteration was made in the date (the 6th October) fixed for the opening of operations of the 3rd Austro-Hungarian and our 11th Armies. We hoped by this means to have a good effect on the determination of the Bulgarians, and we were not disappointed.

THE GREAT RELIEF OFFENSIVES IN THE WEST, END OF SEPTEMBER, 1915

A more serious interruption to our plans seemed at the outset to threaten from events which occurred in the French theatre of war at the time of the deployment against Serbia.

The failure of the long-expected attacks to materialize had led us in August to doubt whether the attempt at relief, now that it could no longer be of use to the Russians, would be undertaken at all. For a time we were disposed to regard the enemy's advancing preparations for attack as a feint. However, from the beginning of September onwards, more and more frequent reports

The West and the Serbian Campaign, 1915

went to show that we had to expect an early attack by the British, supported by the French, in the neighbourhood of Lille, with a simultaneous offensive by the French alone in Champagne.

In Flanders and Artois, on a front of over 50 miles as the crow flies, the 6th Army of the Crown Prince Rupert of Bavaria (Chief of Staff being Major-General Kuhl) held the line with sixteen divisions from south of Ypres, immediately east of Armentières, west of Lens, east of Arras, to a point 10 miles from the latter town.

In Champagne, the 3rd Army, under General von Einem, with seven and a half divisions, held, on a front of fully 30 miles, positions which ran from north of Rheims to Massiges. In touch on the left, as far as the Argonne, stood the right wing of the 5th Army of the German Crown Prince, with two divisions in line.

On the 21st September drum fire began against the 6th Army, and on the 22nd against the 3rd and the right wing of the 5th, of an intensity similar to that which we had for the first time employed on a large scale at Gorlice-Tarnow.

Reinforcements from the scanty general reserve had already been sent to the threatened armies, and were now sent in greater numbers. The 3rd and 6th Armies received heavy batteries and one infantry division each, the 3rd having a brigade of infantry in addition.

The bombardment raged with almost undiminished fury in Champagne until the 24th, and in Flanders until the 25th September. On those days the infantry attacks began on both fronts.

Although the terrible gunfire had caused hitherto unheard-of destruction both in and far behind our positions, in addition to very heavy losses in men, the French

Critical Decisions at General Headquarters

were unable to gain any vital advantages on the 24th in Champagne. The English, on the other hand, on the first day of their attack, by the employment of gas, succeeded in occupying our foremost positions at Loos over a breadth of $7\frac{1}{2}$ miles. They were, however, unable to develop this success. Incessant counter-attacks of the brave defenders not only prevented this, but also recovered substantial portions of the lost positions. The French, who attacked the 6th Army on both sides of the Scarpe in conjunction with the English, achieved no successes worthy of mention at all.

The position in Champagne on the 25th September was much more serious. Continuing their offensive, the French on this day, on and to the east of the Souain–Somme-Py road, with seventeen divisions, drove the remnants of two German divisions, on a front of 15 miles, with a depth of $2\frac{1}{2}$ miles, back into their rear positions, which unfortunately had also been shot to pieces. A serious crisis arose, leading the Staff of the 3rd Army to consider the advisability of a further withdrawal of the whole army front. Such a step would of necessity have led to very serious consequences, firstly in the moral effect, which would inevitably have been general, secondly in the tactical results on the neighbouring fronts, and finally by giving space to the enemy masses, which were crowded helplessly together against our present positions, to escape from their momentarily intolerable situation.

Fortunately the proposed withdrawal was never carried out. On the urgent advice of the Chief of Staff of the neighbouring 5th Army, Major-General Schmidt von Knobelsdorf, the consideration of the matter was adjourned until the arrival of G.H.Q., who were on their way to the Western front, and after their arrival at noon

The West and the Serbian Campaign, 1915

on the 25th September, there was no further question of any voluntary withdrawal. There were still reserves available. They at once threw into Champagne one of the last divisions of the general reserve from Alsace, and the 10th Army Corps, the Guards Corps going to the 6th Army. Both these corps had just reached Belgium from the East. Lieut.-Colonel von Lossberg, who had hitherto occupied a prominent position in the Operations Department of G.H.Q., was appointed as Chief of Staff of the 3rd Army. In addition, the forward reserves of General von Heeringen's 7th Army, on the Aisne, where it was clear that no attacks were in prospect, were withdrawn and sent to the 3rd Army.

This additional strength sufficed to some extent to break the weight of the enemy's first attacks on the fighting fronts, but it was insufficient to repel the whole offensive, which lasted for many days. The heavy fighting wore down the strength even of formations freshly thrown in, all the more quickly because heavy rain had set in on the evening of the 25th September, turning the shell-torn battlefield into a marsh. True, the difficulties thus caused were no doubt even more noticeable in attack than in defence. The enormous numerical superiority against which we had to contend is well illustrated by the fact that there were thrown in against the 3rd Army no less than thirty-five French divisions, with 2,000 heavy and 3,000 field guns. Behind them were numerous cavalry divisions, of which considerable portions actually took part, ready to attack.

Accordingly, in the first half of October, G.H.Q. had many worn troops replaced by fresh divisions, drawn from quiet sectors of the front, until the arrival of further forces from the East relieved them of the task. Apart from the modest initial successes above-mentioned,

Critical Decisions at General Headquarters

the enemy had no further advantages of any importance to record. The fighting did not, however, die down in Flanders until the 13th, or in Champagne until the 20th October.

" The greatest battle of all time," as the commander of an English Guards division described it in divisional orders on the eve of the battle, had been fought. But it had not achieved the success contemplated by the French C.-in-C., General Joffre, in his battle orders.*

They had not driven the Germans out of France,

---

* The order ran as follows :

" G.H.Q., Western Army,
" September 14th, 1915.

" To GENERAL OFFICERS COMMANDING :

" The spirit of the troops and their self-sacrifice are the most important condition of the attack. The French soldier fights all the more bravely, the better he understands the importance of the offensive operation, and the more he trusts in the measures taken by his leaders. It is accordingly essential that officers of all ranks from to-day onwards should explain to their subordinates the favourable conditions under which the next attack undertaken by the French forces will take place. The following points must be known to all ranks :

" 1. It is necessary for us to take the offensive in the French theatre, in order to drive the Germans out of France. We shall both free our fellow-countrymen from their twelve months' slavery, and wrench from the enemy the valuable possession of our occupied districts. In addition, a splendid victory over the Germans will induce neutral countries to reach a decision in our favour, and will force the enemy to slacken his attacks on the Russians in order to meet our offensive.

" 2. All possible steps have been taken to secure that this attack can be undertaken with substantial forces and tremendous material resources. The incessant improvement in the defensive arrangements of our inner lines, the ever more extensive employment of territorial troops at the front, and the increasing number of British troops landed in France, have enabled the C.-in-C. to withdraw from the front a large number of divisions, whose strength is equal to that of several armies, and to hold them in readiness for the attack. These forces, as also those that have remained in the line, are fully equipped with new weapons. The number of machine guns has been more than doubled. There are large supplies of ammunition for the field artillery, and all worn guns have been replaced. The mechanical transport has been increased, both for supplies and for troop movements. Special efforts have been

The West and the Serbian Campaign, 1915

not a single one of their countrymen had been freed from his twelve months' "slavery," and a splendid victory had not been won over the Germans. The only effect one must admit is that, not the attack, but the anticipation of it, and the preparation to meet it, had an influence on the German operations against Russia. But this fact cannot be credited to the battle, being a simple

devoted to the heavy guns, the most important weapon of attack. A great number of large calibre batteries have been combined and prepared, with a view to the next offensive operations. The ammunition provided for every gun is larger than the largest consumption yet known.

" 3. The present time is particularly favourable for a general attack. On the one hand, Kitchener's armies have completed their disembarkation in France, and on the other, the Germans have in the last month withdrawn troops from our front for employment against the Russians. Behind their thin trench lines the Germans have but scanty reserves.

" 4. The attack is to be general. It will consist of several large, simultaneous attacks, on very wide fronts. The English will take part with large forces, and the Belgian troops will also join in. So soon as the enemy is shaken, the troops on hitherto inactive sectors of the front will also attack, to complete the enemy's confusion, and force him to break up. All attacking troops will not merely have to take the first enemy trenches, but will have to force their way through, without rest day and night, across the second and third lines into the open country. The synchronization of the attacks, their weight and extent, will prevent the enemy assembling his reserves of infantry and artillery at one point, as he was able to do north of Arras. These circumstances ensure success.

" The communication of this order to the troops will not fail to raise their spirits to the necessary level. It is accordingly essential that it be communicated cleverly and in a convincing manner."

On the 21st September General Joffre added in a new order:

" The enormous force of the blow which is to be dealt by the French and British troops is to be explained before the attack to all regiments, in substantially the following manner:

" There are told off for the operations:

" 35 divisions under General de Castelnau, 13 divisions under General Foch, 13 English divisions, and 15 cavalry divisions (including 5 English).

" Three-quarters of the French forces are thus taking part in the general battle. They are supported by 2,000 heavy and 3,000 field guns, whose ammunition supplies are far greater than those held at the beginning of the war.

" All the conditions of a certain success are present, especially when one recollects that only 15 divisions and 300 guns took part in our last attacks in the neighbourhood of Arras."

result of waging war on many fronts. The "greatest battle of all time" became a terrible defeat for the attackers. Tremendous sacrifices in men and material were made for a result which was nothing in comparison to the objectives aimed at, and in itself amounted to but little, for it was of no importance from the general point of view whether a few narrow sectors of the German positions had to be withdrawn a few miles or not. The defensive system remained absolutely unshaken. In the then condition of relative strength, no more could be achieved.

Nor could we have done any more with all the additional men we might have brought up by breaking off the Eastern operations earlier. The troops and material available would not even then have been sufficient for counter-attacks, or attacks on other fronts, with large objectives. And to have made any sacrifice for the sake of local successes was not at that time in our interests. Without involving any prejudice to the aims which we could, on a sober calculation of all the conditions, reasonably pursue in the East, the reinforcements arrived in the West at exactly the right moment for the task allotted to them there. Had they arrived earlier they might have ensured that the small indentations in our front should be smaller still, but that was of no importance for the general position, while their earlier recall from the Eastern front would have crippled the operations in progress there, the prospects of which were most emphatically described by the commanders on the spot as extraordinarily good.

The earlier arrival of reinforcements from the East would, however, certainly have spared both leaders and men in France from terrible experiences. What G.H.Q. had to endure at that period requires no description.

The West and the Serbian Campaign, 1915

Finally, it must not be forgotten that the German soldier on the Western front is entitled to most of the credit for the fact that the reinforcements from the East came up in time. His marvellous resistance in the pitifully shattered positions in Flanders and Champagne warded off the danger of their reaching the front line too late.

Amid death and terror he clung firm, in accordance with his battle orders, to the spot he had to defend, in countless cases even when there had long been no officer or N.C.O. left to set him an example. Not content with that, he attacked with magnificent self-sacrifice the enemy masses surging over and around him, whenever opportunity arose. Thus were formed firm islands and islets in the sea of destruction created by the enemy artillery. Against these, the first waves of the enemy infantry attacks were broken, but the masses following them pressed forward unceasingly. Blocks and bunches of men formed, in which the German artillery tore tremendous gaps, while it became impossible to maintain order. Enemy reinforcements failed. The more men were brought up, the worse the position became. The offensive was throttled by its own mass.

No language could be too strong to describe the achievements of the German troops in the Champagne battlefield in those days. Every great deed hitherto done in war paled beside their heroism.

This tribute to the German soldier involves no depreciation of his enemies. To be defeated in a fight against heroes is no disgrace. If the French and English cannot be placed on the same level as the defenders, they certainly did their duty nobly. Their losses are the best proof of this. The lack of success was due to no failure of theirs. It was probably mainly due to the plan of operations. The French had not sufficiently realized that, with the effective weapons of to-day, forces can only be advantageously massed for combined action within narrow limits, and that advantage turns to disadvantage when these limits are not observed. It is certain that the old phrase as to the impossibility of being too strong at the decisive moment will never lose any of its strength, but it is equally certain that numerical superiority alone can never ensure a favourable decision.

In spite of their sorry experiences, not only in the Arras battle, but also in the winter battle in Champagne, the French leaders seem to have clung to the conviction that a break through positions fortified by up-to-date means, and defended by troops of the quality of those, especially the Germans, employed on the Western front, was still possible if very superior numbers could be employed. They may have been confirmed in their views by the success of Gorlice-Tarnow, coupled with the exaggerated Russian reports of the " masses " brought up by the Germans in that battle. These reports would not, however, have mentioned that the attack in Galicia was not undertaken until the Germans felt certain that they were opposed by troops whose *moral* was absolutely rotted by a merciless campaign. In truth, this is the chief factor in the solution of the problem so often discussed during the war, whether attempts to break through with the object of forcing a decision constituted a wise policy or not. Against an enemy in good military and moral condition they were certainly not to be recommended. Accordingly, in the whole course of the war, breaks-through only succeeded where this condition was not present.

It would, further, be quite unjust, in describing the

The West and the Serbian Campaign, 1915

heroic deeds of the German soldiers in the defensive battles in the West, to forget the equally fine achievements of their leaders. Little as these came into prominence when compared with the performances in large offensive operations, they really surpassed them. Never in the whole history of warfare have human nerves been subjected to harder tests than those applied to the leaders in these engagements. They came through the test magnificently. Equal praise must be given to the N.C.O.'s in the trenches and elsewhere, and to the highest officers at headquarters.

THE CROSSING OF THE DANUBE

While the great battle in France was developing and raging, the deployment and preparations for attack in South Hungary pursued their allotted course. Instead of the one division that was to come from France, another that was on its way from Russia to the West was diverted to the South-East. That was the sum total of the influence on the Serbian campaign of all that the English and French had sacrificed in the West.

In the course of the month of September, the Serbian bank was repeatedly shelled for purposes of deception, without any further steps being taken, but on the 6th October the bombardment preparatory to the real crossing was begun, the crossing following on the 7th. The 3rd Austro-Hungarian Army crossed on the line Kupinovo–Belgrade, and the left half of our 11th Army at Ram, the right following on the next day at Semendria. Feints by the troops on the Drina and at Orsova riveted the attention of the enemy at those points. Tactically, they were completely taken by surprise. The assurances

Critical Decisions at General Headquarters

of the Entente that the Central Powers could only be pretending to attack, and that they would reinforce the Serbians in ample time, had lulled the Serbian G.H.Q. into a sense of security. Their main forces were assembled to meet the Bulgarians. It was not until, at the beginning of October, the gravity of the danger threatening from the North was recognized that more or less unsystematic troop movements in that direction were undertaken.

Accordingly, the 3rd Austro-Hungarian and our 11th Army, while they were often bravely opposed, were nowhere resisted with real determination. The speed of their advance was reduced, not so much by the enemy's resistance as by the difficulties of ensuring supplies. Thus, the bridging material for the 11th Army could not be brought up until the hill country around Grotzka, between Belgrade and Semendria, had been cleared. Then bridging work was prevented for several days by one of the notorious Danube storms, called the Kossowa. It was not until the 21st October that we succeeded in building two bridges for this army.

On this day, the heads of our columns stood roughly on the line Ripani, south of Belgrade, Kaliste, south-east of Pozarevacz. Two Austro-Hungarian Landsturm brigades had crossed the lower Drina and reached Sabac. The 1st Bulgarian Army had reached the Timok valley between Zajecar and Kniazevac, and its left wing was fighting round Pirot. The 2nd Bulgarian Army was approaching, between Vrania and Kumanovo, the sector of the Vardar which it had already cut at Veles. The railway communications of the Serbians to Salonica were thus broken. All the armies were complaining bitterly of the great difficulties caused by the lack of roads, and still more by the condition during wet weather of such roads as there were. This was especially the case with

The West and the Serbian Campaign, 1915

the 3rd Austro-Hungarian Army, which, even without that disadvantage, found it more difficult to overcome the enemy resistance than the neighbouring army, which consisted wholly of German formations.

G.H.Q. feared that the lagging progress of the 3rd Austro-Hungarian Army would lead to a general slowing-up of the operations, and accordingly urged upon the Austro-Hungarian G.H.Q. the reinforcement of the army from the Isonzo front. The latter, however, felt unable to adopt this suggestion, as the enemy on the Italian front possessed a superiority of two to one.

The position on the left wing of the 11th Army, too, was not wholly satisfactory. The Austro-Hungarian group at Orsova, not, it is true, a very large one, had not yet succeeded in crossing the river. As a result, the preparations for opening communications with Bulgaria, which the shortage of munitions and equipment that was already making itself felt among the Bulgarian forces made most urgent, could not be carried out. In order to clear up the situation, the Chief of the General Staff decided on the 20th October, to bring reinforcements from the French theatre of war, a step which was rendered possible by the slackening which had meanwhile become apparent in the great offensive activity of the enemy in the West. The Alpine Corps, which had just arrived in France from the Tyrol, and which was so splendidly fitted for mountain fighting, was sent to the Banat. It had been withdrawn from the Tyrolese front, as not being required there in the winter. Before, however, this corps had disembarked, the assistance of some small German forces had succeeded in getting the Orsova group forward and thus opening up the Danube route. The Alpines were thus not required at that point, and could be sent to the right wing of the 3rd Austro-Hungarian Army, to help that to advance. The advance continued at all points, in spite of temporary stoppages at one point or another through difficulties of supply or resistance by the enemy. At times considerable persuasion was required to induce the 1st Bulgarian Army to advance.

Nish fell on the 5th November. The inner wings of the two Bulgarian armies occupied the capital of Serbia. The southern army, the 2nd, had crossed the line Leskovac, Vrania, Kumanovo, in the direction of Prishtina. It held the district of Veles. South of Strumitza weak attempts at attack by the French, who had meanwhile landed at Salonica, were easily beaten off. The main body of the 1st Bulgarian Army had reached the district to the east of Alecsinac, while its right wing, to which the German forces that had crossed at Orsova had attached themselves, had arrived at Paracin. Tied down to its road transport, it had fallen behind the eastward column of the 11th Army, which was already to the south-west of Paracin in the Morava valley. From here the front of the 11th and of the 3rd Austro-Hungarian Armies ran via Kralievo to Cacak. Still further to the west, the Austro-Hungarian brigades that had come across the lower Drina were at Uzice, and one Austro-Hungarian division that had, after all, come from Bosnia lay to the east of Visegrad.

After suffering very heavy losses in the fighting up to this point, the Serbians were now retreating on the whole front in the general direction of the plateau of Kossovo ("the plain of the blackbirds"), near Prishtina. They offered no determined resistance save to the southern half of the 2nd Bulgarian Army, whose swift advance threatened to cut off their retreat to Albania, the only line of escape that still remained open to them. At-

The West and the Serbian Campaign, 1915

tempts to hasten the advance of this army by sending portions of the 1st Bulgarian Army to its aid had no success. The roads and the problem of supply presented insuperable obstacles to all troop movements that could not be thoroughly worked out long beforehand. For this reason it proved impossible to employ German forces on the southern wing, as was repeatedly urged by the Austro-Hungarian G.H.Q. In addition, there was no ground for the fear that the Serbians might break through at Veles in order to join the Entente troops that were advancing from Salonica up the Vardar. That this might be attempted was within the bounds of probability, but it could have no prospects of success in face of the pressure of the main body of Mackensen's forces, which could operate from the north against the flank and rear of any such movement. Signs, too, of the breaking up of the Serbian Army became ever more clearly recognizable on the line of their retreat. If they were not given breathing space, their end would come in a few weeks. Their escape to Albania, it is true, could not be wholly prevented, but it could be rendered more difficult by accelerating the advance of a column of the 3rd Austro-Hungarian Army along the road from Kralievo, through Rashka, and that of the Bulgarians up to and beyond Prishtina in the direction of Mitrovitza. The topographical conditions compelled the pursuing armies simply to keep on the march along the few roads that were still available. But there was little to be feared from a flight into Albania. In that wild mountain country, the Serbians could not take with them artillery or transport, or wheeled vehicles of any description. Again, they could find no food there, nothing indeed but a population largely hostile to them, and unlikely to neglect the opportunity to rob them of anything they had left.

Critical Decisions at General Headquarters

In the light of this position, Mackensen's army group received orders on the 5th November to continue the operations. A request to the same effect was sent to the Bulgarians for their 2nd Army, which was not placed directly under the Field-Marshal. The concentric advance that was ordered would of necessity rapidly reduce the space available for operations, thus forcing substantial portions of the 11th Army into the second line. It was to this that the Austro-Hungarian G.H.Q. had referred in suggesting the reinforcement of the Bulgarian 2nd Army by German troops. It has already been explained why this could not be done. The opportunity that thus arose of restoring the German formations forced out of the line to their old strength by giving them good food and rest in more comfortable quarters in the valleys and in the Banat was very welcome. They were all the more in need of this care, as they had up to the present borne the main burden of the Serbian campaign, for the special features of which they were not adequately equipped.

While the columns of the allied armies climbed up in the course of November to the Kossovo plateau, under indescribable difficulties of marching, increased by bad weather, and soon also by difficulties of supply, the question arose for urgent decision what measures, apart from mere defence, were to be taken against the Entente forces that had landed in Salonica from Gallipoli, Egypt and Northern France to relieve the Serbians. They had been disembarking since the beginning of October. As the Greek Government had not consented to this, their action involved a serious breach of international law, which deprived the Entente even of ostensible justification for any further outcry against the march through Belgium as an act of incredible oppression. Greece did not, however, dare to oppose the invaders

The West and the Serbian Campaign, 1915

by force of arms. The defenceless position of her open coasts and towns against the English and French naval guns, and the fact that the Greek people would starve if they were deprived of imports by sea, were decisive to their attitude. Germany's allies, however, were disposed to take this as a ground for regarding Greece also as an enemy, and it was not without difficulty that another point of view was enabled to prevail. This was to the effect that, while Greece was certainly compelled by the letter of international law not to acquiesce in a breach of neutrality, so that her acquiescence amounted in itself to a breach of neutrality, yet the duty of self-preservation prevailed over the rules of international law, and that this duty had forced Greece to act as she had. Neither the Central Powers nor Bulgaria were then in a position to give Greece any military assistance, or support in her food problems. It was, indeed, satisfactory enough that we succeeded in maintaining the friendly attitude of the Greek Government, having regard to the position of the country, its history, and the unlimited influence that the Entente were able to bring to bear on the Greek people. Germany had certainly no reason, without any perceptible military advantage, and merely to serve the political ambitions of her allies, to procure herself a new enemy, and above all an enemy whose mere existence would be bound to have a tremendous influence on the operations which had just begun against Serbia. In the end neither Austria-Hungary nor Bulgaria were able to deny the force and conviction of this argument. It was further generally recognized that, in the future also, everything was to be avoided that might drive Greece into the ranks of our enemies.

After the Entente troops, as already mentioned, had

Critical Decisions at General Headquarters

been defeated by the Bulgarians in the hills to the south of Strumitza, they abandoned their advance in this direction, and marched instead up the Vardar valley. In the middle of November, the heads of their forces were on the left bank of the Cerna, facing formations from the 2nd Bulgarian Army, which had been diverted to meet them. The movements of the enemy were very slow. The inactivity of the troops in general led to the conclusion that they were very unwilling to obey orders given merely for political reasons, to risk their lives for Serbian interests. Nevertheless, if they were reinforced and advanced further, they might imperil our success in Serbia. Accordingly, in the first ten days of November, Bulgaria and the Central Powers, whose obligations were up to now confined to the operations against Serbia, agreed, after the pending operations against Serbia had been carried through, to take the offensive, again acting together, against the Entente. The Germans certainly thought it well to have it made clear that this agreement was not to be binding if the Entente extended their undertaking to a large scale Balkan operation; if that happened, it would have to be considered afresh whether an attack from our side was worth while, or whether it would not be better to limit ourselves to defending what we had gained.

In this matter G.H.Q. acted consistently with its general attitude to the Serbian undertaking. It regarded it as emphatically a subsidiary operation. The object of the campaign would be completely achieved with the now impending complete defeat of the Serbians, which would remove the threat to the Austro-Hungarian flank, and open the way to the Near East. This last circumstance even gave ground for hope that the enemy would abandon further attempts to force the Dardanelles, and in

The West and the Serbian Campaign, 1915

any event such attempts could no longer have much prospect of success. From the standpoint of the general conduct of the war, the only thing left to do would be to secure the advantages gained. If the opportunity arose incidentally to do military or moral harm to the Entente, it should, of course, not be missed. The idea, however, of seeking the decision of the war in the Balkans was wholly unsound. The German troops necessary for this could not be spared from the main theatres of war. The Entente could send a division to Macedonia more easily than the Germans could a battalion. But even if the necessary forces could have been made available, their effective employment would have been rendered extremely difficult by the nature of the country, the difficulties attending the restoration of the only railway communication, and the probability that its capacity would remain permanently very limited. The employment in that inhospitable country of even a single German soldier more than was necessary, or for a moment longer than was necessary, to achieve our aim, that is, the security of our gains, could only be justified by some advantage of far-reaching importance to the decision of the war.

Holding the views above stated, the Chief of the General Staff found himself to some extent in disagreement with the army chiefs of our allies. They both attached importance to the presence of German troops in the Balkans in as great strength and for as long a time as possible. In addition to the purely military advantages which they stood to gain by this, they hoped also for a furthering of their political aims. It was obviously useful for them to be able, as a result of the presence of strong German forces, to have portions of their own troops available for particular aims of their own. This motive was especially noticeable in the case of the Austro-Hungarian G.H.Q. One must admit that the occupation of Montenegro, carried out by them in January, 1916, was of military importance as a protection to our flank, but the accompanying advance into Central Albania clearly had no value. Both these steps, however, occupied troops which could have been much better employed in Galicia or on the Isonzo.

This divergence of views on fundamental questions relating to the conduct of the war possessed elements of danger that were not to be underestimated, and which were increased by the coolness that had existed from the first in the relations between Austria-Hungary and Bulgaria. The position was not improved when the two armies were brought into closer contact, and the points of difference brought about actual friction. The Bulgarian leaders were greatly hurt by the tendency, apparently firmly rooted among the Austrians, to regard, and at times even to treat, their allies in the Balkans less as allies than as auxiliaries of inferior standing. Austro-Hungarian G.H.Q. complained bitterly of the Bulgarians' thirst for territory and of their arrogance. I make no attempt here to decide which party was in the right. In any case, the unhappy relations between the two allies did not assist the conduct of operations, and frequently called for the mediation of the third party in the alliance. So far this had always been successful, but it was doubtful whether it would always be available at the right moment when the attention of the Chief of the General Staff was more fully taken up with other theatres of war.

Having regard to this situation, the Chief went into the question whether it would not be advisable to give an officially recognized and, therefore, more binding

The West and the Serbian Campaign, 1915

form to the command of the campaign, which in fact lay in German hands, but was exercised formally on the basis of complete equality. The new form would bring us the valuable advantage of the right of supervision and the unconditional veto, but it was to be feared that it would not secure more willing co-operation from our allies, but would be more likely to have the opposite effect. In addition, to emphasize publicly Germany's prominence in the alliance would have an unfavourable effect on the respect commanded by the Austro-Hungarian Government in the interior of the Dual Monarchy. The position would have been different if such a régime had prevailed from the outbreak of war. At the present time its introduction would have been taken by ill-disposed persons, of whom there were many in Austria-Hungary, as an expression of distrust. Finally, we thought we were justified in expecting that the experience gained up to date in the campaign would enable us to avoid serious friction in the future. Accordingly, although both Bulgaria and Turkey favoured the proposal, the Chief of the General Staff let it drop.

The subsequent course of events in the Balkans fully confirmed the correctness of the view taken by G.H.Q.

The advance of the 3rd Austro-Hungarian and our 11th Army to the decisive point in the neighbourhood of Prishtina did not, unfortunately, keep to its programme. In the end, the advance could only be maintained by the withdrawal of half of each of the armies in the neighbourhood of the railways, and the handing over of their supply columns to the troops that remained on the march, in order to enable the latter to continue. The distant co-operation of these troops, however, had its effect on a despairing attack delivered by the

Critical Decisions at General Headquarters

Serbians on the 22nd November at Ferizovic, depriving it of all hope of success once it had failed to break immediately through the brave Bulgarians. The Serbian Army moved quickly to its fate. In the last days of November and on the 1st December it was repeatedly defeated by the Bulgarian troops pursuing it towards Prizren, being in part taken prisoner and in part scattered. Weaker Serbian groups, with which the heads of the 3rd Austro-Hungarian and our 11th Armies came into contact, met with the same fate. Only a few miserable remnants escaped into the Albanian mountains, losing the whole of their artillery and everything else that they could not carry. There was no longer a Serbian Army. The Bulgarians continued the pursuit with small bodies across the Djakova–Dibra line, occupied Ochrida, and dispatched a column to Monastir. A few small German infantry and cavalry formations were attached to this column, both for purposes of deception and to secure the presence of capable and acceptable negotiators in the event of any encounter with Greek troops. To the north of the Bulgarians, portions of the 3rd Austro-Hungarian Army, repelling without difficulty some Montenegrin battalions that had moved across the frontier, advanced on Ipek, Rozaz and Bjelopolje.

The English and French troops dispatched from Salonica had not succeeded in altering the closing act of the Serbian drama. As soon as they realized this, they withdrew, in the latter half of November, the portions of their armies that had advanced over the Cerna back behind the sector, and now held against the main body of the 2nd Bulgarian Army a line running from the Cerna, west of Kavadar, behind the Vardar to Mirovca, and thence to Lake Doiran. Their condition led to the conclusion that, in spite of the shortness of their rear

The West and the Serbian Campaign, 1915

communications, they had not succeeded in satisfactorily solving the question of supply.

The plan of a combined attack upon this force by German and Bulgarian troops, under the supreme command of Field-Marshal von Mackensen, had already of necessity been given up, for the time being, in the middle of November. On closer examination it had appeared that, before the restoration of the Vardar valley railway via Nish to Kumanovo (end of December), it would be impossible to supply more troops in that district besides the Bulgarians who were already there. Even these were only just able, and that irregularly, to bring up enough to cover their requirements in foodstuffs and other essentials. The plan was certainly taken up again for a moment at the end of November, on apparently reliable reports that the Entente did not intend to hold Salonica, for the Chief of the General Staff certainly did not propose to let slip the chance of a victory apparently so easy and certain. It was intended to limit the number of the troops as far as possible, and to carry nothing that could possibly be dispensed with, in order to reduce the difficulties of the enterprise. But this plan was not carried out. Acting on advice from German G.H.Q. to seize independently any opportunity that arose, and on the news that a retirement (probably the result of reports as to the advance of the German-Bulgarian column on Monastir) was in progress among the Entente troops, Bulgarian G.H.Q., in full knowledge of the position, ordered an attack of the 2nd Army on the 5th December. The enemy were thrown back, and retreated southwards on the whole front, suffering considerable further losses as they went. They were unable even to maintain a covering position level with Lake Doiran, the Bulgarians

Critical Decisions at General Headquarters

threatening to outflank it by swift and skilful reinforcement of their troops to the east of the lake. The Entente troops fell back in bad order to Salonica, where they eagerly took up their position in the fortified lines which had been under construction since the beginning of October.

At the request of German G.H.Q., the 2nd Bulgarian Army in their pursuit did not cross the Greek frontier. The army was already suffering considerable want, which it was impossible to remedy, as the allies had made no timely provision to deal with the situation, and the enemy in falling back had completely destroyed such few communications as there were, including the railway line in the Vardar valley. It could not be expected that the Bulgarians under such conditions could achieve any rapid successes against prepared positions, and this all the less because the entry of the Bulgarians alone into Greek territory would have forced even the Greek Government to take active steps against them, and because the enemy were being continually reinforced from Gallipoli. The operation seemed thus to be developing into an undesirable adventure.

At the end of December, 1915, and the beginning of January, 1916, the question of an attack on Salonica was again thoroughly examined more than once. The Austro-Hungarian G.H.Q. was more favourably inclined towards the proposal than the Bulgarian, although the former were unable to provide troops for the enterprise. The Bulgarians appeared less enthusiastic, as they had already completely achieved their main war aim, the conquest of Macedonia. This circumstance alone made the whole undertaking somewhat unsafe. It is not customary among Balkan troops to fight well in a cause of which they cannot see the direct advantage for their

The West and the Serbian Campaign, 1915

own people. Accordingly, when Field-Marshal von Mackensen reported in the middle of January that, in view of the difficulties of supply, a fully prepared offensive against Salonica could not be begun before the middle of April, it was ordered that, while the main grouping of the troops for the offensive was to be carried out, the troops concerned were in the first place to construct permanent positions.

G.H.Q. took up a less favourable attitude to the continuation of the offensive against Salonica with the aid of any substantial body of German troops so soon as it appeared that such an offensive was no longer necessary to compel the Entente to renounce their designs in the Dardanelles. This was the case at the beginning of January. On the morning of the 8th January, 1916, the last English soldier left Gallipoli. More German troops than were absolutely necessary for the support of the Bulgarian fronts could no longer be left in the Balkans. They could only have served particular political aims of the Austro-Hungarians or the Bulgarians, and not the general aims of the war, not to mention any German aim. The entry of the Bulgarians into Salonica would of necessity have had a very unfavourable effect on Greek feeling towards the Central Powers. In all probability a campaign against Greece would have become inevitable. The only advantage that Germany could have reaped from such a campaign would have been to secure submarine bases in the Peloponnesus, certainly a substantial advantage, but by no means sufficient to outweigh the inevitable disadvantages. It was certain that our allies would have made further large demands upon our resources for the campaign, which would have been highly unwelcome to us. We were also reluctant to be faced by the increased Austro-Hungarian claims in the Balkans, which would have been certain to follow any Bulgarian successes. At the very least grave differences between the allies were to be feared. The possession of Salonica must have been very tempting to both of them. It was further to be feared that the attention of the Austro-Hungarians would be attracted to the Balkans far more than was desirable in the interests of the main fronts, a danger, indeed, that already existed. It is true that the expulsion of the Entente would have had the very desirable result for the Bulgarians that they would have been free from any direct danger, but that was only of very doubtful advantage for the general conduct of the war. The Entente troops that would be released in this way would be available for employment in other theatres of war, while the Bulgarians would not. They were not fitted for such employment, nor was their Government bound to supply them. Any alteration of the convention on this point would have been very difficult to secure under the pressure of Bulgarian public opinion, which was wholly unfavourable to such foreign undertakings. The Bulgarian people could only be favourably influenced in their attitude by feeling that they were still threatened and under a duty to fight, and by having an attractive war aim before their eyes. From the general point of view of the Central Powers there was little objection to the development of trench warfare in the Balkans, which was so greatly feared by Austria-Hungary and Bulgaria. If the Bulgarians kept strong detachments of the Entente forces occupied by these means, they would be rendering a great service to the common cause. This was quite possible. One could justifiably hope that the Entente would not, by a voluntary evacuation or by the employment of in-

The West and the Serbian Campaign, 1915

sufficient forces, expose themselves to a second severe moral defeat such as they had just suffered at the Dardanelles. On the other hand we had no need to fear a defeat, even if the Bulgarians were left with the smallest possible support of German troops. The lie of the ground was extraordinarily favourable to defence in the lines now held by Mackensen's Army Group. If the enemy had already failed, under similar conditions, to achieve any decisive success in the Vosges, in the Carpathians, or on the Isonzo, in spite of great efforts, the same result could be confidently expected here, where the climate and many other circumstances favoured the defence.

In the permanent positions the 1st Bulgarian Army, under General Bojadieff, with two Bulgarian infantry divisions and one brigade of cavalry, occupied a line from Lake Ochrida, through Monastir, where there was a German detachment attached to the army, further along the Greek frontier southwards and south-westwards from Prilep. It had thrown out covering forces on the flanks in Albanian territory to Dibra and Elbasan. The 11th Army, under General von Gallwitz, with two German and two and a half Bulgarian divisions, held the Greek frontier from Natja as far as Belasica Planina, to the north of Lake Doiran. In reserve behind this army the German Alpine Corps lay around Veles and Stip. The 2nd Bulgarian Army, under General Todorow, had moved with three Bulgarian divisions on to the Strumitza–Jenikioj–Petric–Nevrokop line. The German troops not included here, who had crossed the Danube in October, were in part in rest camp in Southern Hungary, and in part already back on the Western front. Instead of the one complete German division demanded by Bulgaria in the convention, we had sent

Critical Decisions at General Headquarters

to the Black Sea, with their consent, merely a strengthened brigade of the 101st division; the position there made this reduction possible. The German troops remaining in the Balkans with the Bulgarians did everything that lay in their power to assist their allies in the conduct of trench warfare, for which they were temperamentally less fitted, and insufficiently trained and equipped. If success was only slow in this, the main fault lay with the difficulties experienced by the teachers in making themselves understood by their pupils owing to the differences of language.

The crossing of the Greek frontier from the permanent positions was for the time being only permitted to airmen, in reprisals for an Anglo-French air raid on Monastir, and in cases where the tactical position imperatively demanded. This restriction was due to consideration for the difficult position of the Government and the King of Greece, a consideration similar to that which had weight in many decisions taken during the Balkan campaign. It was never allowed to prevail over military arguments, but the Chief of the General Staff thought it wise to give effect to it wherever this was possible without injury to military interests. In difficult circumstances the Government and the King had faithfully kept the promise they had given to Germany, and she had not so many friends in the world that she could allow herself to throw one away, least of all one who had shown herself capable of disinterested action.

MAP V

Operations in Serbia in the Autumn of 1915

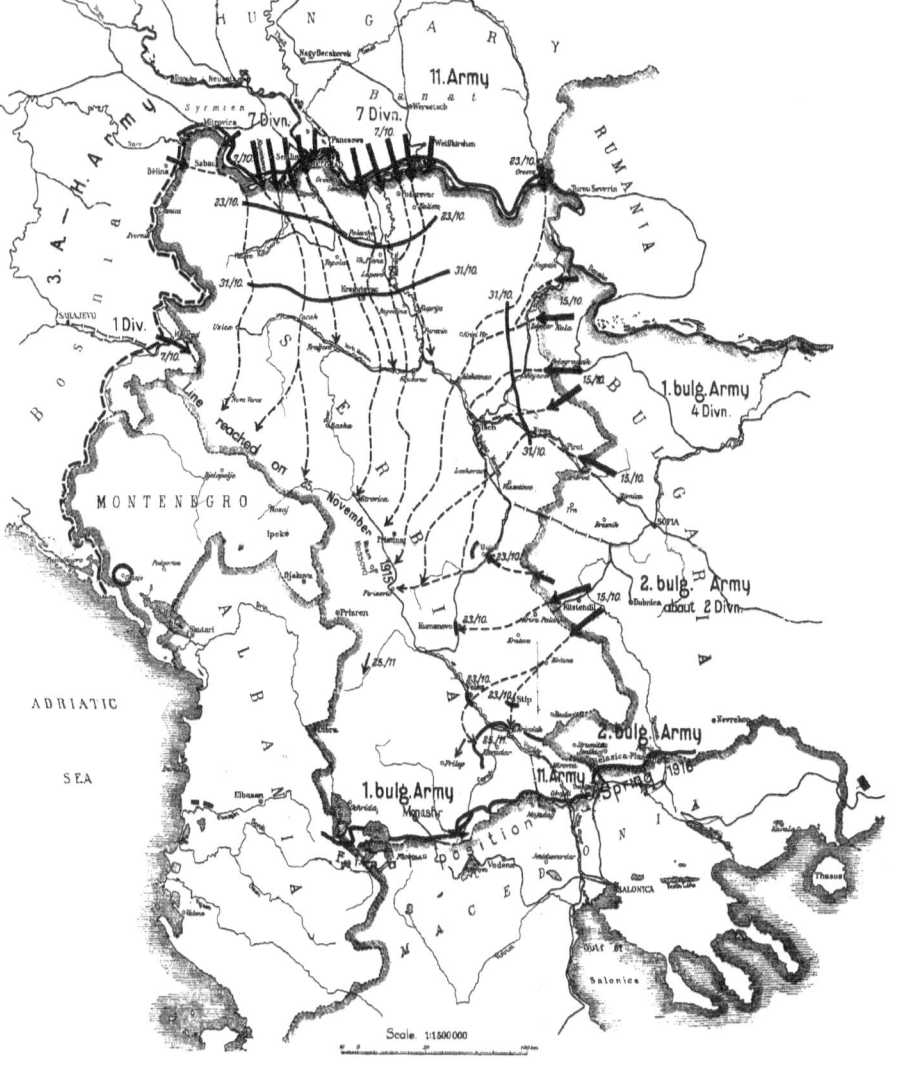

CHAPTER VIII

THE POSITION AT THE END OF 1915

THE campaign of 1915 had taken a course other than might have been expected at the beginning of the fighting season.

We had been compelled to abandon our intention of conducting the operations in the West in such a way that the French and English would lose all hope of changing the situation in their favour before France bled to death. The very moderate achievements of the Allied Army, due far more to the domestic circumstances of the Dual Monarchy than to the enemy, had prevented its realization. We had, therefore, been compelled, so far as the Western theatre was concerned, to be satisfied with holding the line we had won. Thanks to the wonderful bearing of the German troops our defence had been brilliantly successful, a defence which can surely have had no equal in the past and which the future will find it hard to match. The tremendous moral impetus which the field-army received from the spirit prevailing among the vast majority of the people at home played an overwhelming part.

In the East we had reached the goals we had set before us. They had not included the total destruction of the Russian Armies. We had kept within the limits of the possible in confining ourselves to paralysing the offensive power of the colossus so effectively that recovery would hardly be possible.

If the troops, both officers and men, of the Central Powers did their duty in the East serious danger from that quarter was no longer to be apprehended. Distant, but clearly recognizable, clouds already announced the approach of the revolutionary storm which was to burst over the realms of the Czar.

The alliance with Bulgaria and the destruction of the Serbian Army had opened the road to the south-east. Any future menace from that army or from the direction of the Dardanelles seemed to have been removed once and for all.

The position of Austria-Hungary had been relieved to a quite extraordinary degree. The Serbian danger was a thing of the past, the Rumanian had been reduced to a minimum. The tactics adopted against Italy had been magnificently justified and there was no ground for doubting that they would continue to prove successful in the future.

From these successes we had to draw the appropriate lessons for the conduct of the operations in the coming year.

The Austro-Hungarian General Staff, as a result of *their* consideration of this matter, did not hesitate in the middle of December, 1915, to contemplate an offensive against Italy. In order to have Austro-Hungarian forces commensurate with such a task at their disposal they asked us to leave nine German divisions, besides the German troops already in Galicia, in order to release Austro-Hungarian formations from the Galician front. On the Italian front they planned to attempt a breakthrough from the Tyrol in a south-easterly direction, with the right wing approximately on a line from Trent

The Position at the end of 1915

to Schio. The Austrian Staff thereby hoped to make the enormous salient described by the enemy lines in north-east Italy untenable, and perhaps cut it off altogether. As soon as this operation had rendered Italy "utterly harmless," we were promised that the forces thus released—forces estimated by that Staff, in any case much too generously, at 400,000 men—should be transported for a decisive blow on the Western front.

This project contemplated an operation which must, once at least during the war, have certainly attracted the attention of every General Staff Officer who took a look at the map of the Italian theatre of war. It was very inviting.

Looked at from the special Austro-Hungarian point of view the lights blotted out the shadows. Free from cares as regards all other fronts, the Dual Monarchy could concentrate its whole strength against Italy. In that country it saw its own private enemy. Against it advantages were to be obtained which lay outside the sphere of interests of the great ally in the North. Such a victory was not to be shared with another.

But from the point of view of the war as a whole the matter appeared in a different light. To put another nine German divisions into the front line in Galicia would have further enabled our enemies in the West to complete and augment their equipment and meant complete inactivity, so far as we were concerned, on the German fronts. We could not even estimate when that situation would end. We could not allow the troops in the West, who had already endured and suffered heavily from that situation for more than a year, to go on doing so indefinitely. Their admirable courage, supported as they were in every conceivable way by the High Command, did not show the slightest signs of wavering.

Critical Decisions at General Headquarters

But we could not take the responsibility of subjecting them to this new trial, especially as it meant requiring further sacrifice for the sake of an operation, the prospects of which, on a cool examination of all the circumstances, seemed necessarily small if only Austro-Hungarian forces were to be employed in it. We could not trust the execution of so great an undertaking to our ally alone after her performances in Galicia and Serbia.

It is true that it might have been possible to employ the nine German divisions, which the Austrian Headquarters demanded, directly in the proposed offensive on the Tyrolese frontier, instead of putting them into line in Galicia, as was suggested. They would have brought the winning of a great victory tangibly nearer. But even that would not have been sufficient to justify the sacrifice of German blood and all it meant. Only such a victory as would have definitely decided the war against Italy could have justified *that*. From the point of view of the war as a whole it was really immaterial whether the Italians held their lines on the Alps and the Carso Plateau, as at the moment, or withdrew them to a position from Lake Garda to the mouth of the Po, or even further back. It was quite certain that Rome would not be compelled to abandon the war by any reverse, however severe, in the extreme north-eastern corner of the country. She could not possibly do so against the wishes of the other Entente Powers, on whom she was entirely dependent for money, coal and food. If Italy did not go out of the war, no forces of the Central Powers would be released for the French front, still less so as we descended into the plains from our existing positions in the Eastern Alps and the Carso mountains, which were ideal for defence against superior numbers. Lastly, to continue the offensive

The Position at the end of 1915

against the Western Alps, more than three hundred miles away, was quite beyond the powers of the Alliance. Only there would it begin to have a really uncomfortable effect on the Western Powers.

The Chief of the General Staff laid these views before the Austro-Hungarian Headquarters in the following telegram of December 16th, 1915 :

" As your Excellency's proposal in the course of our conversation yesterday raises a question which I have had continuously in mind, I am able to give you my views on the subject in detail to-day. Your Excellency expresses the view that Germany is not doing anything for the war against Italy.

" I do not exactly know on what reasoning that view is based. Everyone knows that from the first German troops have been doing what has been for Austria-Hungary very useful work against Italy. Even Rome knows it well enough. Germany has only declined to declare war herself on Italy. The grounds for that refusal have been discussed in detail earlier, and been recognized as sound on all sides. Even to-day Germany would not hesitate for a moment to take part in active operations against Italy if her participation would be advantageous and if her means permitted it, having regard to the fact that she is bearing the whole burden of the war against Belgium, France and England, and by far the greater share of the burden against Russia and Serbia. The answer to this last question will be found in the following considerations.

" Your Excellency is planning a thrust from the region of Trent on a front of about thirty miles—therefore up to and beyond a line approximately from Schio to Feltre—for which purpose eight to nine Austro-

Hungarian divisions, to be relieved by German troops, are to be brought from the Galician front.

"There is no doubt that if such an operation were successful it would have a very great effect. Yet all my ripe experience goes to show that quite five and twenty divisions will be needed for its execution, which can be neither a strategic nor tactical surprise, since the deployment is limited to a single railway. My doubts as to whether your Excellency can be in a position to collect, from the Italian front as well as the Galician divisions, such a force on the selected sector, are all the greater inasmuch as the nature of the country there, the present season and the very strong positions held by the Italians, mean that only troops of specially high offensive value can be considered. I do not know whether it may be possible to get up the heavy artillery which will be required—we put this at not less than a battery for every 160 yards of front on the sector to be attacked—as well as the copious supplies of ammunition it needs.

"If an offensive force of the strength mentioned and the requisite artillery cannot be concentrated, and if supply cannot be assured in continuous and abundant measure, on purely military grounds we can only oppose the operation with all our might. As the Carpathians and Masurian Lakes battles in January and February of this year showed us only too well, it would have no prospect of decisive success and only two certain consequences.

"On the one hand it would make an enormous, possibly a fatal, hole in the reserves of the Austro-Hungarian Army. On the other it would impose a state of complete inactivity on the German fronts after the withdrawal of the nine divisions to the special Austro-Hungarian front. In the long run that could only be borne if we

The Position at the end of 1915

could hope that the operation would bring a definite decision in the war. Your Excellency believes you may expect such a decision. Unfortunately I cannot share your opinion. Even if the blow succeeds it will not be fatal to Italy. Rome will not necessarily be compelled to make peace because her army has suffered a heavy defeat in the extreme north-east of the country. She certainly cannot make peace against the wishes of the Entente, on whom she is absolutely dependent for money, food and coal. Nor do I believe that it would have the slightest influence on England and Russia if she threatened them that she would have to desert them or regaled them with pictures of her misery. On the contrary, I think it very probable that if the worst came to the worst these two pillars of the Entente would not be deeply grieved to see a partner who did so little and asked so much out of the business altogether. He would still be their slave.

"After this explanation your Excellency will not be surprised if I recommend that the Austro-Hungarian General Staff should hand over to the German High Command all the troops it can make available, after making provision for the unconditional security of their positions against any attack on the Italian frontier and in Galicia, as compensation for the German divisions attached to the army group south of the Pripet.*

---

* According to the agreement between the two General Staffs, the security of the sector of the Eastern front south of the Pripet was entrusted exclusively to Austria-Hungary. The leaving of two German divisions in the Southern Army east of Lemberg was justified by the fact that two Austro-Hungarian divisions were attached to Prince Leopold's Army Group in the German sector of the Eastern front. But we had received no such compensation in the north for the German troops left behind with Linsingen's Army Group or those on the right wing of Prince Leopold's Group south of the Pripet. These troops amounted to more than four divisions.

Critical Decisions at General Headquarters

" There is no intention of using any such accession of strength for offensive purposes, but these forces might be put to very good use by releasing German units from the front which would then be available for active operations. I have not yet definitely decided where these active operations are to take place."*

The Austro-Hungarian G.H.Q. thereupon let its proposal drop through, insisting that they held fast to their view that a decisive victory against Italy was possible. As no new or better grounds were put forward there was nothing to make the Chief of the General Staff change his mind. Indeed, it was rather the other way when the Austrian Staff simultaneously announced that they could not regard the Balkan campaign as closed. There was, therefore, definitely no question of an operation in the Italian theatre in view of the fact that they were not sufficiently strong.

The Chief of the General Staff raised no objection to the operation in the Balkans contemplated by Austria-Hungary. It aimed at the occupation of Montenegro, and the defeat of the weak Italian detachments which had meanwhile landed in Northern Albania. The proposal was inspired mainly by political considerations. But it could not be said that it had no military importance. The use of Montenegrin territory by the Entente as a base for operations against Serbia or Montenegro

---

* There was no necessity to enter more closely into this question in the telegram as, after my conversation with the Austro-Hungarian G.H.Q., there could not have been the slightest doubt that these " active operations " would in no case take place on the Eastern front, in the holding of which Austria-Hungary participated. Still less was it necessary to emphasize that there was no intention of employing Austro-Hungarian troops for these operations.

We gave the Austro-Hungarian G.H.Q. more detailed information of our intention to open operations in the Meuse sector at the end of January, 1916.

The Position at the end of 1915

was always possible, though not exactly probable in view of the character of the country. The results at which the Austro-Hungarian G.H.Q. aimed could be obtained with ease and certainty. According to all reports no prolonged resistance was to be expected from Montenegro; the heroic days of the race were apparently a thing of long ago. The dependence of the force the Italians had landed on its sea base and its very bad communications in Albania, not to mention its weakness in numbers, promised little more in the way of opposition. Every victory won by Austria-Hungary by her own efforts was bound to have a welcome effect on the *moral* of her army and the nation. It is true that there was always a danger that Austria-Hungary would lock up forces in this enterprise in a way that might adversely affect the conduct of the war as a whole. The Austro-Hungarian G.H.Q. were, therefore, repeatedly and emphatically warned of this and also given a firm hint that the new undertaking gave them no right to delay the release of the German units in line south of the Pripet.

The necessity for some such warning arose out of the course of events in Galicia. On December 24th, 1915, the Russians attacked the Southern (General Count von Bothmer's) Army and the Austrian 7th Army under General von Pflanzer-Baltin on the whole front from Burkanow on the Strypa to the Rumanian frontier east of Czernowitz, and continued their stubborn efforts into the middle of January, 1916. Though they did not obtain the slightest success against the Southern Army and, thereupon, soon desisted, the fighting fluctuated for a long time on the front of the Austrian 7th Army, against which the enemy directed his chief pressure. Although the enemy was not in materially superior numbers this army only maintained its positions with difficulty. Its reserves had been insufficient and, further, inward defects had revealed themselves. In the end, it is true, the hostile attacks were, on the whole, beaten off. But it was to be assumed that the same internal conditions prevailed among the other Austro-Hungarian Armies on the Galician front, and this compelled us to devote serious attention to these revelations.

The Austro-Hungarian operations in Montenegro and Albania progressed quickly and successfully, as we anticipated. The Montenegrins had been overthrown by the middle of January, and in February the Italians were repeatedly defeated in a number of small actions and thrown back over the Vojusa.

In the so-called New Year's Battle, to which I have just referred, the Russians had for the most part employed half-trained troops, with few officers, and those of little value, for an attack at an unfavourable season of the year. We could therefore only assume that in so doing they had some special and urgent object in view. The only object of that kind, as far as the Chief of the General Staff could judge, was the hope of influencing the attitude of Rumania. If that judgment was right it was all the more urgent to adhere to our view that no great new enterprise should be embarked upon before our relations to that State were cleared up.

Rumania's attitude to the Central Powers had been obscure from the first day of the war, and after the death of King Charles I. in August, 1914, became suspicious. Every time Austria-Hungary suffered a reverse it got worse, until it was hardly more than veiled hostility—only to become almost friendly as soon as a victory was won over Russia.

Neither the German nor the Austrian General Staff

The Position at the end of 1915

had any doubt that the political leaders of Rumania intended to follow the same course which had led to such cheap victories in the last Balkan war. They only intended to take part in the mighty struggle when they could do so without risk. Accordingly they were postponing the day of decision and taking the greatest pains to avoid committing themselves in any way to either side.

This waiting attitude was facilitated by the fact that German policy had not succeeded in peace time in obtaining the confirmation of the treaty concluded with Rumania by the Rumanian Parliament, an event which would alone have given it legal sanction. On the other hand, this attitude was rendered difficult by the very active party in the country which was unconditionally pro-Russian and pro-French. This party was boisterously demanding Rumania's adhesion to the Entente, and in this they were receiving distinguished support from adroit diplomatists working with unlimited supplies of money.

In anticipation of these developments the German General Staff had ceased to place any serious reliance in peace time on Rumania's adhesion if war broke out. Nevertheless, the vacillating attitude of that country was having unpleasant consequences for the military operations of the Central Powers. Austria-Hungary was always very sensitive to the situation in that quarter. Our communication with Turkey and Bulgaria was seriously hindered, at times almost interrupted. Rumania interpreted the principles of international law as regards neutrality in a way that could not be regarded as less than benevolent to the Central Powers, but was none the less very questionable. This became more noticeable after the Entente began the attack on the Dardanelles. As early as the spring of 1915 we had had

Critical Decisions at General Headquarters

to look into the question whether it was advisable to compel Rumania by force of arms to adopt an attitude more in keeping with her moral obligations. We had decided against such a step. As long as the Russian pressure on Austria-Hungary in Hungary and Galicia continued in full force no operation against or through Rumania was possible. The forces required could not be made available, even though the powers of resistance of Rumania could only be considered small in view of her lack of arms and ammunition.

The question came up for consideration again when, at the end of the summer of 1915, it had to be decided whether we should seek to clear our path to the southeast through Rumania or through Serbia. The Chief of the General Staff chose the Serbian route. It was true that Bulgaria, our new ally, saw no objection whatever to an attack on Rumania. Quite the contrary. The healthy hatred in every Bulgarian heart against the treacherous foe in the Balkan War would have made her only too anxious to participate in other circumstances. On the other hand, her yet more ardent desire to recover possession as speedily as possible of the old Bulgarian territory torn from her by Serbia, as well as her defective military equipment, made it necessary to adopt the shortest route. That route led through Serbia. Even apart from those considerations we should have been compelled to decide in favour of it. Bulgaria was not in a position to undertake operations against Rumania as long as her southern and western flanks were not secured against Greece and Serbia. The internal situation in Austria-Hungary just after the beginning of the Italian offensive made it imperative that she should be relieved of the Southern-Slav danger, which was always potential so long as Serbia had not been overthrown.

The Position at the end of 1915

Moreover, there had been a material improvement in Rumania's attitude after our break-through at Gorlice–Tarnow. Her frontiers had been thrown open more almost every day. The rapid overthrow of Serbia had intensified this favourable development. We got as far as negotiating for the delivery of large quantities of Rumanian corn, which was calculated to relieve the approaching food and fodder famine in Germany, and still more in Turkey. The equally urgent demand for oil seemed likely to be met from Rumanian sources.

Of course no one at German G.H.Q. allowed the accommodating spirit shown by the Rumanian authorities to blind them to their true feelings. All of us were perfectly clear that it was solely due to the compulsion of circumstances, and could become the reverse as soon as those circumstances changed. We therefore clung fast to our notion that matters must finally be cleared up as regards Rumania.

It was principally with that object in view that the bulk of the troops withdrawn from Mackensen's Army Group in November and December, 1915, and January, 1916, were retained in Southern Hungary. When the Tsar of Bulgaria visited G.H.Q. at the beginning of 1916, the Chief of the General Staff came to an agreement with General Jekoff, the Bulgarian acting Commander-in-Chief, that an ultimatum, with a short period of grace, should be issued to Rumania, and, if no satisfactory reply to this was returned, joint operations were to be undertaken. It was certainly doubtful whether it would have been possible for the Bulgarians to carry out the obligations they had undertaken. The shortage of everything, from which their troops on the Greek frontier were suffering, and the very low capacity of their communications between that region and the Danube were serious obstacles.

Critical Decisions at General Headquarters

The compact was never put into execution. Rumania carried out in exemplary fashion the terms of the corn agreement, which had meanwhile been concluded. Besides, she reinsured herself as regards the Entente, with whom she concluded a similar agreement. The latter, however, did not alter the fact that the supplies we received from Rumania warded off a severe famine in Germany, and especially Turkey. Moreover, other economic relations were once more established.

The result of all this was that the political tension became less acute, a change which justified certain hopes for the future, in the opinion of the diplomatists. But we did not succeed, and there was, in fact, no prospect of our succeeding, in persuading Rumania by diplomatic methods to throw in her lot once and for all with the Central Powers. The diplomatists believed that even the employment of the last of these methods, an ultimatum, was bound to fail. The mere issue of an ultimatum would mean a temporary interruption of the corn deliveries, and if it were followed up by an allied attack on Rumania these deliveries would stop for an indefinite time. Having regard to the economic situation in Germany and Turkey such a turn of events was seen to be disadvantageous to us. The attack we had planned was abandoned for the present. Our renunciation was rewarded by the complete fulfilment of the agreement with Rumania, which made our position secure as regards food and raw materials, the receipt of which was considered indispensable at that time.

How difficult it is to organize the delivery of supplies of this kind from a conquered country received ample illustration from our experiences in Rumania—and the Ukraine—later on.

In that respect our reasoning was perfectly just.

The Position at the end of 1915

But there is another question whether in the end it would not have been still better for the general course of the war if we had cut the knot with the sword. Those who incline to that view must be reminded that the ground on which they stand is quite weak. Could the Central Powers have held out if neither food nor oil had been supplied by Rumania in 1916 ? Would Germany have been able to maintain her line on the Western front in 1916, if she had faced the battles of Verdun and the Somme, with a large part of her reserves, small enough in themselves, by the Black Sea ? He who cannot answer that question unconditionally in the affirmative must be guarded in his opinion.

Nor must it be forgotten that Rumania's entry into the war on the side of the Entente was finally brought about by an event which was not foreseen and could not have been foreseen—the breaking of the Austro-Hungarian front in the summer of 1916 by an enemy who, for the Eastern theatre, was certainly not superior.

In the discussion of the Serbian campaign it was mentioned that it also put an end to any threat from the Dardanelles. After the English and French had withdrawn troops from that theatre for the defence of Salonica they dared not wait for the relief measures, which, in the first place by the supply of raw material, Germany organized for Turkey immediately after the opening of the Danube and the railway, to produce their effect. At the beginning of January they completely evacuated Gallipoli once and for all. It was to be anticipated with certainty that after his terrible experiences and so serious a moral defeat, the enemy would not again attempt any enterprise in that quarter. The evacuation released forces which were large for a country like Turkey, which

Critical Decisions at General Headquarters

was very exhausted after nearly six years of continuous war. The Turkish Staff, always ready to make sacrifices, offered them for use in Europe.

For the present, however, such employment seemed to be purposeless. For the next few months in the European theatre nothing could be expected of troops which, according to German standards, were insufficiently equipped, badly clothed and untrained. Further, there were insurmountable technical railway difficulties in the way of their transport. Moreover, the internal situation in Turkey, and more particularly the Arab danger, made it imperative that they should be transferred to the Asiatic provinces of Turkey to relieve the pressure of the Entente in that quarter. Accordingly we decided to do without them for the time being, and only suggested that such troops as could not be employed in Asia, owing to the low capacity of the one railway—and that not continuous—which communicated with that theatre, should in any case be brought up to a standard which would enable them to be brought to the European battlefields later on.

As regards operations in Asia the Chief of the General Staff proposed a further attempt on the Suez Canal. As the English were directing all their efforts to the capture of Bagdad at the end of 1915, such an attack seemed to have certain prospects and would serve to draw off British troops from Salonica, as well as from Mesopotamia. The employment of the troops to be used against the Suez Canal for the defence of Bagdad was impossible, owing to the difficulties of supply and transport. As regards that front we had to confine ourselves to wait for the appearance of the divisions which had started on their march thither some months before, the arrival of the war material which was in course of transport, and

The Position at the end of 1915

the effect of the presence of Field-Marshal Baron von der Goltz, who was also on his way there.

On the Armenian front also there was nothing for it but to wait—even though a Russian offensive was known to be imminent. Only small reinforcements could be despatched—and that quite by degrees—to that theatre, in view of the enormous distance, the bad communications, and the supply difficulties in a country which had been drained of its resources. It was known that preparations for this offensive had been set on foot immediately after the arrival of the Grand Duke Nicholas, that is, in the late autumn, when, as a result of the defeats on the Eastern front in Europe, he had exchanged his command there for the command in the Caucasus.

It has been said above that the Chief of the General Staff was unable to agree with the views of his Austro-Hungarian colleague as to the future plan of operations. His own conclusions rested on considerations which he expressed as follows in a document written at Christmas, 1915, to serve as a basis for the report to His Majesty the Kaiser :

" France has been weakened almost to the limits of endurance, both in a military and economic sense—the latter by the permanent loss of the coalfields in the north-east of the country. The Russian armies have not been completely overthrown, but their offensive powers have been so shattered that she can never revive in anything like her old strength. The army of Serbia can be considered as destroyed. Italy has no doubt realized that she cannot reckon on the realization of her brigand's ambitions within measurable time and would therefore probably be only too glad to be able to liquidate her adventure in any way that would save her face.

Critical Decisions at General Headquarters

"If no deductions can be drawn from these facts, the reasons are to be sought in many circumstances, the details of which there is no need to discuss. But the chief among them cannot be passed over, for it is the enormous hold which England still has on her allies.

"It is true that we have succeeded in shaking England severely—the best proof of that is her imminent adoption of universal military service. But that is also a proof of the sacrifices England is prepared to make to attain her end—the permanent elimination of what seems to her the most dangerous rival. The history of the English wars against the Netherlands, Spain, France and Napoleon is being repeated. Germany can expect no mercy from this enemy, so long as he still retains the slightest hope of achieving his object. Any attempt at an understanding which Germany might make would only strengthen England's will to war as, judging others by herself, she would take it as a sign that Germany's resolution was weakening.

"England, a country in which men are accustomed to weigh up the chances dispassionately, can scarcely hope to overthrow us by purely military means. She is obviously staking everything on a war of exhaustion. We have not been able to shatter her belief that it will bring Germany to her knees, and that belief gives the enemy the strength to fight on and keep on whipping their team together.

"What we have to do is to dispel that illusion.

"With that end in view, it will not, in the long run, be enough for us merely to stand on the defensive, a course in itself quite worthy of consideration. Our enemies, thanks to their superiority in men and material, are increasing their resources much more than we are. If that process continues a moment must come when the

The Position at the end of 1915

balance of numbers itself will deprive Germany of all remaining hope. The power of our allies to hold out is restricted, while our own is not unlimited. It is possible that next winter, or—if the Rumanian deliveries continue—the winter after the next, will bring food crises, and the social and political crises that always follow them, among the members of our alliance, if there has been no decision by then. Those crises must and will be overcome. But there is no time to lose. We must show England patently that her venture has no prospects.

"In this case, of course, as in most others involving higher strategic decisions, it is very much easier to say what has to be done than to find out how it can and must be done.

"The next method would be an attempt to inflict a decisive defeat on England on land. By that I do not mean here the island itself, which cannot be reached by our troops. Of that the navy is profoundly convinced. Our efforts can therefore be directed only against one of the continental theatres where England is fighting. As far as our own continent of Europe is concerned we are quite sure of our troops, and are working with known factors. For that reason we must rule out enterprises in the East, where England can only be struck at indirectly. Victories at Salonica, the Suez Canal, or in Mesopotamia can only help us in so far as they intensify the doubts about England's invulnerability which has already been aroused among the Mediterranean peoples and in the Mohammedan world. Defeats in the East could do us palpable harm among our allies. We can in no case expect to do anything of decisive effect on the course of the war, as the protagonists of an Alexander march to India or Egypt, or an overwhelming blow at Salonica, are always hoping.

Critical Decisions at General Headquarters

Our allies have not the necessary means at their disposal. We are not in a position to supply them, owing to the bad communications, and England, which has known how to swallow the humiliations of Antwerp and Gallipoli, will survive defeats in those distant theatres also.

" When we turn from them to the European theatre, where England can be struck at on land, we cannot close our eyes to the fact that we are faced with an extraordinarily difficult problem.

" In Flanders, north of the Lorette ridge, the state of the ground prevents any far-reaching operations until the middle of the Spring. South of that point the local commanders consider that about 30 divisions would be required. The offensive in the northern sector would need the same number. Yet it is impossible for us to concentrate those forces on one part of our front. Even if, as was planned, we collected a few more divisions from the German sectors in Macedonia and Galicia, in violation of our military and political convictions, as well as common prudence (the Army Headquarters Staffs report that it is not feasible at all on the front north of the Pripet), the total reserve in France would still amount to little more than 25 or 26 divisions. When all these are concentrated for the one operation all other fronts will have been drained of reserves to the last man. The dangers that involves for our most sensitive points—Champagne, the Woevre, Lorraine—as well as the risk of being unable in any case to come to the help of our allies in an emergency, are more than anyone dare undertake to face, in view of the fact that as a rule the modern purely frontal battle means a slow start. Moreover, the lessons to be deduced from the failure of our enemies' mass attacks are decisive against

The Position at the end of 1915

any imitation of their battle methods. Attempts at a mass break-through, even with an extreme accumulation of men and material, cannot be regarded as holding out prospects of success against a well armed enemy, whose *moral* is sound and who is not seriously inferior in numbers. The defender has usually succeeded in closing the gaps. This is easy enough for him if he decides to withdraw voluntarily, and it is hardly possible to stop him doing so. The salients thus made, enormously exposed to the effects of flanking fire, threaten to become a mere slaughter-house. The technical difficulties of directing and supplying the masses bottled up in them are so great as to seem practically insurmountable.

"We must equally discountenance any attempt to attack the British sector with comparatively inadequate means. We could only approve that course if we could give such an attack an objective within reasonable reach. There is no such objective. Our goal would have to be nothing less than to drive the English completely from the Continent and force the French behind the Somme. If that object, at least, were not attained, the attack would have been purposeless. But even if it is reached, our ultimate aim will not yet have been secured because England may be trusted not to give up even then, and further, France herself would not have been very hard hit. For that purpose a second operation would have to be undertaken. It is very questionable whether Germany would be able to dispose of the forces required. The idea of procuring them on a large scale by raising new formations cannot be entertained for this winter. In view of the pressing shortage of officers with sufficient training, such a step is not of immediate military value, and threatens to impose a dangerous strain on the situation at home.

Critical Decisions at General Headquarters

"The upshot of this discussion is that the attempt to seek a decision by an attack on the English front in the West cannot be recommended, though an opportunity of doing so may arrive in a counter-attack. In view of our feelings for our arch enemy in this war that is certainly distressing, but it can be endured if we realize that for England the campaign on the Continent of Europe with her own troops is at bottom a side-show. Her real weapons here are the French, Russian and Italian Armies.

"If we put these armies out of the war England is left to face us alone, and it is difficult to believe that in such circumstances her lust for our destruction would not fail her. It is true there would be no certainty that she would give up, but there is a strong probability. More than that can seldom be asked in war.

"It is all the more necessary that we should ruthlessly employ every weapon that is suitable for striking at England on her own ground. Such weapons are the submarine war and the conclusion of a political and economic union between Germany and not her allies only, but all States which are not yet entirely under England's spell. This review is not concerned with the formation of such a union. The solution of that problem is the exclusive sphere of the political leaders.

"The submarine war, on the other hand, is a weapon to itself. It is the duty of those who are conducting the war to explain their attitude on this question.

"Submarine warfare strikes at the enemy's most sensitive spot, because it aims at severing his oversea communications. If the definite promises of the naval authorities, that the unrestricted submarine war must force England to yield in the course of the year 1916, are realized, we must face the fact that the United

The Position at the end of 1915

States may take up a hostile attitude. She cannot intervene decisively in the war in time to enable her to make England fight on when that country sees the spectre of hunger and many another famine rise up before her island. There is only one shadow on this encouraging picture of the future. We have to assume that the naval authorities are not making a mistake. We have no large store of experiences to draw on in this matter. Such as we have are not altogether reassuring. On the other hand, the basis of our calculations will be materially changed in our favour if we can increase the number of our submarines and make progress with the training of their crews. For all these reasons there can be no justification on military grounds for refusing any further to employ what promises to be our most effective weapon. Germany has every right to use it ruthlessly after England's unconscionable behaviour at sea. The Americans, England's secret allies, will not recognize that, but it is doubtful whether, in face of a determined diplomatic representation of Germany's standpoint, they will decide to intervene actively on the Continent of Europe. It is even more doubtful whether they could intervene in sufficient strength in time. If we refuse to adopt unrestricted submarine warfare, it means that we are abandoning what all competent experts assure us is a sure advantage of inestimable value for a drawback which is serious but only problematical. In Germany's position that course is not permissible.

"When we come to the question how we are to proceed against England's tools on the Continent, Austria-Hungary is pressing for an immediate settlement of accounts with Italy. We cannot agree with that proposal. If we adopted it, it would advantage Austria-Hungary and her future prospects only, and not directly the prospects of the war as a whole. Even Italy's desertion of the Entente, which is scarcely thinkable, will make no serious impression on England. The military achievements of Italy are so small, and she is, in any case, so firmly in England's grip, that it would be very remarkable if we let ourselves be deceived on that score. Moreover, Italy is that one of our enemies whose internal conditions will soon make her further active participation in the war impossible, provided the Austro-Hungarian Army continues to do its duty at all. No one knows whether an attack on her would accelerate or delay this beneficent process. On that account it is better to leave her alone, especially as any further concentration of Austro-Hungarian troops on the Italian front is undesirable in view of her task in the East.

"The same applies to Russia. According to all reports, the domestic difficulties of the giant Empire are multiplying rapidly. Even if we cannot perhaps expect a revolution in the grand style, we are entitled to believe that Russia's internal troubles will compel her to give in within a relatively short period. In this connection it may be taken for granted that she will not revive her military reputation meanwhile. We need not be anxious about that. On the contrary, it is probable that any such attempt, and the losses it must involve, would only hasten the process of disintegration. Moreover, unless we are again prepared to put a strain on the troops which is altogether out of proportion—and this is prohibited by the state of our reserves—an offensive with a view to a decision in the East is out of the question for us until April, owing to the weather and the state of the ground. The rich territory of the Ukraine is the only objective that can be considered. The communications towards that region are in no way

The Position at the end of 1915

sufficient. It is to be presumed that we would either secure the adhesion of Rumania or make up our minds to fight her. Both are impracticable for the moment. A thrust at Petersburg, with its million inhabitants—whom we should have to feed from our own short stocks if the operations were successful—does not promise a decision. An advance on Moscow takes us nowhere. We have not the forces available for any of these undertakings. For all these reasons Russia, as an object of our offensive, must be considered as excluded. There remains only France.

"Fortunately, these views, based more on negative grounds, are supported by the corresponding positive grounds.

"As I have already insisted, the strain on France has almost reached the breaking-point—though it is certainly borne with the most remarkable devotion. If we succeeded in opening the eyes of her people to the fact that in a military sense they have nothing more to hope for, that breaking-point would be reached and England's best sword knocked out of her hand. To achieve that object the uncertain method of a mass break-through, in any case beyond our means, is unnecessary. We can probably do enough for our purposes with limited resources. Within our reach behind the French sector of the Western front there are objectives for the retention of which the French General Staff would be compelled to throw in every man they have. If they do so the forces of France will bleed to death—as there can be no question of a voluntary withdrawal—whether we reach our goal or not. If they do not do so, and we reach our objectives, the moral effect on France will be enormous. For an operation limited to a narrow front Germany will not be compelled to spend herself so completely that all other fronts are practically drained. She can face with confidence the relief attacks to be expected on those fronts, and indeed hope to have sufficient troops in hand to reply to them with counter-attacks. For she is perfectly free to accelerate or draw out her offensive, to intensify it or break it off from time to time, as suits her purpose.

"The objectives of which I am speaking now are Belfort and Verdun.

"The considerations urged above apply to both, yet the preference must be given to Verdun. The French lines at that point are barely twelve miles distant from the German railway communications. Verdun is therefore the most powerful *point d'appui* for an attempt, with a relatively small expenditure of effort, to make the whole German front in France and Belgium untenable. The removal of the danger, as a secondary aim, would be so valuable on military grounds that, compared with it, the so to speak 'incidental,' political victory of the 'purification' of Alsace by an attack on Belfort is a small matter."

At Christmas, 1915, it was decided to give effect to the views which had crystallized out of this process of reasoning. However, even before a beginning could be made we were compelled to abandon an important part of our plans.

When the unrestricted submarine campaign was to be opened in February the Chancellor raised his voice against it. He demanded a postponement of several weeks—to the beginning of April—so that he might have time to make another attempt to come to some agree-

The Position at the end of 1915

ment with the United States. We protested that we should have nothing to expect from the negotiations, in view of America's attitude hitherto, and that no moment could be more favourable for the opening of submarine activity than the period of excitement preceding the approaching presidential election, but the Chancellor brushed these aside, as well as our anxiety that a later start would prejudice the success of the submarine campaign. In this he was supported by the changed attitude of the Chief of the Naval Staff, Vice-Admiral von Holtzendorff, who had now come round to the view that a short postponement would not materially prejudice our ultimate aim—to paralyse England in the course of 1916—because the new construction coming forward in the meantime would make good the loss of time.

A decision was given in favour of a further postponement of the unrestricted submarine campaign. For the time being our submarines were only permitted to attack armed enemy merchant ships, without a previous summons to stop. No notice was taken of the Chief of the General Staff's hint that this method would be quite useless, and give no real results, because the inevitable mistakes of the submarine commanders in deciding whether a particular ship was armed or not would lead to complications with neutrals.

However, as it turned out, it was not only a question of postponement. Before the agreement with America envisaged by the Imperial Chancellor had been concluded, the torpedoing of an unarmed vessel, the *Sussex*, raised the very case that might have been anticipated. In a Note which was as unprecedented technically as in its tone, America demanded that, for the future, submarine warfare must be carried on only in those forms which

Critical Decisions at General Headquarters

had been prescribed by international agreement for cruiser warfare. After this, even the greatest optimists could hardly remain in doubt as to what attitude the United States would adopt. Further regard to her wishes was not only useless but positively dangerous in consequence of the loss of time.

Accordingly, in April the Chief of the General Staff again demanded that an immediate start be made with the unrestricted submarine campaign. He laid all the greater emphasis on this because the Chief of the Naval Staff insisted that he must adhere to his well-known view as regards the offensive co-operation of the naval forces in the war in any other form than by the submarine campaign. The employment of the High Seas Fleet could only be considered under exceptionally favourable tactical conditions. Otherwise the disparity of numbers would mean no hope of victory, but rather the danger that an enterprise aiming at a decision would end with a serious weakening of the fleet. In that case not only would the protection of the coast be jeopardized, but also our command of the Baltic, which it was as vital to maintain, on account of the imports of ore from Sweden, as the security of our shores.

The result of the only great naval battle of the war, as may be observed here in anticipation of the objection, does not give the lie to that view. It was put to the test in the battle near the Skagerrak a few weeks later, on May 31st, which took the form of a chance, or accidental encounter. It brought immortal laurels for the German war flag, so quickly faded, but it certainly did not prove that the opinion of the Chief of the Naval Staff as to the present use of the German fleet was wrong. Whether, as has often been alleged, a surprise attack by our fleet, aiming at a decision in the first days of the war, would

The Position at the end of 1915

have produced any other result must remain open to doubt.

On the question of the submarine war the political leaders did not adopt the view of the Chief of the General Staff. They could not be brought round to it, even by his insistence on the fact that the opportune employment of the unrestricted submarine war was a wholly essential ingredient in our war plans and hopes. They proved it by informing the American ambassador of Germany's abandonment of the unrestricted submarine campaign without telling the Chief of the General Staff of their intention beforehand. When he heard of this he considered it his duty, having regard to all the circumstances, to accept the *fait accompli*. Had he persisted, against the Kaiser's wish, in his request to be relieved of his office and for the appointment of a successor, it would have been construed as a demonstration against an Imperial order already given, and the opposition on this question between the military and political leaders would have been revealed to the outside world—to the detriment of Germany.

It was too late to effect any essential change in the situation, and in any case so much time had been lost that it had become extremely doubtful whether any decisive results could be obtained in the current year, that is, before the bad weather set in in August.

In these circumstances it was more to the point to avoid the danger of America's entry into the ranks of our open enemies, and therefore to postpone the decision as to the adoption of the unrestricted submarine campaign until we could see better how the operations in progress on land should turn out. Any other attitude would have been justified only by definite assurances by the naval authorities. They could not be given, however. For that reason we also turned down the proposal, which was put forward at various times during the summer of 1916, that experiments should be made by giving our submarines full freedom of action in circumscribed areas, such as the English and Irish Channels. These would have been half measures. Results of really decisive military value could not have been expected, whereas a break with America would have been a certainty.

CHAPTER IX

THE CAMPAIGN OF 1916

VERDUN (SEE FIG. 4, PAGE 231)

A CONSIDERABLE time before the decision dealt with in the preceding chapter—an offensive in the Meuse sector, with Verdun as the objective—was made known to the commands concerned, extensive preparations for feint attacks had been made according to instruction in Upper Alsace by Gaede's Army Detachment, for the purpose of misleading enemies and friends alike, and the same thing, though on a smaller scale, was done in the 4th, 5th, 6th and 3rd Armies. These operations were continued when the preparations for the operations in the Meuse region started in earnest after Christmas, 1915. In this way we succeeded in keeping the enemy for a long time in uncertainty as to the sector to be chosen for attack. The first more or less definite information on the subject seems to have reached him in the closing days of January or early in February through incautious remarks let fall in Berlin social circles and communicated by some renegade. This circumstance proves once more how indispensable it is that the closest secrecy regarding future plans be observed, even among one's own people.

The working out of the operations was influenced in a marked degree by consideration of the physical peculiarities of the country in question and the nature of its soil.

The ascent from the Woevre plain—a wet winter and early spring had turned it into a swamp—to the precipitous eastern slopes of the Meuse "Heights" was so difficult as to be out of the question, so far as the main operation was concerned. There was no prospect of success until we had cleared the way for it by an attack on the Heights themselves. The overwhelming obstacle to the attack from the south was the barrier of trackless hills, with their dense undergrowth, which, if practicable at all for close bodies of troops or motor transport, could only become so after much tedious work on clearing.

The same conditions applied to the Argonne sector.

Had the attack been made still further west, in the Aisne district or in Champagne, it would not have corresponded to our strategic conception. It would have become a break-through operation on the familiar plan. But this we were particularly anxious to avoid; in fact, it was absolutely necessary to avoid it, in view of the general situation and the limitations of the resources at our disposal. Our object, which was to inflict on the enemy the utmost possible injury with the least possible expenditure of lives on our own part, could not be achieved on the other side of the Argonne. There the enemy had ample space in which to evade the blow, while we had not sufficient troops to follow up our blow indefinitely.

Thus there remained as the theatre of operations only the region north of Verdun on both sides of the Meuse, from the foot of the Argonne in the west to

The Campaign of 1916

the Orne valley in the east. The breadth was between thirty and forty miles. To make full use of the opportunities for attack it afforded it would have been necessary to employ a far greater number of troops and much more artillery and ammunition than we had at our disposal. It had been impossible to raise the strength of the Army Reserve on the entire Western front to more than twenty-six divisions or so. It had, indeed, been thought for a time that the necessary increase of the Reserve might be brought about by straightening out individual sectors, above all the projecting salient between Arras and the district south of Laon. Experiments made on the spot proved, however, that any such hope was fallacious. This front was already held so lightly that not more than two or three divisions could be economized in this way. The resulting increase in the Reserve was not considered to be of sufficient importance to compensate for the numerous drawbacks which must have been the consequence of following such a course. For the construction of the new positions there was not nearly enough labour available on the spot. To supply it we would have been compelled to make still further demands on the homeland, already suffering from a serious shortage in this respect. And the same difficulty existed with regard to the materials required for the construction of our positions. Moreover, it was not to be expected that in a few weeks it would be possible to build lines of a strength in any way comparable to those which had taken more than twelve months to construct. Valuable, in fact irreplaceable, technical material would have been lost, and important railway connections behind the front would have been interrupted and cut. The Chief of the General Staff regarded these considerations as having so much weight, that he did not hold it admissible to allow any deviation from the principle of not abandoning a strategic position once it had been gained, except in return for sure and definite advantages.

At least a third of the Army Reserve had to be kept behind those sectors of the front against which it was considered likely that relief offensives would be made; and since the whole German front—the Army Reserve excluded—had to be held with only about one man to the yard, this precaution seemed necessary. The reserves in the West could no longer be materially increased by the addition of units from other theatres of war. Apart from units the transfer of which had already been decided upon, none, according to reports from the staffs of the Army Groups on the spot, could be spared. If the prescribed limits in this respect were overstepped, great perils would have had to be risked.

The recruiting position in the Empire, our concern for the maintenance of the economic structure of the country, as well as the shortage of officers, no longer allowed us to raise new formations of well-mixed troops. We had to impose strict limits on ourselves in that direction, in order to meet the extremely urgent demand for fresh artillery and aviation units.

The question whether further demands on the forces of our allies were to be recommended was thoroughly considered. In any case, the idea was not feasible. Turkey had as yet no troops available which it was possible to train, equip and transfer to France. The Bulgarians were not pledged to render assistance outside the Balkan peninsula. Their troops, even had it been possible to bring them to the Western or the Eastern front, would assuredly have shown them-

The Campaign of 1916

selves reluctant to serve there. Moreover, any reduction of their forces in the Balkans would, it was feared, produce an unfavourable effect on the attitude of Rumania, and also of Greece. Lastly, the Austro-Hungarian troops, as a whole, could not be considered as specially cut out for the very hard fighting on the Western front, if indeed they were sufficiently trained. The gratifying fact that they were offering a stout resistance on the Italian front against very great odds is only superficially a proof to the contrary. A considerable share of their successes must be attributed to the inferior fighting capacity of the Italians, and to the favourable nature of the *terrain*. Even with the employment of Austro-Hungarian troops on the Western front the danger of reverses in the West, and in the East as well, would in all probability have by no means vanished. The possibility of such consequences outweighed the advantages promised by co-operation, the more so as Austria-Hungary, in the opinion of German G.H.Q., absolutely needed all her really trustworthy troops, in other words those having a German or a Magyar reserve, to secure the safety of her own fronts. Moreover, all her armies put together barely sufficed to fulfil the special obligations—to look after the Serbian and Italian fronts and do her share in the East—which she had undertaken. Still, despite German pressure, the Dual Monarchy had not succeeded in bringing up their armed forces even proportionately to the same strength as those of Germany. To repair their own internal organic deficiencies quickly enough was apparently not possible for the Austrians—at any rate, during the course of the war. No doubt, however, very much more might have been done in this direction if the governing circles in Austria-Hungary had seriously

Critical Decisions at General Headquarters

devoted themselves to making an end, once and for all, to their habit of " muddling through." The Austro-Hungarian General Staff could not do that by themselves. Besides, they got in the way of relying on the fact that in the long run Germany would be compelled to come to the rescue.

ATTACK ON THE EAST BANK OF THE MEUSE

According to the figures already given, there were on the Western front seventeen or eighteen assault divisions available. Of these, nine were needed for the first attack on the right—eastern—bank of the Meuse, if it was to be carried out with the necessary determination. Some more had to be kept in readiness for the relief of the battle units, in order to give the operation that effect of continuity which was part of our plans. The form of the front itself showed that this was the only place where the main attack could be delivered. The sharp salient formed by the enemy's front north-east of the armoured fort of Douaumont offered from the outset encircling possibilities such as are rarely to be found in a war of position. There was also the hope of being able to maintain the important advantage of producing an enveloping effect as the operation proceeded.

The danger that as we got forward on the east bank of the Meuse we should come under a harassing, long-range flanking fire from the enemy artillery on the west bank was recognized.

The danger could be minimized only by pushing forward our positions, and, therefore, by an attack on that side. For this we had but a relatively small force

The Campaign of 1916

available, as the calculations given above will show. It was very doubtful whether this force, whether it waited for the beginning of the assault on the east bank or made its attack even earlier, would have met with success. For it would have had to take, purely frontally, a strong, well-constructed position, occupied by an enemy in superior strength, and, further, to make the attack on a very narrow front. Moreover, the lie of the land was in no way favourable to operations on the west bank. If the attack should fail here, there was the danger that the exposure of our flank on the east bank would presumably be permanent, as we had not sufficient troops to go on repeating the attempt.

The conditions for the western attack might be materially improved if it followed after the attack to the east of the river. We could certainly count on a big initial success for our powerful thrust on the east. Its effect must make itself felt on the other bank, to the extent that the French, in order to check it, would probably be forced to use the nearest troops in line on the west bank. Consequently a certain weakness was to be expected there. More important still, there appeared to be the possibility, even if our attack on the east bank should result in an advance of but a few miles, of effectively outflanking the foremost French lines west of the Meuse. This was calculated to make the attack west of the river much easier. The Chief of the General Staff decided for that reason to let the western attack start later than the main attack. That arrangement had the further advantage that the troops it was previously proposed to employ for the operation west of the river would not yet be tied to the ground, and would therefore be available in the event of a hostile relief offensive on another part of the front.

Critical Decisions at General Headquarters

All previous experience showed that such relief offensives must always be reckoned with. Shortly before Christmas, 1915, the Headquarters Staff of the Army of Lieut.-General the Crown Prince Wilhelm, whose Chief of Staff was General Schmidt von Knobelsdorf, received definite orders (though, for reasons of secrecy, these orders were verbal at first) to attack the French positions north of Verdun on the right bank of the Meuse. The 3rd Army in Champagne, which had formed part of this Army Group since the autumn fighting in 1915, was again detached from it, in order that the Headquarters Staff might not be involved in events which had but slight relation to the heavy task entrusted to it. On the other hand, General von Strantz's Detachment in Lorraine (Woevre), General von Falkenhausen's—in Lorraine (on the right bank of the Moselle), and in Lower Alsace—as well as Gaede's —in Upper Alsace, were attached to it. They stood in such close relation to the group on the Meuse that everything happening to them was bound to react there immediately and *vice versa*.

Besides the troops already on the spot, nine thoroughly rested and specially trained divisions were assigned to the Staff of this Army Group for the operation, so that each division had less than a mile and a half of front to attack. Further, a large number of divisions were also kept in readiness for the relief of exhausted units. Finally, it was decided to bring up immediately three picked divisions in case that situation, to which reference has been made, should arise in which, as the operations on the right bank proceeded, a thrust on the left might appear helpful and promising, and the position on the rest of the front seemed to permit it. An extraordinary amount of artillery of the largest

The Campaign of 1916

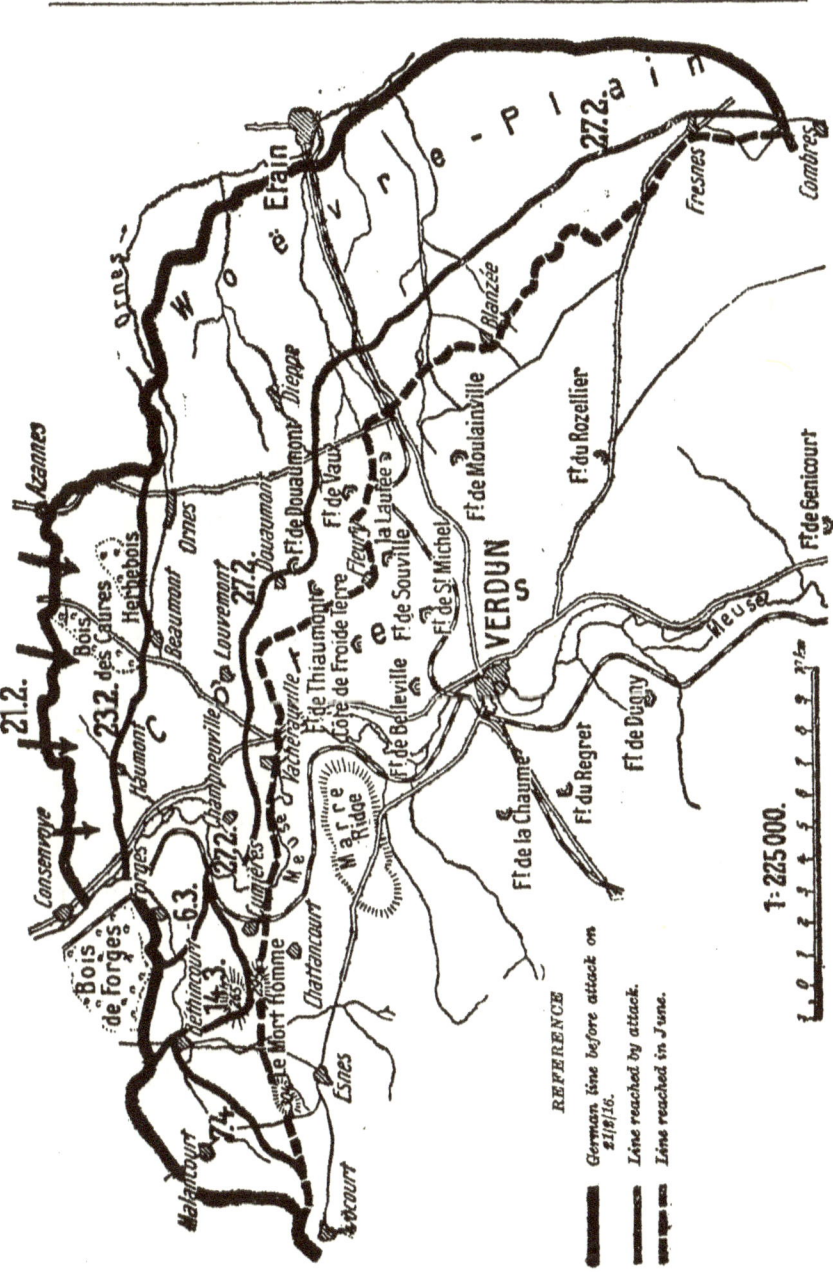

Fig. 4.—The Battles on the Meuse, 1916.

Critical Decisions at General Headquarters

calibre was allotted both to the troops on the sector selected for the offensive and those on the adjacent sectors on the west bank of the Meuse and in the Woevre, which at the outset were to give artillery support only. The supply of ammunition considerably exceeded the quantity which all previous experience suggested as likely to be needed. Similarly, every demand for labour and equipment was complied with.

In order to divert the attention of the enemy from all these preparations, the other armies in the West were charged with the task of keeping him busy by small enterprises on their sectors. In this they acquitted themselves in exemplary fashion.

On the 9th of January the 3rd Army attacked at Maisons de Champagne, on the 12th of February at Ste. Marie à Py, and on the 13th of the same month at Tahure. On the 28th and 29th of January the 2nd Army had a fine success at Frise, south of the Somme. The 6th Army struck on the 26th of January at Neuville, on the 8th of February to the west of Vimy, and on the 21st of February east of Souchez. Gaede's Army Detachment pushed forward into the French lines near Obersept on the 13th of February. Everywhere the appointed objectives were reached, and the enemy suffered heavy losses. The relatively slight German losses sustained on these occasions were justified, for it is highly probable that these operations materially contributed to mask our plans. In return, it was only in the nature of things that larger operations other than the main attack already planned should be discountenanced. When the 3rd Army inquired whether it was still to undertake a big attack on its sector, it was informed accordingly, and the following remarks were added in explanation of the plans to be followed

The Campaign of 1916

in the Meuse sector: " Our precise problem is how to inflict heavy damage on the enemy at critical points at relatively small cost to ourselves. But we must not overlook the fact that previous experience of mass attacks in this war offer little inducement to imitate them. It would almost seem as if the questions of command and supply in these attacks were insoluble."

On the day appointed for the opening of the attack the condition of the ground in the Meuse district, soaked with continuous rain, prevented any movement of the troops, while the poor visibility in the cloud-laden sky made artillery work impossible. Not till the middle of the month did the weather improve sufficiently to admit of the bombardment starting on the 21st of February.

The successful infantry attack on the following day was carried out with an irresistible impetus, and the enemy's first lines were simply overrun. Nor could the advanced fortifications, constructed in peace, stop the brave attackers, although these works were not much damaged by our artillery. On February 25th the 24th (Brandenburg) Infantry Regiment stormed the Fort Douaumont, the strong and reputedly impregnable north-eastern pillar of the Verdun defence system. Simultaneously the enemy gave way in the Orne valley as far as south of the Metz-Verdun road, so that the German front here also moved forward to the foot of the Heights of the Meuse. From many signs it was clear that this powerful German thrust had not only shaken the whole enemy front in the West very severely, but that its effects had not been lost on the peoples and the Governments of the Entente.

However, the Headquarters Staffs of the Army Groups considered it necessary to stay the forward movement against the Heights. Violent—one may say desperate—counter-attacks by troops collected in extreme haste from all parts of the front had begun. They were repulsed everywhere with very heavy loss to the enemy. The situation might have changed, however, had we not brought up our artillery, which had been unable to follow fast enough over the still barely passable roads, and assured the supply of ammunition and food.

ATTACK ON THE WEST BANK OF THE MEUSE

Meanwhile the enemy had with astonishing rapidity brought a number of powerful batteries of artillery into position behind the Marre ridge, on the western bank of the river. Their half-flanking effect made itself severely felt on our assault troops. The discomfort caused by these guns had to be stopped. This could not possibly be effected from the right bank of the Meuse, for here we had our hands full in dealing with the enemy forces immediately confronting us. The only means available—as had been foreseen and prepared for—was to push forward the German front on the left bank so far that its artillery could deal with the Franco-British guns on the Marre ridge more effectively than before. We now had troops available to carry out this necessary movement. Apart from a weak attempt in Champagne, there had been no relief attacks by the enemy in any other sectors, and our observations showed that no preparations for any immediate attack of this sort were in hand. Indeed, it had become highly improbable. The French had nearly got together the whole of their reserves from the rest of their

The Campaign of 1916

front, and had quickly handed over to the English the sector near Arras, formerly held by them, in order to provide the wherewithal to hold their positions in the Meuse sector. The English had been compelled, by taking over the Arras sector, to extend their line so much, that nothing on a big scale from this direction was to be apprehended. To be sure, the formation of Kitchener's conscript armies in England was proceeding vigorously. Thus it was to be anticipated that the forty to forty-two English divisions, whose presence on the Continent had been established, would be nearly doubled at no very distant date. Whether, and when, these new troops would become fit for use in an offensive was still, however, a matter of uncertainty.

In these circumstances the question that had to be considered by G.H.Q. was whether to intimate that the continuance of the operation on the Meuse would be abandoned, and a new enterprise started on another front. This measure would have meant a complete departure from the views on which the attack north of Verdun was based. Nor was there any reason for doing so. We had hitherto achieved what we had set out to achieve, and there was every reason to hope we should do so again in the future. As a matter of fact, that is what actually happened. No offensive elsewhere had particularly good prospects. The enemy still held their line in great strength. The English, for example, had from seven to eight men to every yard of their front. Success was to be gained against positions so strongly held as these only by employing the artillery we had concentrated on the Meuse. Further, it would have meant a great loss of time, and the enemy would assuredly have taken advantage of this to transfer his reserves likewise. It was therefore decided to renounce the idea of changing the scene of operations.

The attack carried out on the 6th of March and in the succeeding weeks on the west bank succeeded to this extent, that the French were thrown out of their foremost lines with heavy casualties every time. Owing to the peculiar confirmation of the country we could not use these successes to bring our artillery far enough forward, and consequently the preparatory work here had to be continued. Intense fighting lasted for the whole month of April on the western bank. Not till our occupation of the main portion of Hill 304, on the 7th of May, was there any momentary pause in our attack in this sector.

The conduct of the actions in the Meuse sector was at first directly in the hands of the H.Q. Staff of the Crown Prince's Army Group itself. But with the extension of operations some relief of the burden on this Staff became necessary. Accordingly, in March, while preserving its control, we put General von Mudra (Chief of Staff, Major Kewish) in command on the right bank, and on the left General von Gallwitz (Chief of Staff, Colonel Bronsart von Schellendorf [Bernard]), whose command of the 11th Army in Macedonia was taken over by Lieutenant-General von Winckler.

In April General von Mudra was succeeded by General von Lochow (Chief of Staff, Major Wetzell), and in July Lieutenant-General von François (Chief of Staff, Major von Pawelz) took General Gallwitz' place.

As already stated, there had been a temporary cessation of our attack in the western sector; but it must not be assumed from this that things had become absolutely quiet there. Here, as on the eastern bank, the fighting raged continuously and more fiercely than

The Campaign of 1916

ever. The French saw to that with their practically incessant counter-attacks. The artillery battle never stopped. The raids of the defenders were generally relieved by big thrusts carried out by forces far superior to those of the attackers. For example, a particularly resolute thrust was made on the 22nd and 23rd of May, in the region of Douaumont, and for a time our hold on the armoured fort was in danger.

For our part, we usually confined ourselves to sending our opponents home with bloody pates, recovering from him such small patches of ground as he might have gained here and there, and, where necessary, effecting slight improvements in our positions. Nevertheless, this fighting without visible or—for the man at the front—tangible result afforded the sternest test imaginable of the capabilities of the troops. With very few exceptions they stood the test most brilliantly. The enemy nowhere secured any permanent advantages; nowhere could he free himself from the German pressure. On the other hand, the losses he sustained were very severe. They were carefully noted and compared with our own which, unhappily, were not light. The result was that the comparison worked out at something like two and a half to one : that is to say, for two Germans put out of action five Frenchmen had to shed their blood. But deplorable as were the German sacrifices, they were certainly made in a most promising cause. The operations developed in accordance with the plans on which their execution had been based. To be sure, crises arose occasionally : as when the enemy slackened in his convulsive efforts, and we had to decide whether increased pressure would pay at that point, or whether it were better to shift our attack to somewhere else ; or, again, whether it would be more profitable to refrain from

Critical Decisions at General Headquarters

heavy attacks, or whether, finally, we should make up our minds to risk large forces in order to improve our own positions.

A crisis of the kind last-mentioned was caused by the fight around Douaumont already referred to. It had shown that the German lines there must be further advanced very appreciably if the fort was to be secured permanently. That, however, considering the local conditions, could only be brought about by means of an attack on a large scale. We had therefore to decide for it. The position on the rest of the front was favourable to such a decision. The long-pending attack for the relief of the Meuse sector was announced. In the sectors of the 6th, 2nd and 7th Armies, as also of Falkenhausen's Army Detachment, preparations for an offensive on the part of the enemy had been observed. Those on the purely French fronts could certainly be regarded only as feints. In the light of recent events on the Meuse, it was not credible that the French themselves could be strong enough to attempt a big enterprise. But the movements on the English front, which was being continually reinforced from the homeland, demanded more serious attention. This was especially the case as regards the Somme area, where the preparations had assumed a definite shape. The 2nd German Army stationed there had been materially strengthened by the transference of troops and artillery. Notwithstanding these withdrawals and the reliefs which had to be held in readiness for the Meuse sector, our army reserve was always strong enough to furnish sufficient troops to reply by a lusty counter-thrust to any possible enemy attack. It was not yet clear whether the French would be able to take part in an English attack. It was now hardly possible for them to concentrate a decisive

The Campaign of 1916

superiority. However, thanks to their reckless inroad on their colonies, they still disposed of more than enough man-power to bring at least a portion of their reserves up to strength and to make them fit for an offensive. In order to interrupt this process, a fresh German success on the Meuse was imperative.

The end of May saw the beginning of the operations designed for this purpose. In the first place, the Cumières positions on the left bank were taken. During the first days of June the armoured fort of Vaux, with the outworks in its neighbourhood, was captured by our brave troops after long and—even for the Verdun battle—extraordinarily stubborn fighting. On the 23rd of June the village of Fleury, standing on a rock, and the armoured works of Thiaumont were stormed. Splendid feats of arms were accomplished. Once more they provoked furious but futile counter-attacks, which must have cost the enemy dear. After these had been crushed, it was resolved to proceed during the next few weeks with the preparation of our attack on the works in the inner line of defences—Souville, La Laufée. We had thus good prospects of securing enveloping positions, the possession of which would make the citadel and its neighbourhood a hell for the French, and also materially reduce the German casualties.

But before going into the further development of events on the West front, it is necessary to devote attention to what was happening meanwhile in the other theatres of war.

THE RELIEF OFFENSIVE IN THE EAST IN MARCH, 1916

At first we had had practically no explanation of the total absence of relief offensives on the part of the

Critical Decisions at General Headquarters

enemy on the Western front during the first weeks of the operations on the Meuse. Not till later did the absorption of so many French troops in the Verdun fighting solve this riddle. Up to the 17th of March the French must have put in at least twenty-seven infantry divisions, fresh, or newly brought up to strength; to the 21st of April, thirty-eight; to the 8th of May, fifty-one, and to the middle of June far more than seventy. Thereafter, owing to the necessity of having to replenish their beaten units, they were left without the means to attempt anything decisive on other fronts. On the German side, however, it had not been even necessary to send half as many into the battle, and this comparison strengthened G.H.Q. in its conviction that its intentions in the operation on the Meuse could be realized.

Even more surprising than the continued absence of attempts at a relief offensive in the West was the opening of a relief offensive on quite a big scale on the northern portion of the Eastern front in the second half of March.

Since the battles at Dvinsk had been broken off in November, 1915, everything had remained quiet at this point. On the 18th of March, however, the Russians attacked in the Lake Dryswjaty–Postawy sector, and on both sides of Lake Narotsch, in very strong force and with an immense expenditure of ammunition. During the next few days their efforts were extended to several points of practically the whole front as far as south of Riga. They were continued with extraordinary tenacity until the beginning of April. They might, however, be described as bloody sacrifices rather than attacks. Helpless in their massed formation, their storming columns of badly-trained men, led by officers

The Campaign of 1916

as bad, suffered frightful losses. All success was denied them, save for one casual local break-through south of Lake Narotsch, and the ground lost was retaken by us without difficulty in a counter-attack. By way of reinforcement, the Army Group which was attacked required only a single division, which was stationed south of the Niemen, at Baranovici. Nor was this division asked for by the Headquarters Staff of the Army Group in question. It was offered by General Headquarters itself.

There was no doubt whatever that these attacks by the Russians were simply carried out under pressure from their Western allies and for the sake of helping them. No responsible leader, unless under constraint from outside, would have let such inferior troops attack well-built positions like those held by the Germans. Even if the enemy had met with initial successes, they could not have been turned to good account, owing to the state of the roads at that time of the year. The general impression, from the course which the fighting took, was that G.H.Q.'s opinion of autumn, 1915, that the offensive power of Russia was paralysed, had been confirmed. That impression was in no way altered by the fact that, individually, the Russians fought with their habitual contempt of death. That alone can never win successes against modern weapons in the hands of reliable troops. After these experiences it must have been evident that something quite improbable would have to happen if any faith could be placed in the capacity of the enemy to win real victories on the Eastern front. Further, that opinion was justified by the fact that the Russians had far more than two-thirds of their whole fighting strength—over a million and a half—opposed to the six hundred thousand men on the German front north of the Pripet, and there were no indications of any kind to suggest that a transfer to the front of our allies in the south was in progress.

THE AUSTRO-HUNGARIAN OFFENSIVE IN THE TYROL IN MAY, 1916

Unfortunately, however, that "something quite improbable" materialized. Despite our warnings, the Austrian General Staff clung to the idea of an offensive from the Tyrol front to the south-east. They could not find it in their hearts to let slip what appeared to be so inviting an opportunity of settling accounts with the Italians. Moreover, there was a special temptation in the thought of being able to carry out the project with their own resources, without the German advice they regarded as "patronizing."

When the Chief of the General Staff heard, through rumour, of the plan, which was not officially communicated to him, he tried to deter the Austrian G.H.Q. from proceeding with the scheme by demanding the heaviest Austro-Hungarian artillery for the operations in the Meuse sector. This heavy artillery was of very little use for trench warfare in Galicia and Italy, but indispensable for an offensive from the Tyrol. However, the Austrian Staff did not agree to give it up, and it did not seem an appropriate time to protest in another form. After all, it was Austria-Hungary's business how she used her own troops on a front she was holding by herself. We told our ally often and emphatically, that the security of the Eastern front must not suffer through any of their many projects.

The Campaign of 1916

Thereafter they could not easily lose sight of what was an absolutely vital necessity to them. We trusted, also, to the fact that transfers of troops from one seat of war to another, which might disturb the equilibrium, could not escape the attention of the numerous German liaison officers with our ally, and would be reported in good time. In both of these expectations the Chief of the General Staff was deceived.

On the 14th of May the Austrian General Staff informed us that, weather permitting, they proposed to launch an attack on the Tyrol front from the Adige to the Sugana valley.*

On the very next day the attack, for which the troops had been ready for six weeks, but detained by the snow, began. They got forward rapidly at first, though having to grapple with very difficult country, and soon had to overcome a number of strong works constructed in peace time. The Italians were unable to withstand the heavy artillery fire and the vigorous attacks of the pick of the Austro-Hungarian armies, so long as they were still fresh. By the end of May the centre of the attack had reached the region of Asiago and Arsiero, but the wings were still a long way behind. The right, which had got as far as Mori, in the valley of the Adige, had made practically no progress. The left had just about reached Strigno in the Brenta valley. The troops —too few for the length of front attacked—were now exhausted. It was difficult for the artillery to follow them. Even by the 27th of May the Austrian G.H.Q. had been compelled to ask us to give up a division of the Austrian 12th Corps, which was in Prince Leopold's Army Group, for the Italian front. As this corps had a purely Rumanian reserve, which could hardly be

* See Fig. 3, pages 92 and 93.

employed against Italians, and had, moreover, shown itself to be untrustworthy in the autumn of 1915, this suggestion furnished significant indications as to their critical situation on the battle-front.

Meanwhile the Italian counter-attacks had begun. Conducted with superior numbers, drawn partly from the Italian Reserve Army around Vicenza and partly from the Isonzo, they brought the offensive to a complete standstill. It became clear early in June—and, indeed, before things grew lively in the southern half of the Eastern front—that our ally could neither continue their offensive, remain in the salient they had reached, nor yet take advantage of the weakening of the Italian Isonzo front, due to the transfer of troops to the Tyrolean front. As regards this last alternative, the Austrian Staff even doubted whether, in case of an Italian attack, they would succeed in holding their own Isonzo positions, which had also been unduly denuded for the benefit of the Tyrolese operations. But before the necessary conclusions could be drawn from this unpleasant situation, the blow fell like a bolt from the blue in Galicia on the 4th of June.

BRUSSILOFF'S OFFENSIVE, JUNE, 1916

After the failure of the March offensive in Lithuania and Courland, the Russian front had remained absolutely inactive. Up to the beginning of June, as far as it was possible to judge from the very accurate reports the Headquarters of the Central Powers received, not a single battalion or battery had been moved from the front north of the Pripet to the Austro-Hungarian sector south of the marshes. As a matter of fact, no transfer

The Campaign of 1916

of troops on a scale worth mentioning did take place. We could thus feel confident that our allies, as formerly, were opposed by an enemy but slightly superior. Later calculations were to show that the Russian superiority amounted to a few divisions. However that may have been, in any case there was no reason whatever to doubt that the front was equal to any attack on it by the forces opposing it at the moment. This view was also held with complete conviction by the Headquarters Staff of the Linsingen Army Group, which had control of the most northerly section of the Austro-Hungarian front. General Conrad von Hötzendorf had given a very strong expression of the same opinion in a conference on the situation held in Berlin on the 23rd of May. He declared that a Russian attack in Galicia could not be undertaken with any prospect of success in less than from four to six weeks from the time when we should have learnt that it was coming. This period at least would be required for the concentration of the Russian forces, which must be a necessary preliminary thereto. In somewhat disquieting opposition to the important assertion was the energy with which, on this same occasion, timely German support from north of the Pripet was demanded, in case of need, for the Austro-Hungarian front. This promise was most willingly given, on the supposition that some movement of Russian troops from north to south must have taken place. However, before any indication of a movement of this sort had been noticed, to say nothing of announced, a most urgent call for assistance from our ally reached the German G.H.Q. on the 5th of June.

The Russians, under the command of General Brussiloff, had on the previous day attacked almost the entire front, from the Styr-Bend, near Kolki, below Lutsk, right to the Rumanian borders. After a relatively short artillery preparation they had got up from their trenches and simply marched forward. Only in a few places had they even taken the trouble to form attacking groups by concentrating their reserves. It was a matter, not simply of an attack in the true sense of the word, but rather of a big-scale reconnaissance, which would show the hard-pressed Italians that their ally was trying to help them. As became known later, July 1st was the date the Entente had in view, a date appointed by their new Supreme Command, for the big simultaneous offensive on the Eastern and Western fronts.

A " reconnaissance " like Brussiloff's was only possible, of course, if the General had decisive reason for holding a low opinion of his enemy's power of resistance. And on this point he made no miscalculation. His attack met with splendid success, both in Volhynia and in the Bukovina. East of Lutsk the Austro-Hungarian front was clean broken through, and in less than two days a yawning gap fully thirty miles wide had been made in it. The part of the 4th Austro-Hungarian Army, which was in line here, melted away into miserable remnants.

Things went no better with the 7th Austro-Hungarian Army in the Bukovina. It flowed back along its entire front, and it was impossible to judge at the moment whether and when it could be brought to a halt again. On the other hand, the Southern Army stood its ground on the Strypa, and north of it the 2nd Austrian Army held firm in its positions west of Tarnopol and east of Brody, as did the 1st Austrian Army up to

The Campaign of 1916

its left wing, which was involved in the collapse of the 4th Austrian Army on the Ikwa.

All the available reserves of the sectors still holding, especially the Germans in the Southern Army and Linsingen's Army Group, were immediately flung into the threatened fronts. Nevertheless, when the losses of the allied armies, both in men and in *matériel*, and the details of the behaviour of the troops in the battle were made known, there was no doubt that but for strong German support we should have seen a complete collapse of the whole front in Galicia.

The mere holding of ground in Galicia had but slight importance for G.H.Q. In fact, it was practically limited to seeing that the continued exploitation of the oil wells was assured. On the other hand, a fresh Russian invasion of Hungary or another threat to Silesia could not be allowed. The realization of either of these events was bound to bring about the speedy exhaustion of the Central Powers.

We were therefore faced with a situation which had fundamentally changed. A wholesale failure of this kind had certainly not entered into the calculations of the Chief of the General Staff. He had considered it impossible.

The simplest way of dealing with the situation appeared to be to concentrate hastily a strong German Army Group in Poland, West Galicia, or Hungary, and proceed to a counter-attack with far-reaching aims. The Austrian General Staff strongly recommended that proposal. But however attractive this idea appeared in theory, it was barely possible in practice.

The great superiority of the enemy on the German portion of the Eastern front has already been referred to.

Apart from the surpassing efficiency of the German troops, the equilibrium could only be maintained if those troops were supported by really well-built positions supplied with an abundance, but not a dead-weight, of mobile material. There were no such positions further back, and on that account, for us to withdraw our front with a view to shortening it in order to release troops, promised no results. We had even to anticipate that all the troops we intended to draw from Hindenburg's Army Group would have to be sent to Prince Leopold's Army Group, as the latter had no country behind it as suitable for defence with reduced numbers as that in which its lines lay at the moment. Lastly, the technical difficulties of evacuating the present front, in the face of an enemy with threefold superiority in numbers, and even then crouching to spring, were so formidable, that we shrank from the idea. We were faced with the danger that the old proverb, about the pack of hounds which will always manage to kill the game in the end, however badly trained they are in themselves, would once more come true.

Consequently it was credible enough when the Staffs of the two Army Groups reported that they might gradually be able to release troops for the Galicia front, but that they could not surrender them, anyhow not within the time required, to form an offensive group, as the Austrian General Staff proposed.

This group could only have been formed by bringing very strong forces simultaneously from the West. This would involve delay during which the last line of resistance left to the Austrians in the East would be broken down. It would, in fact, have been necessary to carry on the war against Russia without our allies. For this, however, the troops available from the West were

The Campaign of 1916

inadequate even if it were decided to withdraw behind the Meuse or to the frontier. Even a constant shifting of the centre of gravity of our attack could never compensate for the disadvantages which must inevitably follow such a sudden cessation of our pressure in the West.

The proposal of the Austrian G.H.Q., therefore, could not be accepted.

The converse was equally unacceptable: the idea of our simply leaving the East to look after itself, sending no reinforcements from the Western front, but carrying on the war here with the greatest possible pressure, and awaiting the development of events in the Russian theatre of war. It would have been presumptuous to rely on a failure of the Russian leadership similar to that of the autumn of 1914. They had learnt too much in the meantime for this. Also, as a result of the loss by our allies of far more than 200,000 men in three days, the mere numerical superiority of the Russians had become too great. There was, therefore, no hope of forcing a decision in the West before the military and political break-down of Austria. Such a break-down meant in any circumstances the loss of the war.

There remained the adoption of the system of direct assistance which all the German Staffs in the East unanimously urged.

Those German reserves on all fronts which could be in any way spared without actually endangering the front itself, were to be thrown with all possible speed into Galicia and Volhynia so as to bring the Russians to a standstill where they threatened most, and to strengthen the Austrian line where it seemed most brittle. Only by this means could we hope to succeed in welding the different parts of our ally's army, not

Critical Decisions at General Headquarters

yet hopelessly shattered, into a weapon capable of co-operating effectively with our own; only in this way could we check the disorder which had already spread considerably along the lines of communication of the southern half of the Eastern front, and which was threatening to frustrate all efforts to save the situation.

There is no doubt that even so limited a withdrawal of reserves made the position on the Western front much less favourable. The intention of nipping in the bud, by means of a heavy counter-attack, the offensive then being prepared by the English had to be dropped. The reserves of men and ammunition which were being held in readiness for this were too seriously reduced by the claims of the East. We could, however, rely on our brave troops in the West to weather the gathering storm even without this help. On the Meuse it was necessary, as a result of the plan of operations in hand, to keep the development of the situation within bounds that corresponded to the forces available.

On the 8th June the Chief of the General Staff informed Austrian G.H.Q. that German G.H.Q. was prepared to help within the limits imposed by these considerations. It was regarded as the most urgent task to bring to a standstill the Russian troops attacking in the Lutsk area, because there was imminent danger of their rolling up those parts of the Austrian 1st and 2nd Armies that were still holding. The enemy advance in the Bukovina seemed for the moment less menacing. In the mountains the pace would be bound to slacken greatly of itself. Accordingly, four or five German divisions—one from each of the Army Groups of Prince Leopold and Hindenburg, and three from the Western front—were to be united with some of the sounder Austrian troops in the neighbourhood of Kowel, under

The Campaign of 1916

the command of General von Linsingen, with Colonel Hell as Chief of Staff, to undertake a combined offensive to the south-east. The necessary conformity of action on the part of the Austrian 1st Army with this attack-group was ensured by placing the former under the command of Von Linsingen's Army Group. It was further stipulated that in future the German Staff, in addition to the control of the operations, should be ensured full insight into the internal condition of the Austrian troops under their command. Hitherto the Austrian G.H.Q. had persistently refused the encroachment of the authority of the German Command on the Austrian sphere of authority which these measures involved. They had maintained that it would undermine their prestige in the eyes of their own army, and that the German Command, who did not understand the peculiar circumstances of the Dual Monarchy, could not produce better results from its troops, and would have serious friction with the local authorities and the people. These considerations had been weighed on the German side. There is no doubt that to a certain extent they were justified. The facts that had come to light, however, as to the conduct of our ally in carrying out the Italian " Excursion " excluded henceforward any such consideration. As it appeared, the Galician front was not only weakened by the withdrawal of troops for the benefit of the Italian front, but even its capacity for resistance had been reduced below any reasonable standard by the withdrawal of its strong complement of artillery, the importance of which for unreliable troops is well known, and further, the loss, partly by exchange and partly by the addition of unreliable reserves, of a considerable part of its most reliable elements. This explained the collapse. There must be no repetition of these occurrences. To prevent it the Chief of the General Staff demanded a second guarantee by uniting the front between the Pripet and the Dniester under the command of Field-Marshal von Mackensen. This placing of full powers in the hands of the Commander of a part of the front, the arrangement we were now proposing in the Field-Marshal's case, had many objections as regards the unity of command. However, in view of the seriousness of the situation and the personality of the Field-Marshal, it was thought that these could be laid aside. But the Austrian G.H.Q. flatly refused to consider this plan, maintaining that to put it into practice in the present situation would involve a *diminutio capitis* for themselves which would have a harmful effect. As this argument could not for the moment be refuted, and as, moreover, north of the Dniester the 2nd Austrian Army alone was not under German control, the appointment of the Field-Marshal was provisionally abandoned. For the same reason it was still found impossible at the end of June to give a similar position to Field-Marshal Hindenburg, as had been intended. On the other hand, the German General von Seeckt was appointed Chief of Staff to the Austrian 7th Army, which occupied the sector south of the Dniester as far as the Rumanian frontier. The Austrian G.H.Q. finally pledged themselves not to carry out any important operations without first coming to an agreement with German G.H.Q.

The impetus, unusual for Russian troops, with which the offensive was launched in the first few days, soon slackened. Where they were opposed by German or even by the sounder Austrian divisions, they were brought to a complete standstill. The Russian failure

The Campaign of 1916

to have adequate reserves at hand was their own undoing. Not until the enemy command realized the full extent of their success, which came as a surprise even to them, were orders given to hurry up with all possible speed some of the masses of men that were accumulated in front of Hindenburg's Army Group. At the beginning of the attack by Linsingen's Army Group on the 16th June, which was launched on an extensive scale from Kovel, Vladimir Volynsk and Gorochov, the enemy in the Lutsk area had advanced two days' march beyond the Styr. He never got an inch further here, although with ruthless sacrifice of life he drove his reinforcements, now gradually beginning to come up, again and again against the allied lines.

On the contrary, in several places we succeeded in driving him back appreciably, true, only after heavy fighting during the second half of July, and after bringing up further German troops. These had again to be drawn for the most part from the West, as the weakening of the Russian front facing Hindenburg's Army Group was not realized, to an extent at all approaching the reality, until later. Prince Leopold's Army Group was not in a position to supply any further reinforcements. General von Woyrsch's Detachment, which belonged to this group, had in the middle of June been actually attacked by an enemy superiority of five to one. They had brilliantly repulsed the enemy, but it was certainly to be expected that he would before long renew his attempts to break through the shortest line of communication behind the German Eastern front, and seize the railway junction at Baranovici. By the end of the month he brought up no less than thirteen divisions from the north against this narrow front, only one less than the strength of the reserves withdrawn at the same time from before Hindenburg's Army Group for the front south of the Pripet, five or six times as long.

Like Woyrsch, the very lightly-held position of Linsingen's left wing on the Styr below Kolki was expecting a big attack. The Russians had apparently realized the impossibility of making any further progress in the neighbourhood of Lutsk. They were occupied with the formation of shock groups, to be used against the Styr sector and the north wing of the Austrian 2nd Army. This army had during the June fighting actually evacuated the position it had hitherto held on the Ikwa, but had already formed a new front on the line Salotsche-Werben, which it was stubbornly defending.

In this it was brilliantly supported by the behaviour of the Southern Army of General Count von Bothmer, which held out unflinchingly in its original trenches on the Strypa, even when the Russians south of the Dniester, in the headlong course of their victory, not only occupied the whole of the Bukovina, but at the end of June reached Tlumatsch and Kolomea, right on the flank of the Southern Army. At the same time the enemy in the mountains was pressing on to the passes towards Hungary. Both the Jakobeny and Tartar passes had to be considered as seriously threatened. The sectors concerned had also been already strengthened with German reinforcements. The Tlumatsch sector had received a division from Macedonia and part of the Southern Army. Detachments to the strength of about a division, made up of reinforcements from various parts of the Western front, had been pushed into the mountains. This stiffening had, however, proved insufficient to have any lasting influence on the general retirement. Several times when their neighbours gave way, they, too,

The Campaign of 1916

were washed back by the flood of the Russian masses. Often the great distances made it impossible to bring them in time to the places where they were needed. The front required further attention. The Chief of the General Staff suggested the trial of " reliefs " on similar lines to those adopted with Linsingen's Army Group in the Lutsk area. At the beginning of July a new Austrian army, the 12th, was to be formed out of weak detachments from the Italian, Western and North-Eastern fronts, and stronger ones from Linsingen's Army Group, the Austrian 2nd Army and the Southern Army, and to be sent to the Dniester above Halitsch, where it was to join with the inner wing of the Southern and Austrian 7th Army on what would as far as possible be a surprise counter-attack along the Dniester. To facilitate unity of purpose for the three armies they were to be united to form an army group. The command was to be given to the Austrian heir-apparent, Field-Marshal Archduke Charles, as it was hoped that his appointment would spur Austria-Hungary to special efforts on this front. The Archduke was given a German Chief-of-Staff by the transference of General von Seeckt from the staff of the Austrian 7th Army to the new army group.

In these measures just discussed, consideration of the attitude of Rumania was already playing a part. With every forward step of the Russians this attitude grew less favourable. The frontiers were again closed. News came to hand of the renewal of serious negotiations on the question of joining the Entente. Statements were known to have been made by the King and Queen, and by several leading men, which left no doubt as to their real feelings and intentions. Moreover, it was known that the war material necessary for Rumania's entry

Critical Decisions at General Headquarters

into the war was actually on the way through Russia, but that several weeks must elapse before it could be delivered. Finally it was thought that Rumania's entry into the war need not be expected until the end of the harvest, and then only if Austria's position grew still worse in the meantime. Otherwise the very cunning politicians in Bukarest would find it difficult, with Bulgaria in their rear, to throw for such high stakes.

The obvious plan to forestall the threatening Rumanian attack by an attack of our own was not feasible in June. Nor was it so, we may add at once, in July, or even August. The troops and material required for the difficult offensive over the Southern Carpathians and the Transylvanian Alps were more urgently needed elsewhere. Still less could they be held ready for defensive action on the Hungarian South-East frontier. The allied Command already decided to conduct the war against Rumania north of the mountains by means of a counter thrust. The preparations for this began soon after the Russian break-through at Lutsk. Austria, in view of her position, was only able to take a minor part. All the keener was the activity on the German side. The reorganization of units was at once begun, and these were specially trained and equipped for the theatre of war for which they were intended. Further, the improvement of the very inefficient railways in and approaching this region was undertaken by German railway troops to ensure a quick advance in case of need. The necessary reconnaissance for possible operations was taken in hand.

The above review of the position of the Central Powers in the middle of 1916 requires for its completion a supplementary account of the events that had occurred meanwhile in the Balkan and Asiatic theatres of war.

The Campaign of 1916

EVENTS IN THE BALKANS IMMEDIATELY PREVIOUS TO
THE SUMMER OF 1916. MAP 5

In Albania no change of importance had taken place since January. The Austrian thrust in February had reached and passed the Skumbi sector, but a further advance against the Italians in their prepared positions behind the Vojusa had been abandoned. The resources available had proved inadequate. Austrian G.H.Q. also required a large part of them before long to carry out their plans on the Italian front. The enemy gained no advantage from this. Apparently the difficulty of the ground hindered him just as much as it had already hampered the Austrian operations.

Neither had the situation in Macedonia materially changed. The attack on Salonica had been finally abandoned in March. The enemy had meanwhile so strengthened themselves, and their positions, that very great resources would have had to be thrown into the scale to ensure a success which at the best could have borne no just proportion to the means involved. From the point of view of the war as a whole, it remained more advantageous to know that between two and three hundred thousand men were being chained to that distant region than to drive them from the Balkan peninsula, and thence to the French theatre of war. That any serious danger could arise to our defence on the Macedonian front was regarded as outside the bounds of possibility. The German–Bulgarian positions were favoured in a quite unusual way by the nature of the country, and in accordance with the circumstances were fortified with exceptional strength. The Bulgarian troops could be relied upon to fight well henceforward in defence of Macedonia, to them sacred ground. The example of the few German stiffening troops with whom they fought in close comradeship had a good effect. An enemy offensive had no hope of success unless it were followed up in great strength. If, however, the necessary masses were thrown in, the difficulties of supply must become insuperable. In both cases there was no clear objective within reasonable reach for an enemy offensive. It could only have become effective if it were pressed as far as the interruption of the Nisch–Sofia–Constantinople railway. To reach this, more than one hundred and fifty miles of most difficult and pathless mountain country had to be crossed. It was out of the question that the enemy would embark on such an enterprise. As a matter of fact, they did not seriously venture on it for more than two and a half years. When in September, 1918, they at last advanced to the attack, they knew quite well that no resistance would be offered. The German troops had been withdrawn from the Macedonian front, and the Bulgarians had meanwhile been completely demoralized by political intrigue. In view of this state of affairs, G.H.Q. did not approve the plans of Mackensen's Army Group for further improving our position, in case of an enemy attack, by pushing forward the Bulgarian 1st Army on its right wing beyond Florina. The considerable consumption of troops this would certainly entail was not desirable. Also, it did not seem out of the question that such a penetration of Bulgarians into Greece would cause an unfavourable outbreak of national feeling, and cause Greece to join the Entente. To avoid this, the Greek Government had actually ordered the demobilization of the army.

The Campaign of 1916

This, however, had not gone so far as to make a serious encounter with Greek troops impossible.

The Turkish fronts in Asia, apart from Armenia, were not so safe as the Balkans, but were still sufficiently secure for no alarm to be felt.

ASIA IN THE SUMMER OF 1916

The exceptional mildness of the winter of 1915–16 had made it possible for the Russians to attack in Armenia as early as January. The very inferior Turkish 3rd Army, suffering in many ways from lack of supplies, was everywhere pressed back. On the 16th of February the capital, Erzerum, had to be evacuated. In the middle of April the important port of Trebizond also fell into Russian hands. Thus nearly the whole province of Armenia was lost. The Turks re-established themselves on a line from Platana on the Black Sea through Zighana, north-west of Baiburt, and through Mamakhatun to Bitlis and along Lake Van. They had suffered such heavy losses, and their service of reinforcements worked so unsatisfactorily, that further progress of the enemy had to be anxiously expected. Until the middle of the year, however, there was no sign of this. The Russians had the same difficulties to contend with as the defence.

In the Irak region the hopes that had been built on the arrival of Field-Marshal Baron von der Goltz and the reinforcements that he had brought with him were unexpectedly fulfilled in the last weeks of 1915. The Anglo-Indian Army of General Townshend, marching on Bagdad, was forced to retreat in the battle at Ctesiphon, a few miles from the gates of Bagdad, and

Critical Decisions at General Headquarters

then surrounded by the Turks in Kut-el-Amara on the Tigris. Very vigorous but over-hasty attempts at relief on the part of the English along the Tigris, and the Russians, utterly regardless of Persian neutrality, through Persian territory, could do nothing to avert their fate. At the end of April Townshend had to surrender. A few days later Field-Marshal Baron von der Goltz succumbed to spotted fever, caught while visiting Turkish hospitals. This surrender was a great triumph for the Turks. Unfortunately they were too weak and too badly equipped to take advantage of it in Irak, where the summer heats had already set in. It was also not thought advisable to attempt a serious thrust on the Tigris, so long as the Russian Army was not pressed back. The van of this army had already reached Revanduz and Khanikin in Western Persia. They found themselves, however, in such a difficult position for further action, that at the end of June they withdrew east again without waiting for the Turkish attack that had been planned.

It had not yet been found possible to begin the intended fresh advance from Palestine against the Suez Canal. It had not been possible during the cool season of 1915–16 to bring up the necessary material with sufficient promptitude. Further, a serious Arab rising against the Turkish Government had crippled the power of the latter in this region. First kindled in The Hejaz by English intrigue and English money, this rising quickly spread over the Arabian peninsula, and also unsettled the Arabian population of Syria, as well as the Bedouin tribes of the Syrian Desert as far north as the Euphrates. Appearing as it did in the guise of religious mummery, it furnished a conclusive proof that Turkey's attempt by the proclamation of the so-called

The Campaign of 1916

"Holy War" to rouse the Mohammedan population against the English had, on the whole, miscarried. The threads of religious kinship stretched to Persia, Afghanistan, India, Northern Africa and Egypt, but nowhere was the feeling strong enough to overcome the fear of England's arm. Only in Cyrenaica, where the Italians were the enemy, did the movement gain appreciable importance, and did, indeed, influence the course of events on the Italian front.

The internal condition of the Turkish Empire had grown worse through the want of sufficient food in the centres of population, which was due not so much to lack of actual supplies as to the undeveloped state of the means of transport. A serious crisis in Constantinople was fortunately averted by the timely delivery of Rumanian wheat. In other spheres, too, such as those of finance and recruiting, the length of the war was making itself severely felt, although on the German side no means was left untried that seemed likely to stop this evil, or at least to mitigate its consequences. It is impossible to praise too highly the bearing of our allies; not even under these trying circumstances was there ever the slightest wavering. They steadfastly rejected the Entente's repeated attempts to seduce them, and saw to it that so far as was within their reach the Entente activities among the people should not develop into more serious mischief.

THE BATTLE OF THE SOMME, 1916. FIGURE 5, page 264.

We left the French theatre of war at the point when before Verdun the great German success of the 23rd of June against Thiaumont had been won. On the following day the long-expected and hoped-for enemy offensive was begun in front of the 2nd Army—General Fritz von Below, with Major-General Grünert as Chief of Staff—on both sides of the Somme, after artillery preparation and gas attacks. It was directed against the German sector from north of Gommecourt to south of Chaulnes. Not only the English, but the French also took part. At the point of attack the positions north of the Somme were held by five divisions, those south of the river by three. Close behind were three divisions in reserve, ready to be sent into the line immediately. A third division, which, however, had been heavily engaged on the Meuse, was in the third line. The requests of the Commander of the 2nd Army for reinforcements, made in the last weeks during which the attack was expected, had been met as fully as possible. In artillery and aircraft it had, indeed, been impossible to meet his demands completely, in view of the situation in Galicia. The heavy diversion of troops to this front had necessitated the abandonment of our intention of breaking the enemy attack by a counter-thrust planned on a large scale. The necessary forces for this were not available in the West. Nor could they be withdrawn from the Meuse battle-field, as owing to the peculiarities of this area it was not safe, even after the defensive had been resumed, to reduce our forces there below a certain limit. Nowhere was it more important not to give the enemy any opening for an advance than on the Meuse, where the most important German lines of communication still lay almost within his reach. In view of the lack of adequate troops for a counter-attack, it had also been necessary to reject the suggestion that it might be expedient shortly before the attack began to withdraw the German positions at the point of attack, which were fairly well known to the enemy. This would have reduced our losses for the moment, and would have hampered the enemy. He would have been forced to bring forward his artillery and prepare the attack afresh. In the end this manœuvre would merely have amounted to an exchange of excellent positions for others less good and to a brief postponement of the decision which the Chief of the General Staff was anxious to bring about without delay. There was little to be gained on the German side by a temporary postponement of the issue, but much to lose, since a continuance of the existing state of tension would further prejudice freedom of decision and movement.

The artillery preparation of the enemy continued almost without interruption until the 1st of July. Vast masses of ammunition, for the most part of American origin, were hurled into the German lines. All obstacles were completely swept away, and the trenches themselves were for the most part flattened out Only a few, particularly solidly built, could stand before this savage hail of shell. Still worse, however, was the way in which in many cases the men's nerves suffered under this seven days' fire.

The French attacked with seven divisions in the first line and five in the second south of the Peronne–Albert road, on a front of about ten miles, the English with twelve divisions in the first line and four infantry, as well as several cavalry divisions behind, north of the road on a front of about fifteen miles. With this superiority it was inevitable that the enemy, when, on 1st of July, the storm at last broke, should score the usual initial successes.

The gains of the English were even less than usual. North of the Bapaume–Albert road they did not advance

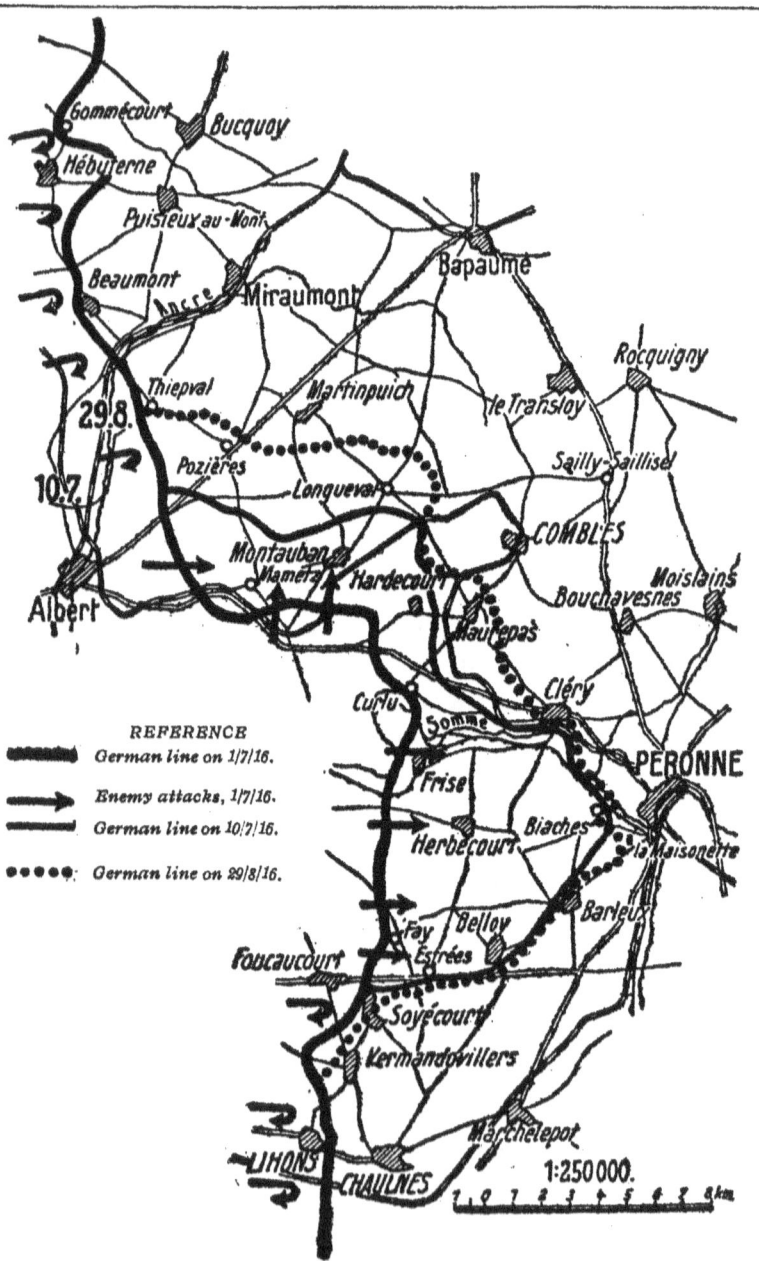

Fig. 5. The Battle of the Somme.

The Campaign of 1916

a yard, south of the road not appreciably beyond the first German line. The French gains were greater: the whole of the German first line from Fay to south of Hardecourt, north of the Somme, was lost. In several places the attack penetrated the second line. Even in this sector there was no question of the intended breakthrough having succeeded. The position became more serious when the local command allowed itself to be persuaded by the French successes to evacuate the German second-line between the Estrées–Foucaucourt road and the Somme, where it was still in our hands, in order to facilitate the withdrawal of the troops in the line Biaches–Barleux–Belloy–Estrées, who, it is true, had suffered severely from the enemy fire, and their relief from the main reserves sent up from G.H.Q. This allowed the enemy during the first weeks of the battle to take us in the flank on the north bank, which was very serious for the German troops there, who were heavily engaged on their front, and was of great importance for the further advance of the enemy. This uncertainty as to the way to conduct a defensive battle was quickly overcome. After this, the attack south of the Somme was unable, until the end of August, when this battle came to an end, to achieve any successes worth mentioning, although in the first days of July wave after wave broke upon the German lines. For the rest the French offensive fury soon calmed down south of the Somme after those first few days of storm. Lack of reserves did not permit the French Command to attack on both banks at the same time. They decided, therefore, in order to preserve touch with the English, to transfer the centre of gravity of the attack to the short French front north of the Somme.

Here and on the English front the battle was stub-

Critical Decisions at General Headquarters

bornly continued. In July and August it developed into one of those battles of *matériel* in which on both sides hitherto unexampled masses of artillery and ammunition, and, on the enemy's side, of men were expended. On the German side we were, for good reasons, extraordinarily economical in our use of men. Nevertheless, the number of the troops accumulated on the scene of the battle soon became so great, that it was no longer possible to direct the battle from one place. For this reason the command of what had hitherto been Second Army Headquarters, under General Fritz von Below, with Colonel von Lossberg as Chief of Staff, was limited to the sector north of the Somme, while General von Gallwitz, with Colonel Bronsart von Schellenberg as Chief of Staff, was transferred from the Meuse area, took over the command of the newly-formed 1st Army, and at the same time that of Gallwitz's Army Group, in which the two armies were combined.

Once again the unsurpassed fighting qualities of the German soldier were shown up in the strongest light. Always inferior numerically, he gave ground step by step before the fury of the enemy artillery only where a stand had, in fact, become impossible. He was always ready to win back lost ground from the enemy, and to take advantage of every weakness. The losses in this stubbornly contested struggle were heavy on both sides, but those of the enemy were unquestionably the heavier. If by the evening of the second day of the battle it was quite certain that the break-through planned by the English and French would not succeed, G.H.Q. knew with equal certainty, after the first week, that the enemy was also to fail to reach his objective in the tactics of attrition to which he had been compelled to resort after the miscarriage of the break-through.

The Campaign of 1916

As with the losses the numbers thrown into the attack were so greatly out of proportion to those employed in the brave defence, that, however long the operations lasted, loss of *moral* or fatigue were bound to affect the enemy first. In fact, the only result of the eight weeks of desperate enemy effort was that at the end of August the German front was pressed back on a front of thirteen miles both sides of the Somme nowhere more than four miles. And even then the German reserves on the West front had not been exhausted.

The clever propaganda of the Entente, which unfortunately was making itself felt within the Empire, has made out the Battle of the Somme to be a serious disaster for Germany. It is true our losses were very heavy. In reality, however, it had had comparatively little influence on the further course of the war, in no way proportionate to the sacrifices of the Entente, or to the result that for many months the Entente were practically crippled.

The events on the Somme have no connection with those of August on the Italian front, which led to the loss of the right bank of the Isonzo. Even if the Battle of the Somme had not been fought, G.H.Q. would not have sent any German troops to Italy for purposes of defence, because in the light of past experience they could not hope to exercise any favourable influence on the achievements of Austria.

In Galicia the most dangerous moment of the Russian offensive had been passed before the first shot of the Battle of the Somme was fired. The events that followed, in any case, had no decisive influence on the numbers of the reinforcements sent East. The position there was regarded as still very serious, but no longer critical. It is improbable that the decision only to withdraw just sufficient forces from the West for the work in hand would have been altered if the Battle of the Somme had not taken place.

The only tangible gain, then, of this battle to the enemy remains in its effect on the situation on the Western front. As a matter of course, an expenditure of strength such as the enemy favoured demanded the use of correspondingly strong forces for the defence. The operations in the Meuse area were not yet, however, immediately affected. On the 11th July we were still able, by a strong thrust, to advance our line on the east bank almost to the works of Souville and La Laufée. After this it was the tension of the whole situation, and especially the necessity to husband our *matériel* and ammunition, which necessitated the abandonment of any big German offensive operations on the Meuse. The Headquarters of the Crown Prince's Army Group were instructed to carry on the offensive calmly and according to plan, so as to give the enemy no good reason for concluding that he could hope for its cessation. This, too, was quite successful, for the French were unable to bring up reinforcements from the Meuse to the Somme front until September, when, following on the change of Chief of the General Staff, the "Verdun-offensive" had been completely abandoned.

More than three-fifths of the entire French forces were ground in the mill of the Meuse area before August, 1916. That they were able, in spite of this, to take part in the operations on the Somme, must be attributed as regards *personnel* to the unexpectedly extensive use of colonial troops, as regards *matériel* entirely to American support. The part played by America in this way was also important, in that she alone made it possible for the English to carry on the Somme struggle as long as they did.

The Campaign of 1916

This participation did not indeed violate the letter of international law, but it meant a slap in the face for real neutrality. On the one hand, America was seeking to prevent Germany from using every weapon against her deadly enemies, partly by appeals to international law coupled with veiled threats of war, partly by protestations of her peaceful intentions. On the other hand, the Great Republic not only shut her eyes to the grossest violations of this same international law by these same enemies, but even supplied them on a large scale with the weapons for Germany's destruction. We may think what we like about America's attitude towards the war. The shame which such conduct has brought upon her will never be wiped out.

THE RUSSIAN OFFENSIVE OF JULY AND AUGUST, 1916
(*vide* MAP 6)

For the Russians in the East, the opening of the Battle of the Somme was the signal for redoubled exertions. There is no doubt that in this they were acting on fresh instructions from the Entente. It is scarcely conceivable that their own leaders could still hope for decisive results.

During the month of July and the first half of August there was no complete cessation of the Russian attacks along the vast Eastern front, stretching from the Baltic to the Southern Carpathians, and these were often carried out on several parts of the front at the same time. The sector held by Hindenburg's Army Group was attacked at Riga, Friedrichstadt and Dvinsk, though in most cases only by way of a demonstration. Against Woyrsch's Detachment of Prince Leopold's

Critical Decisions at General Headquarters

Group the enemy hurled himself times without number with the greatest stubbornness. Linsingen's Army Group had frequently to resist his onslaughts on the lower Stochod and the middle Styr. The Austrian 2nd Army had to fight hard at Werben, east of Brody, and round Salotsche. With the Southern Army of Count von Bothmer the fighting was focussed on Burkanow and Butschatsch, both on the Strypa, and, later, at Monasterzyska and Tlumatsch, south of the Dniester. In the sector held by the Austrian 7th Army, the Russians strove to gain access to the mouths of the Carpathian passes during the first ten days of August, and also pressed forward south of the Dniester towards Stanislau. Here, as with Bothmer and the Austrian 7th Army, the attacks did not die down until the middle of August, whereas, with Hindenburg's Army Group, they were practically abandoned by the middle of July, with Woyrsch and Linsingen at the end of this month. From all accounts the Russian losses must have been nothing short of colossal. The poor shooting of their artillery, compared with their achievements in the early days of the war, was unable to give sufficient preparation for the attacks, and the infantry, driven forward in unwieldy massformation, were usually unable to cross the zone of our machine-gun fire. The objectives gained were, therefore, of little importance compared with the strength expended.

In the sectors held entirely by German troops they were absolutely nil.

In Linsingen's Army Group the troops on the Styr were pushed back behind the Stochod. The Austrian 2nd Army had to evacuate the line Werben–Salotsche, which it had held so well, and with it the town of Brody, but re-established a front a few miles west, and bravely held its ground on the line Berestetschko–

The Campaign of 1916

Sokolowka, and the region between Slotschow and Salotsche. In this region it was in touch with the Southern Army, which, after repulsing many attacks in admirable style, was ordered to withdraw from its positions on the Strypa to a line behind the Zlota Lipa, as the retirement of the Austrian 2nd Army and the advance of the Russians in the sector held by the left wing of the Austrian 7th Army, as far as the Zlota Bystrzyca, west of Stanislau, about the middle of August, threatened seriously to endanger the lines of communication of Bothmer's Army.

The attack planned by the Army Group of the Archduke Charles, with the object of forcing the Russian divisions in the Carpathians to withdraw behind the Dniester, and therewith to effect an improvement in the attitude of Rumania, which was rapidly becoming unfavourable, was not carried out. It became necessary to divert the troops intended for this purpose as soon as they came up, to strengthen the more shaky parts of the line, as in general the scanty reserves behind the whole battle front had to be kept ready for immediate employment in any part of the line, if we were to offer effective resistance in those sectors where the Russians attacked from time to time.

Meanwhile, in high political and other circles at home, the desire was being urgently expressed to give Field-Marshal von Hindenburg a wider field of activity. The final aim was to make the Field-Marshal Chief of the General Staff. The Chancellor was an eager advocate and promoter of this movement. Although hopes in the province of military affairs, as well as of winning over the Field-Marshal to support the Chancellor's war policy, might favour this appointment, the primary motive lay in the sphere of domestic politics. Efforts were made to effect the appointment by the methods usual in political campaigns of this kind, allusions in the Press, pressure on those in high places, diplomatic reports and other similar means. The Chief of the General Staff did not hear of this until later. He had, however, to give way, and welcomed the fact that this widening of the sphere of Field-Marshal von Hindenburg's authority so far coincided with the exigencies of the military situation as to open a way for once more concentrating the command of the Eastern front in German hands, which was considered desirable. This had become all the more expedient in view of the fact that the disposal of reserves mentioned above had given rise to differences of opinion as to whether a particular army group was in a position to spare reserves or not. There had been particular friction in the case of Hindenburg's Group. Field-Marshal von Mackensen was no longer available for the purpose in question. For him an important task was waiting in another theatre of war, with which we shall have to deal later. Neither was it possible to appoint him over Field-Marshal von Hindenburg's head.

On the other hand, there was only one leader to be considered whose prestige would ensure respect in the eyes of our ally. The Kaiser accordingly, with the approval of the Emperor Francis Joseph, entrusted to Field-Marshal von Hindenburg the command of the Eastern front from the right wing of the Austrian 2nd Army in the neighbourhood of Salotsche, east of Lemberg, to the Baltic coast, to date from the 30th July. The Chief of the General Staff agreed to this arrangement, as he hoped, wrongly as it turned out, that it would obviate all difficulties as to unity of command. The following were placed under the orders of the new

The Campaign of 1916

Commander of the Eastern front—the Austrian Army already mentioned, the Army Groups of Linsingen and Prince Leopold, and the Army Groups hitherto commanded by Field-Marsahl von Hindenburg, and now taken over by General von Eichhorn. In the first half of August six more divisions were given to Field-Marshal von Hindenburg, for disposal on the front under his command. Two of these came from the Western front, and were in need of recuperation, but could in case of necessity be employed against the Russians. Two divisions were newly formed from troops drawn from different sections of the East and Western fronts. The last two consisted of Turkish troops offered by the Ottoman Command for use in the European theatres of war after the evacuation of Gallipoli by the English at the beginning of 1916. The reasons which prevented use being made of these at that time have already been explained. When these scruples had been overcome, Austrian G.H.Q. had not been able to make up their minds to accept the renewed offer, although the employment of these well-disposed and reliable troops on their front would have been most useful. In the meantime they had been able still further to perfect their training. In the fighting in East Galicia, during September and October, they proved themselves an uncommonly valuable asset to the Southern Army, in whose sector they were placed. Though Field-Marshal von Hindenburg's new front, even before it was strengthened by the six divisions just mentioned, was no longer regarded as in a critical position, after the arrival of these, it should not only have been equal to any call that might be made upon it, but should also have been in a position to send reinforcements anywhere where there was a shortage of men. The commander of the front did not, however, share this opinion. During August he repeatedly and emphatically voiced his misgivings, not only as to the security of his own front, but also of that immediately adjoining it, and of the Rumanian frontier. They proved to be unfounded.

The southern part of the Eastern front, from the left wing of the Southern Army to the Rumanian frontier, remained an independent command under the Archduke Charles. Under his command were the Southern Army, the Austrian 3rd Army, which had replaced the 12th Austrian Army by a change of name, and the Austrian 7th Army. It has already been mentioned that the Archduke's Chief of Staff was a German.

In addition to advantages in the province of strategy and executive command, the Chief of the General Staff hoped to get, by these innovations, a grip on the inner administration of the various units which would enable us to increase the fighting value of the Austrian Army. There had always been a crying need for this, and since the break-through at Lutsk it had become even more vital.

This newly acquired grip did not, it is true, give us any security against a repetition of such strategical mistakes in the conduct of the war as a whole as the Austrian offensive against Italy. There was no means of obtaining unconditional control, as it always remained dependent on the good-will of our allies. Nevertheless, it had become essential to effect some change in the system of "joint command," which had been hitherto, at least, nominally in force. The disastrous consequences of the Tyrol enterprise had destroyed all confidence in this system. The granting to G.H.Q. of a right of supervision could no longer be evaded. The institution of a "Supreme Command of the Central

The Campaign of 1916

Powers" in German hands had therefore become a necessity. When this proposal was submitted through the Chief of the General Staff, Turkey and Bulgaria confirmed their previous attitude by immediate assent. Austria raised the objections already known, which, as has already been pointed out, were from many points of view justified. After the disastrous experiences of the past, however, no decisive importance could now be allowed to attach itself to these. Finally, this was admitted by the leaders of the Dual Monarchy themselves. The formal settlement of these negotiations did not occur, however, until after the change of Chief of the German General Staff took place at the end of August.

Ostensibly the final deciding factor in this change was the declaration of war by Italy and Rumania. But before these developments are further gone into, let us turn our attention to certain events in the realm of politics which stand in close connection with this change.

THE LIBERATION OF POLAND

Since the occupation in 1915 of " Congress Poland " there had been no truce to the differences of opinion as to the ultimate fate of Poland, although the proverb of not dividing the skin until the quarry is slain should have been borne in mind. The Governments of Berlin and Vienna were agreed that complete " liberation from the Russian yoke " must be granted and secured for the Poles. But as to the way in which this liberation was to be effected it was for a long time found impossible to agree. This was inevitable. German policy took this direction only out of necessity, because it could find no better solution to the problem of Poland's future. Austria, on the other hand, was heart and soul for the liberation, from which she hoped to reap great advantage in the future.

The Chief of the General Staff regarded this scheme with distrust. He considered it inexpedient to cut off the St. Petersburg Government from any possibility of again seeking a *rapprochement* with Germany. Moreover, from observation of the Polish-speaking population of his own province of West Prussia, he had come to the conclusion that it was impossible to establish permanently a satisfactory, neighbourly relationship between a Polish State risen from the ashes and the German Empire. The Polish *irredenta* had already caused Prussia much anxiety. This was bound to be increased, if, as a result of this movement, an independent Polish State were set up with all the hope in its own future of a new birth. There is no doubt that Austria would be able, through her connections in Galicia, to exert a paramount influence over the youthful State. This it was to be feared would give rise to friction, which might be fatal to the alliance. The exclusively Western orientation of German policy which would then necessarily follow was, from a military point of view, highly undesirable, involving as it would dealing with great but uncertain powers, instead of powers weak, it is true, but intimately known. It is true that the Prussian troops from the Polish-speaking areas had in general done their duty loyally during the war. That they would continue to do so if they knew that beyond the frontier was a Polish State with quite different ambitions from Germany's was in the highest degree improbable.

Further, nothing could be more likely to prejudice

The Campaign of 1916

calm judgment than the promises of the partisans of Poland's liberation that Germany would thereby gain an immediate increase in military strength from Polish resources. It was scarcely to be expected that the youth of Poland, who have so admirably shown themselves ready to do their duty against the Russian Empire, would flock with any particular enthusiasm to the German standards, which were as abhorrent to them as those of Russia. Even if an army could be raised, it would be impossible to place full confidence in the troops. That such troops are more of a burden, and in certain circumstances a very heavy one, than a help, had been more than proved by the history of the Austrian Army.

When, therefore, the Chief of the General Staff was informed in August that the Imperial Chancellor was in Vienna for the purpose of finally settling the Polish question, he forwarded a protest and succeeded in postponing a decision in the matter. The question was not raised again until after his resignation.

In itself an increase in the forces of the Central Powers would at this time have been most welcome. Southeast of Hungary a new war was ready to burst into flame at any moment.

RUMANIA DECLARES WAR

In discussing the attitude of Rumania it has already been explained that after the great successes of Brussiloff her entry into the war on the side of the Entente was entirely dependent on further disasters to Austria's position. Subsequent events in June and July hardly amounted to this. They were the logical and inevitable consequence of what had already happened. The

Critical Decisions at General Headquarters

Entente diplomatists, however, were able to put their own interpretation upon them for the benefit of the political and military leaders in Bukarest, who were little capable of judging for themselves. In any case, at the end of July the news from Rumania left the Command of the Central Powers no doubt that the decision as to when Rumania would join the ranks of our enemies turned on a hair, and was no longer in the slightest degree dependent upon the action of the Central Powers. It remained for the Entente alone to give the word. Steps had to be taken to meet this situation. The first efforts of G.H.Q. were directed towards postponing the actual break as long as possible. The later it came the better would it be for the Central Powers, for it might be assumed, in the light of recent events, that any gain in time would give both the West and East fronts a better chance to consolidate their line and so put themselves in a better position to spare troops for use against the new enemy without danger to themselves. For this reason German reinforcements from the West were, during the last ten days of July and in August, transferred to those sectors of the Eastern front bordering on Rumania. It was feared that a reverse here, under the very eyes as it were of Rumania, even if of minor importance in itself, might precipitate her entry into the war. As there were signs of hopes in Bukarest that Germany would be unable or unwilling to aid Austria in a war with Rumania, the error of such hopes was emphatically pointed out to the Rumanian Military Attaché at German G.H.Q., and every opportunity was given him to convince himself that Germany had quite sufficient resources at her disposal for this purpose. To emphasize this assurance, those parts of the German 101st Division which had

The Campaign of 1916

been in East Bulgaria since the autumn of 1915 were transferred to Rustchuk on the Danube, that is to say, right on the Rumanian frontier. The Turkish and Bulgarian commands were also instructed to make similar declarations in Bukarest. Austrian Headquarters were induced strongly to urge upon the Austrian Government the importance of going on with the negotiations between the Austrian Government and Rumania as to the price of the latter's continued neutrality, although there was no prospect of their ultimate success.

Simultaneously with these measures to avert, or at any rate to postpone the evil day, preparations to meet it were being made. The necessary redistribution of the German forces was hurried on, as well as the construction of railways for their transport in South Hungary and North Bulgaria. Field-Marshal von Mackensen was informed in July that in the event of war with Rumania he was to take over the command on the Dobrudja frontier and the Danube. Arrangements were made with him as to the conduct of the operations. He received instructions to take in hand the necessary preparations and reconnaissance work as far as possible without attracting attention. Lastly, on 29th July an agreement was arrived at at German G.H.Q. between General Conrad von Hötzendorf, Colonel Gantschew, the Bulgarian plenipotentiary, and the Chief of the General Staff as to the common course of action to be followed in the event of a declaration of war by Rumania. Turkish Headquarters also became a party to this, through Enver Pasha, at a meeting on 5th August at Budapest with the Chief of the General Staff and General Conrad von Hötzendorf.

It was regarded as a foregone conclusion that, if Rumania declared war, she would, in accordance with the "hungry" way of thinking of her leaders and without much consideration for military exigencies, first try to get possession of the most coveted prize, Transylvania. It was calculated that Rumania's main effort would be made in this direction, and that comparatively weak forces of the second and third lines would be left to defend the Dobrudja and the Danube against Bulgaria.

A decision was quickly come to as to the countermove.

Immediately after the outbreak of hostilities a new army under Mackensen was to invade the Dobrudja from Bulgaria, overrun the Rumanian bridgeheads at Tutrakan and Silistria and press forward to the shortest line between the Danube and the Black Sea. It was intended to form this new army from the German 101st Division, part of which was already in Rustchuk, four Bulgarian Divisions (of which three were already in North Bulgaria and one came from Macedonia), and two Turkish Divisions from the neighbourhood of Adrianople. General von Conrad would have liked the armies to advance at once across the Danube instead of into the Dobrudja, so as to bring about an earlier relief in Transylvania. The Dobrudja plan, however, was kept to, as the crossing of the river was not considered practicable until the Rumanian forces in the Dobrudja had been effectively dealt with. Preparations were made on the German side for the abundant equipment of Mackensen's army with such modern weapons, not yet known to the Rumanians, as heavy artillery, mine-throwers and gas. The gradual assembling of men and material was to begin as soon as possible, because, in view of the inadequacy of the communications in the Balkans, there remained a possibility of

The Campaign of 1916

their not being able to advance in time. After Mackensen's army had reached the line agreed upon, strong detachments were to be withdrawn from it and sent to Svistov in Bulgaria, where they were to cross the Danube and march on Bukarest. The technical difficulties of a crossing further downstream were thought too great for this to be attempted. To facilitate the crossing as much as possible, it was decided to send the Austrian heavy Danube bridging-train at once to the arm of the Danube south of the island of Belene, near Sistova, for if the tension in the relations with Rumania came to a head, it would become impossible to get it out of Hungary. The scruples of Austrian Headquarters as to this measure, which certainly meant the exposure of valuable bridging-material to a perpetual risk, were successfully overcome.

While these operations were being carried out by Field-Marshal Mackensen, Austria was to try to hold up the advance of the main Rumanian forces over the mountains as long as possible until the attacking troops, which were to be despatched immediately after the declaration of war, had got into position. Germany had provided five infantry and between one and two cavalry divisions to help in this. Austrian Headquarters intended to send into Transylvania two infantry divisions and one cavalry division, all of which had suffered heavily in the battles on the East front. On arrival these divisions were to be brought up to full strength and recuperated. Further, at the request of Germany, unity of command on the Rumanian front from the Danube to the Bukovina was established by placing the Austrian 1st Army under the orders of General Arz von Straussenberg. The first duty of this General was to organize South Hungary on a clear military

Critical Decisions at General Headquarters

basis, which had not yet been done, and to train into a useful fighting corps the numerous but weak bodies of gendarmerie, excise officers, alarm-troops, Landsturm, Landsturm reserves, mountain-troops and single infantry battalions which were at the disposal of Austria for the defence of her frontier, and to block the mountain roads in readiness for the enemy advance. Unfortunately these precautionary measures of Austrian Headquarters were seriously hampered in the middle of August by the events on the Isonzo front.

When the Italians met with sustained resistance in the higher mountain regions they broke off their counter-attack on the Tyrolese frontier and transferred their reserves to the Isonzo, where they attacked in greatly superior strength at the beginning of August. The Austrians had not been able to reply quickly enough to this change of plan. Indeed, the troops thrown into the Isonzo front after the heavy fighting in the Tyrol no longer possessed the necessary powers of resistance. In any case, the important bridge-head west of Gorizia was lost on the 6th August, and, shortly afterwards, the town itself. The enemy gained ground in many places on the east bank of the Isonzo. This produced a serious crisis. It was even necessary to bring up several divisions from the East front, who were replaced by German troops, to restore the situation. It is unnecessary to point out how this increased the difficulties in the East, not for Austrian Headquarters alone, but for the general prosecution of the war. The evil consequences of Austria's independent enterprise in the Tyrol were increasingly felt; the last of these, Rumania joining the Entente, was still to come.

For this the events on the Isonzo were decisive.*

* (Map 5).

The Campaign of 1916

To the preparations for the war against Rumania belong the operations on the Macedonian front, which after a prolonged lull were carried out in August. It has already been mentioned that it was considered desirable for the improvement of our position on this front to advance our right wing, the Bulgarian 1st Army, out of the Monastir plain to the heights south of Florina and west of Lake Ostrovo. The Bulgarian Command had recently pointed out that a similar advance of the Bulgarian 2nd Army on the left wing as far as the Struma sector would be very advantageous. The Chief of the General Staff had to advise against this suggestion because, in view of the danger of becoming involved in a war with Greece, the losses to be expected were disproportionate to the advantage to be gained. Meanwhile the situation had changed. The Greek Army had for the most part been demobilized. There was, for other reasons too, no longer any danger of an unintentional encounter with Greece. An improvement in our position, as well as a shortening of the Bulgarian line, was now desirable, even if it meant immediate sacrifices, for it would make it possible to hold troops in readiness for use elsewhere, in this case against Rumania. Permission was therefore given for these operations to be carried out. They began on 15th August, and after several battles, with varying results, finally achieved their objective on the 28th of the same month. The usual lull in this part of the Balkan theatre of war then set in for a considerable length of time. In the north-east of the Balkans, on the other hand, the torch of war blazed up all the more fiercely.

On the evening of 27th August the Italian Government declared war on Germany, and at the same hour the Rumanian ambassador in Vienna handed to the Austrian

Critical Decisions at General Headquarters

Government Rumania's declaration of war. While Italy's step was treated as, what indeed it was, a formality requiring no answer, Germany replied to Rumania's action against Austria on the next day with a declaration of war. The situation caused by these declarations of war found G.H.Q. not unprepared, but it took them by surprise. The Chief of the General Staff had not expected war with Rumania until after the Rumanian harvest in the middle of September. The causes of this early move have never been fully explained. Later information leads one to suppose that France's urgent call to Rumania not to delay any longer was an important factor. General Joffre may have hoped in this way to put fresh spirit into those wide circles of the Entente whose *moral* was beginning to waver in consequence of the unsatisfactory progress of the battle of the Somme and the crippling of the Russian offensive in Galicia. In any case, the new ally reaped no advantage by following this advice. It required only a few telegrams from German G.H.Q. to bring the counter-measures to completion which were already well advanced. The Chief of the General Staff of that time was no longer destined to direct the operations.

On the 28th August the Chief of the Military Cabinet, General Baron von Lyncker, appeared with the message that the Kaiser had seen fit to summon Field-Marshal von Hindenburg to a consultation on the following morning on the military situation that had arisen through Rumania's appearance in the ranks of our enemies. To this General von Falkenhayn had to reply that he could only regard this summoning of a subordinate commander, without previous reference to him, for a consultation on a question the solution of which lay in

The Campaign of 1916

his province alone, as a breach of his authority that he could not accept and as a sign that he no longer possessed the absolute confidence of the Supreme War Lord which was necessary for the continuance of his duties. He therefore begged to be relieved of his appointment.

As what the Chief of the General Staff regarded as a vital principle was at stake, a conference with him, summoned by His Majesty, could not hope to reconcile the conflicting views. His request to be relieved of his office was granted in the early morning of August 29th.

At the moment when Field-Marshal von Hindenburg took over the conduct of affairs the general situation was serious.

It had never been anything else, though there had been fluctuations, since September 14th, 1914, remained so to the bitter end, and, owing to the enemy's immense superiority in men and material, could not have been otherwise until his resolution was broken. It is probable that nothing contributed more to the deplorable conclusion of the war than the circumstance that this fact was concealed from the mass of the German people until it was too late to save anything.

Yet in spite of all the assertions that were made later and are diligently spread abroad even to-day, the position was not desperate at the end of 1916.

In the Western theatre the force of the enemy's attack on the Somme, which had attained the utmost concentration of effort, had been broken.

Even if the enemy were to achieve a few successes in getting forward at a terrible cost, there was no doubt that, taken as a whole, their efforts were doomed to failure and that a recurrence of circumstances of such magnitude and so unfavourable for Germany was improbable. Even if we had not been able to bring these attacks to an end or convert them into an advantage by a German attack, this was solely due to the reduction of our reserves in the West, a reduction which had been rendered necessary by the unexpected collapse of the Austro-Hungarian front in Galicia, when G.H.Q. had been unable to get timely notice of the critical transfer of the centre of gravity of the Russian attack from Lithuania and Courland to the region of Baranovici and Galicia.

For the fact that in spite of giving up large forces for the East the Western front not only disposed of sufficient resources to shatter the Somme offensive, but was in a position to furnish the bulk of the troops required to deal with the Rumanian attack, we have to thank the fundamental conception underlying the Verdun operations. To it also must be ascribed the fact that the French—to our great advantage—were able to take only a relatively small part on the Somme. About ninety of their divisions, that is, about two-thirds of their total strength, had been through the mill at Verdun. The German losses there had been not much more than a third of those of the enemy. It is true that in consequence of the decrease in the army reserve the Verdun operations had gradually to be restricted from the beginning of July. The form of those operations made this possible without any special difficulty, and enabled the attack to be resumed at any time. We could still anticipate that such a resumption, even if it took another form, would have attained its purpose of bleeding France white. The proceedings in the French Chamber of Deputies in the summer of 1916 are the best proof, even if belated, of the soundness of that view.

On the Russian front all real danger could be con-

The Campaign of 1916

sidered as over from the moment when we had realized the scale on which the Russians were transferring troops to the south. The most northerly German army group now furnished the reserves which were required to stem the enemy's advance in Galicia. Our view that the Russians would not recover from the blows dealt them in 1915, and therefore could not again become dangerous to German troops, no matter what their superiority in numbers might be, had been proved correct. Of course there was always an element of danger in the failure of some of the Austro-Hungarian troops and the internal weaknesses of that country. It was humanly impossible to eliminate it altogether. We could only reduce it to a minimum by suitable precautions, and that was done to the limits of the possible.

The allied Staffs had done all that was possible to settle accounts with the Rumanians. The issue, which seemed certain as far as human judgment could foretell, no longer depended on them, but on the handling of the situation on the spot.

The Turkish fronts in Asia, definitely a subsidiary theatre of war, required little consideration on a general survey of the whole situation. In any case, things were satisfactory there, apart from Armenia, where, however, a further Russian advance was no longer to be feared. Our anxiety lest the isolation of Russia should be terminated by the opening of the Dardanelles was a thing of the past.

Even better was the situation in Macedonia. The German–Bulgarian front there might be considered as equal to any possible development within a calculable period.

The Austro-Hungarian situation on the Italian front, such as it was left after the unsuccessful Italian offensive

Critical Decisions at General Headquarters

from the Tyrol, was a weak point in the position of the Central Powers. Yet here the advanced season gave us all the more grounds for hoping that we were about to enjoy a long breathing-space, during which we should have to see to it that counter-measures were taken.

Nothing more had been done about the decision whether and when the weapon of submarine war, still held in reserve, was to be used. After the conflict with the political leaders over this question in the spring, the Chief of the General Staff had most carefully avoided outwardly committing G.H.Q. in any way. The very necessity of preventing the enemy from taking counter-measures prescribed that course. Surprise, at least as far as it was still possible to obtain it, was a condition precedent to the effective use of the unrestricted submarine weapon. Besides, the Chief of the General Staff considered it necessary that active operations in the West should be undertaken concurrently with the opening of the submarine campaign. Yet we could not tell at the moment when that would be possible.

The strain on the homeland had, of course, been very great. However, our refusal to raise new formations on a great scale after the summer of 1915 had prevented that strain from reaching the breaking-point. Our recruiting situation was secure for a long time to come, and developing in a regular manner. We could once more consider the question of raising new formations on a larger scale. In spite of that we had succeeded in increasing the output of war material to correspond to requirements without dangerously shaking the economic fabric of the country. It was on the lines then laid down that the maximum production of the year 1917 was reached. They seemed to be capable of completely satisfying all demands that could then have been antici-

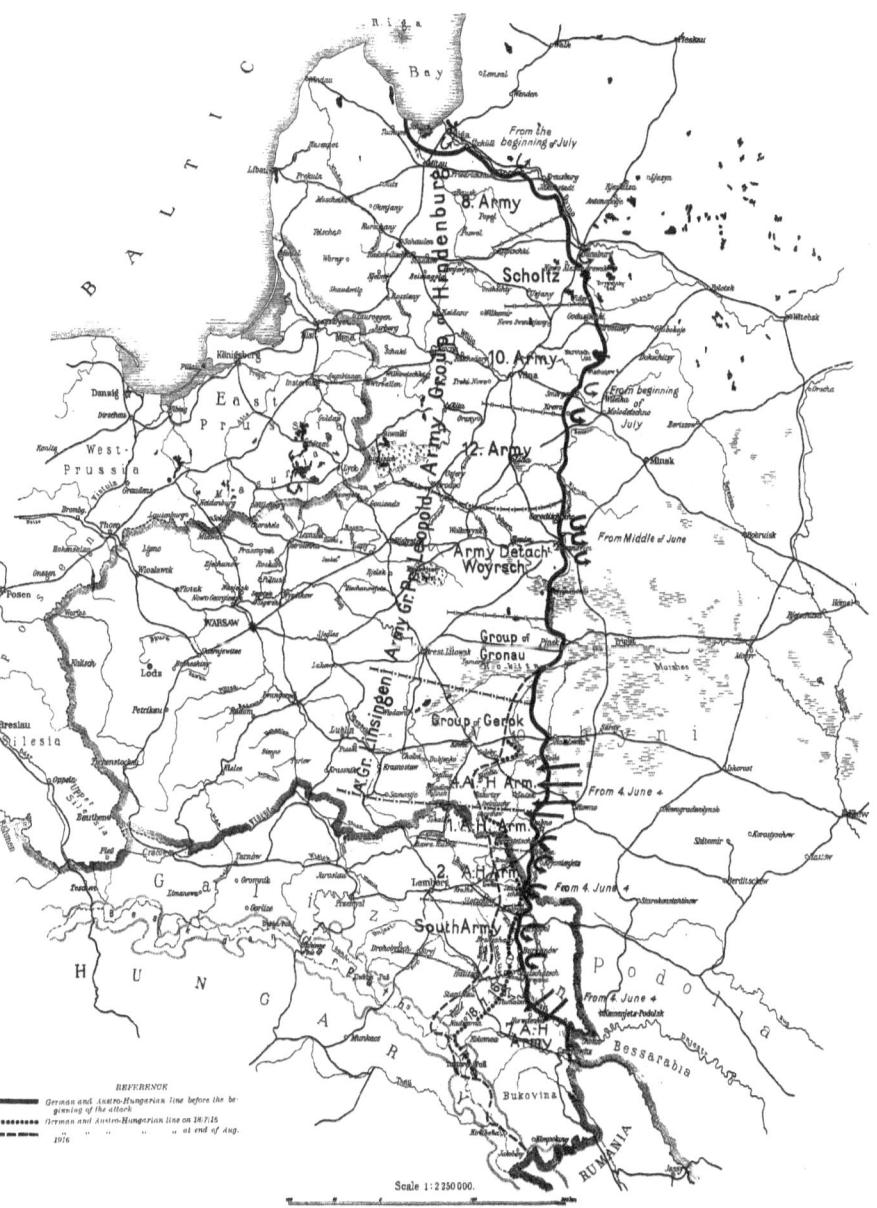

The Campaign of 1916

pated. As a matter of fact they not only did so, but throughout the war our scheme remained the model for munitions production.

Our relations to the Turkish, as to the Bulgarian General Staffs, were never troubled by the slightest friction. Both adhered unswervingly to the alliance and were always ready to adopt without questioning any measure recommended by G.H.Q.

In the same way our personal relations with the Austrian General Staff could not be described as bad; at any rate no signs of anything else could be observed in our intercourse. A certain tension which had arisen in the winter in consequence of an attempt by the Austrian Headquarters to get rid of the influence of G.H.Q. had long vanished, after personal explanations.

In our business relations with the Allied General Staff there was, of course, a line on the far side of which a certain constraint inevitably took the place of friendly understanding. That line was reached when it was a question of imposing reasonable limits, in the interests of the war as a whole, on the special schemes of Austria-Hungary, which went far beyond her resources in men and material. After the deplorable experiences of recent times it had become necessary to introduce formal unity of command and place it in German hands.

This survey of the situation at that time revealed little that was inviting, as well as much that was serious. But there were no grounds for describing it as desperate. At any rate, neither the departing Chief of the General Staff nor his colleagues at the head of the allied Staffs regarded it as such.

The goal towards which we had hitherto striven in our conduct of the campaign was to break the enemy's will

Critical Decisions at General Headquarters

to war, nor had we lost sight of the fact, for it was self-evident, that that goal could in any case be reached only by the offensive and the employment of all our resources—not by merely remaining on the defensive.

In the first weeks of the war we had not succeeded in realizing—though it then seemed very probable that we should—our hope of forcing a decision by overthrowing our enemies by a few great blows, the product of an extreme concentration of effort and complete disregard of all secondary issues. In the winter of 1914-15 the events in the Eastern theatre had prevented us from resuming our effort to achieve our end on the same lines. Subsequently the decay of our first ally's fighting capacity, our own weakness at sea and the attitude of America made it uncertain whether in any case we should be able to adopt that course again.

But it remained unquestionably our ideal.

But we were now engaged in a struggle in which the very existence of our nation, and not only military glory, or the conquest of territory, was at stake. We could not now leave out of account, seeing the way things had shaped themselves, that we might be placed in a position where the decision must be obtained not by the military defeat, in the literal sense, of all our foes, but only by hammering into them that they were in no position to pay the price of overcoming us.

Faced with such a necessity, our duty to secure that the Central Powers should "hold out" during the war acquired a new and outstanding significance. A carefully calculated husbanding of their war resources was of enormous importance, and we had unconditionally to renounce all operations, the demands of which overtaxed our power to hold out.

If the Central Powers did not hold out, or, in other

The Campaign of 1916

words, if they did not maintain their resolution and power to win longer than their opponents, everything they had done on the battlefield hitherto had been in vain. The war would not only be lost, but it would threaten our utter destruction. But if they held out they would win the war in the only way in which it could be won, seeing the strategic situation of Germany and her Allies, opposed by practically the rest of the world. From that point of view it was immaterial for the final result whether the advantages our purely military achievements had brought us were great or otherwise.

These were the considerations which had been the foundation for our prosecution of the war. In spite of the grievous violation of their principles by the enterprise in Italy our conduct of the campaign had stood the terrible tests to which it had been subjected in Galicia and on the Somme. We had a right to presume that it would be equal to the further battles with which it was faced. It did so completely, as everyone knows.

The Chief of the General Staff was accordingly unshaken in his conviction that a favourable termination of the war was not to be obtained in any other way than by force of arms.

Personally, in conformity with his repeated requests to be allowed to resign since the spring, he felt no regret that the burden which had been laid on his shoulders two long years before, at the most critical moment of the war, should be taken off. Owing to the situation which had arisen out of the differences of opinion between the highest authorities on the weightiest questions of policy and the prosecution of the war, a situation which he could do nothing to change, he believed that he was no longer in a position

Critical Decisions at General Headquarters

to do useful service to the Fatherland in his present office.

But it was only with great anxiety that he contemplated the certainty that a change in that office, under the circumstances, must inevitably mean a change of system in the conduct of the war.

APPENDIX

RELATIVE STRENGTHS OF THE OPPONENTS

NOTE:
(1) Only fighting troops are included; L. of C. and recruit formations are excluded.
(2) As the strength returns of the individual units are not available, the numbers are calculated on a basis allowing for gaps. They cannot, therefore, claim absolute accuracy, but they show the comparison well enough.

Appendix

A.—Eastern Theatre

		Germans.	Austro-Hungarians.	Total.	Russians.
1. Middle of September, 1914.	(a) On East-Prussian frontier	140,000	—	140,000	160,000
	(b) On the German-Polish frontier and in Poland—not always in touch	40,000	—	40,000	138,000
	(c) In Galicia	16,000	367,000	383,000	652,000
2. End of December, 1914.	(a) On German frontier east of the Vistula	105,000	—	105,000	320,000
	(b) In Poland, west of the Vistula	385,000	140,000	525,000	847,000
	(c) In Galicia and the Bukovina	12,000	513,000	525,000	521,000
3. End of January, 1915.	(a) On German frontier east of the Vistula	125,000	—	125,000	317,000
	(b) In Poland, west of the Vistula	273,000	146,000	419,000	916,000
	(c) In Galicia and the Bukovina	48,000	525,000	573,000	610,000
4. End of April, 1915.	(a) On German frontier east of the Vistula	366,000	—	366,000	640,000
	(b) In Poland, west of the Vistula	184,000	54,000	238,000	407,000
	(c) In Galicia and the Bukovina	89,000	610,000	699,000	720,000
5. Beginning of June, 1916.	(a) North of the Pripet	560,000	30,000	590,000	1,590,000
	(b) South of the Pripet	30,000	456,000	486,000	650,000

Appendix

B.—Western Theatre

	Germans.	Enemy.
1. Middle of October, 1914	1,700,000	2,300,000
2. Beginning of May, 1915	1,900,000	2,450,000
3. Middle of July, 1915	1,880,000	2,830,000
4. Middle of September, 1915	1,970,000	3,250,000
5. Beginning of February, 1916	2,350,000	3,470,000
6. Beginning of July, 1916	2,260,000	3,840,000

INDEX

A

ALBRECHT OF WURTEMBERG, GENERAL DUKE, 28.
Arz, Straussenberg von, 281.

B

BARTENWERFFER, COLONEL VON, 8.
Bauer, Major, 46.
Below, General von, 60, 112, 261, 266.
Beseler, General von, 12, 125.
Beskiden Corps, German, 109.
Besser, von, German infantry division, 39, 75, 83.
Bethmann-Hollweg, 3.
Bismarck's "Gedanken und Erinnerungen," 14.
Bockmann, Major-General, 60.
Bockmann, Major-General von, 112.
Bothmer, General Count von, 109, 201, 254, 270, 271.
Bojadieff, General, 165, 191.
Brussilow, General, 97, 244, 245, 246, 277.
Bülow, General von, 34, 96.
Bulgaria, Tsar of, 205.

C

CALIPH, Sultan of Turkey, 50.
Castelnau, General, 171.
Charles I., King, 202.
Charles, Field-Marshal Archduke, 255, 271, 274.
Clear, General von, 8.
Crown Prince's Army, 167, 236, 268.
Conrad, General von, 83, 84, 160, 280.
Coupette, Major-General, 46.
Czar, The, 194.

D

DOMMES, GENERAL VON, 7.
Dellmensingen, Major-General Kraft von, 28.

E

EICHHORN, GENERAL VON, 59, 273.
Einem, General von, 52, 167.
Enver Pasha, 77, 279.

Index

F

FABECK, LIEUT.-COLONEL VON, 8, 164.
Falkenhayn, Lieut.-General, 1, 2, 4, 7, 23, 84, 160, 230, 238, 284.
Fischer, Lieut.-General, 52.
Foch, General, 171.
Francis Joseph, Emperor, 272.
Francis, Lieut.-General von, 236.
Freiherr von Freytag-Loringhoven, Lieut.-General, 8.

G

GAEDE, GENERAL, 52, 223, 232.
Gantschew, Lieut.-Colonel, 160, 279.
Gallwitz, General von, 61, 110, 112, 114, 116, 117, 121, 124, 148, 164, 191, 236, 266.
Goltz, Field-Marshal Baron von der, 209, 259, 260.
Gorlice-Tarnow, 174.
Greece, King of, 192.
Grodno, 138.
Groener, Colonel, 8.
Grünert, Major-General, 27, 112, 261.

H

HÄNISCH, LIEUT.-GENERAL VON, 53.
Heeringen, General von, 53, 169.
Hell, Colonel, 59, 251.
Hemmer, Lieut.-Colonel, 109.

Hentsch, Lieut.-Colonel, 8, 165.
Heye, Colonel, 75.
Hindenburg, General von, 10, 18, 27, 54, 59, 250, 252, 253, 254, 269, 270, 271, 272, 273, 284, 285.
Hoeppner, Major-General von, 52.
Hohenborn, Major-General Wild von, 8.
Hohenlohe-Langenburg, Prince von, 160.
Hotzendorf, General Conrad von, 22, 160, 219, 245, 279.
Humann, German naval attaché, 49.

I

ILSE, COLONEL, 28.

J

JAGOW, Imperial Chancellor and Foreign Secretary VON, 23.
Joffre, General, 170, 171, 284.

K

KAISER, THE, 145, 146, 148, 209, 221, 272, 284, 285.
Kewish, Major, 236.
King and Queen, Their Majesties, 255.
Kitchener's armies, 171.
Koeth, Major, 46.
Kövess, General von, 164.
Kuhl, Major-General, 167.

Index

L

LA LAUFÉE, Work of, 268.
Lauenstein, Lieut.-General, 34.
Lauter, General, 8.
Leopold of Bavaria, Field-Marshal Prince, 112, 124, 128, 130, 133, 136, 138, 149, 151, 199, 243, 250, 253, 269, 273.
Linsingen, General von, 60, 75, 109, 151, 199, 245, 247, 251, 253, 254, 255, 270, 273.
Lochow, General von, 236.
Lossberg, Colonel von, 169, 266.
Lyncker, General, 284.
Ludendorff, Major-General, 18, 60.
Lusitania, The steamship, 157.

M

MACKENSEN, GENERAL VON, 27, 31, 86, 116, 119, 120, 121, 122, 124, 125, 126, 128, 132, 133, 134, 136, 138, 139, 147, 148, 160, 165, 179, 180, 187, 189, 191, 205, 252, 258, 272, 279, 280.
Marquard, Colonel, 116.
Marwitz, General von der, 63, 75.
Marschall, Lieut.-General Freiherr, 60, 76.
Massow, Major von, 160.
Moltke, Field-Marshal Count von, 1, 2, 14.
Mudra, General von, 236.

N

NAPOLEON, 56, 210.
Nicholas, Grand Duke, 209.
Nicolai, Major, 8

P

PAWELZ, MAJOR VON, 236.
Pflanzer, General 60.
Pflanzer-Baltin, General von, 201.
Pohl, Vice-Admiral von, 69.
Pollio, 67.
Potiorek, Lieut. Field-Marshal, 57.
Prittwitz, General von, 10.

R

RADETZKY, 97.
Rathenau, Dr. Walter, 45.
Rauch, Lieut.-Colonel von, 8.
Rupert of Bavaria, Prince, 28, 167.

S

SANDERS, GENERAL LIMAN VON, 77.
Seeckt, German General von, 86, 252, 255.
Schellendorff, Lieut.-Colonel Bronsart von, 52, 236, 266.
Schjerning, Surgeon-General von, 8.
Schlieffen, General Count von, 14.
Schoeler, Major-General von, 8.
Scholtz, General von, 112.

Index

Schmidt, Major-General von Knobelsdorf, 52, 168, 230.
Schubert, General von, 22.
Schwerin, Colonel Count von, 112.
Sieger, Lieut.-General, 8.
Souville, Works of, 268.
Stolzmann, General von, 60.
Strantz, General von, 52, 230.
Szurmay, 100.

T

TAPPEN, COLONEL, 7.
Tieschowitz, Lieut.-Colonel von, 8.
Todorow, General, 165, 191.
Townshend, General, 259, 260.
Thomsen, Major, 8, 48.

V

VOIGTS-RHETZ, MAJOR-GENERAL VON, 8.

W

WANDEL, LIEUT.-GENERAL VON, 20.
Wangenheim, German Ambassador Freiherr von, 49.
Wetzell, Major, 236.
Wilhelm, Lieut.-General the Crown Prince, 52, 230.
Winckler, Lieut.-Colonel von, 236.
Woyrsch, General von, 75, 99, 111, 116, 117, 119, 120, 121, 122, 124, 147, 148, 253, 254, 269, 270.
Wrisberg, Colonel von, 21, 43.
Wurtzbacher, Major, 46.

Y

YEKOFF, GENERAL, 205.

Z

ZEPPELIN, COUNT VON, 48.
Zoellner, Major-General, 8.

www.ingramcontent.com/pod-product-compliance
Lightning Source LLC
Chambersburg PA
CBHW030403250426
43670CB00049B/123